Cooking Light with O ORGANICS

Healthy
EVERYDAY FOOD

Soy-Ginger Stir-Fry with Tofu,
page 24

Cooking Light with O ORGANICS

Healthy
EVERYDAY FOOD

simple · organic · over 300 recipes

Oxmoor House

ISBN-13: 978-0-8487-3310-0
ISBN-10: 0-8487-3310-X
Library of Congress Control Number: 2009925694

Printed in the United States of America
First Printing 2009

Be sure to check with your health-care provider before making any changes in your diet.

OXMOOR HOUSE, INC.
VP, Publishing Director: Jim Childs
Brand Manager: Allison Long Lowery
Managing Editor: L. Amanda Owens

Cover: *Asparagus and Tomato Pesto Pasta*, page 20
Back Cover: *Spinach, Olive, and Tomato Pizza*, page 23

Cooking Light® with *O* Organics™
Healthy Everyday Food
Editor: Heather Averett
Project Editor: Diane Rose
Director, Test Kitchens: Elizabeth Tyler Austin
Assistant Director, Test Kitchens: Julie Christopher
Test Kitchens Professionals: Kathleen Royal Phillips, Catherine Crowell Steele, Ashley T. Strickland, Deborah Wise
Photography Director: Jim Bathie
Senior Photo Stylist: Kay E. Clarke
Associate Photo Stylist: Katherine Eckert Coyne
Senior Production Manager: Greg A. Amason

Contributors
Designer and Compositor: Carol O. Loria
Copy Editor: Catherine C. Fowler
Proofreader: Adrienne S. Davis
Indexer: Mary Ann Laurens
Nutritional Analyses: Kate Wheeler, R.D.
Photo Stylist: Missie Neville Crawford
Interns: Emily Chappell, Georgia Dodge, Christine Taylor, Angela Valente

To order additional publications, call 1-800-765-6400.

For more books to enrich your life, visit **oxmoorhouse.com**

To search, savor, and share thousands of recipes, visit **myrecipes.com**

COOKING LIGHT®

Editor in Chief: Mary Kay Culpepper
Executive Editor: Billy R. Sims
Creative Director: Susan Waldrip Dendy
Managing Editor: Maelynn Cheung
Deputy Editor: Phillip Rhodes
Senior Food Editor: Ann Taylor Pittman
Projects Editor: Mary Simpson Creel, M.S., R.D
Associate Food Editors: Timothy Q. Cebula,
    Kathy Kitchens Downie, R.D., Julianna Grimes
Associate Editors: Cindy Hatcher, Brandy Rushing
Test Kitchen Director: Vanessa Taylor Johnson
Assistant Test Kitchen Director: Tiffany Vickers
Senior Food Stylist: Kellie Gerber Kelley
Test Kitchen Professionals: Mary Drennen Ankar,
    SaBrina Bone
Art Director: Maya Metz Logue
Associate Art Directors: Fernande Bondarenko,
    J. Shay McNamee
Senior Designer: Brigette Mayer
Senior Photographer: Randy Mayor
Senior Photo Stylist: Cindy Barr
Photo Stylists: Jan Gautro, Leigh Ann Ross
Copy Chief: Maria Parker Hopkins
Assistant Copy Chief: Susan Roberts
Copy Editor: Johannah Gilman Paiva
Copy Researcher: Michelle Gibson Daniels

Production Manager: Liz Rhoades
Production Editor: Hazel R. Eddins
Cookinglight.com Editor: Kim Cross
Cookinglight.com Intern: Maggie Gordon
Administrative Coordinator: Carol D. Johnson
Editorial Assistant: Jason Horn
Interns: Caroline Ford, Emily Kaple

O ORGANICS™

Senior Brand Manager: Julie Shryne
Marketing Trainee: Melissa Kampling
Chef: Domenica Catelli
Category Director, Books and Magazines:
    Judy Russell
Category Manager, Books and Magazines:
    Gary Sundgren
Category Analyst, Books and Magazines:
    Clive Fernandes
Consultant: Straus Communications
Consultant: Celia Shryne

NEIGHBOR AGENCY

Creative Director: Rand Denny
Art Director: Jason Fontana
Account Supervisor: Michelle Esposito
Account Executive: Adrienne Stephen

Table of Contents

Introduction

Most of us want to combine healthy ingredients and delicious flavor in our dishes. So often, we sacrifice nutrition for flavor, but why should we have to choose? Now we can have our cake and eat it too! The editors of *Cooking Light®* books are proud to introduce *Cooking Light with O Organics™ Healthy Everyday Food,* a collection of more than 300 organic-inspired recipes that will bring nutritious, flavorful food to your dinner table.

This cookbook offers not only many of our all-time greatest recipes, but also an entire chapter devoted to recipes that focus specifically on organic ingredients. *Cooking Light* teams up with the O Organics brand in order to provide the most nutritious, delicious, and organically inspired collection of recipes available.

Within these pages, you'll discover tips about how to purchase the right kind of organic foods and incorporate them into your family's everyday life. With suggestions at your fingertips, you can make smart cooking decisions quickly and easily without sacrificing nutrition or flavor.

We've provided the opportunity for you to include organic ingredients in all of the recipes presented in this book. With such delicious options and beautiful photographs, we hope that *Healthy Everyday Food* will inspire your creativity in the kitchen and bring exciting new dishes to your dining table.

We sincerely hope that you will enjoy discovering new possibilities within your cooking. Whether you're already using organic food in your creations or are looking to add new twists to old favorites, we hope this book will encourage you to eat smart, be fit, and live well.

We hope that *Healthy Everyday Food* will inspire your creativity in the kitchen and bring exciting new dishes to your dinner table.

Organics for Everyone

Why this cookbook?

The organic movement is growing. Organic foods are becoming available and affordable to an ever-growing group of people. At O Organics, we're proud to play a big part in helping make that happen. In fact, that's the very mission of O Organics: making organic food available to everyone. Every budget. Every lifestyle. Every neighborhood. Every member of the family. Organic foods taste great and are better for people and the planet. We encourage you to learn more about the benefits of eating organic foods and to spread the word to your friends and family.

Rosemary and Balsamic Beef with Arugula and Blue Cheese, page 26

Why a Collaboration
with *Cooking Light* ?

The decision to work with *Cooking Light* was easy because we share an interest in health and wellness as well as a passion for food.

Cooking Light provided countless mouthwatering recipes that have met their carefully crafted nutrition standards (see page 248). O Organics brought an understanding of organic foods, an eye towards which recipes could most easily be made with organic ingredients (given current availability and cost), and our own delicious recipes designed with our product line in mind. We had somewhat different perspectives on the use of nonstick pans, so you will find guidelines for proper use on page 256 and can decide for yourself what works for you.

We are pleased with the result of this collaborative effort and hope you will be as well.

History and Definition of Organic Foods

WHAT IS THE HISTORY OF ORGANIC FOOD?

Organic farming is not as new a concept as we are inclined to think, because for most of agricultural history, farming was essentially organic. It wasn't until after World War II that petroleum-based fertilizers and pesticides were developed. In the 1960s and 1970s, a small number of farmers and food producers started to return to a more ecologically based way of farming. Then, only after prolonged efforts on the part of very passionate organic advocates, USDA organic standards came into being in 2002. So now we've come full circle.

WHAT EXACTLY IS ORGANIC FOOD?

The approach to organic farming is fundamentally different from conventional farming methods because it strives to work in harmony with nature. It avoids the use of toxic chemicals; relies on more natural techniques (e.g., composting); and treats animals more humanely, with regular access to the outdoors. This approach helps keep toxic synthetic chemicals away from our food, farm workers, the soil, our waterways, and the air. It's better for people and better for the earth.

At its most basic, organic foods are produced without the use of the following:

THE FOUR NO'S

1. No synthetic pesticides
2. No genetic modification
3. No growth hormones
4. No antibiotics

To get the more detailed story, visit the USDA Web site: **www.ams.usda.gov** and click on National Organic Program.

One of the easiest ways to know if a product is organic is to look for the USDA organic logo. However, because there are different levels of organic, clearly understanding labeling rules will help determine the right choice for you.

On the Package	Percent Organic Ingredient	USDA Organic Logo
100% organic	100%	yes
Organic	95%	yes
"Made with organic ingredients X"	70%	no

IS THERE A DIFFERENCE BETWEEN NATURAL VS. ORGANIC FOOD?

It is not uncommon for people to confuse natural and organic foods. There are no government standards for use of the term natural (except for meat), but manufacturers typically use it to mean minimally processed and made without the use of artificial ingredients. Although there is a short list of synthetic ingredients that are allowed in organic foods (e.g., baking soda, pectin, vitamin C), organic food is generally understood to be natural. And with the stringent requirements noted above, organic is considered a higher standard than natural.

Why Buy Organic?

According to The Organic Center, 43% of consumers choosing organic food do so because of "better taste."

There are lots of lists articulating reasons to go organic. This is ours.

1. Keep synthetic pesticides out of our bodies and the environment
2. Protect young children (who are most vulnerable to pesticide exposure)
3. Provide food that mounting evidence suggests is more nutritious
4. Enjoy food that tastes better
5. Use less fossil fuel (i.e., fewer synthetic fertilizers) that contributes to global warming
6. Promote farming methods that preserve soil fertility for future generations
7. Support farmers and food producers that care about you and the land

"Credible scientific data regularly shows that organic production of food and other products promotes both environmental and human health."

—THE ORGANIC CENTER

ARE ORGANIC FOODS SAFER THAN CONVENTIONAL FOODS?

Emerging scientific research suggests that organic foods are safer than conventional foods. According to the non-profit organization The Organic Center, a 2006 dietary study proves than an organic diet makes a dramatic and immediate difference in how much toxic insecticides people come into contact with. Buying organic food not only decreases your and your family's risk of pesticide exposure, but it also keeps pesticides out of our soil and water and protects farm workers and people who live in agricultural areas.

ARE ORGANIC FOODS MORE NUTRITIOUS THAN CONVENTIONAL FOODS?

Scientists are just starting to answer this question. There have been numerous studies testing the nutrient quantities of organic foods compared to conventional ones, and the results have been encouraging. A review by The Organic Center of research in 2008 found organic foods to be nutritionally superior in two-thirds of cases in which it was compared to conventional food grown under the same conditions.

To see scientific studies on the benefits of organic foods, go to The Organic Center's Web site: **www.organiccenter.org.**

Where Can I Buy Organic Foods?

THERE ARE MANY DIFFERENT PLACES TO BUY ORGANIC FOODS

Farmers Markets—Farmers markets carry produce grown locally and in season. They are typically open once or twice a week and can make for a wonderful weekend outing.

Roadside Stands and U-Pick Farms—Usually located in rural areas, these places provide an opportunity to learn about growing practices firsthand and to feel a personal connection with those who grow the food as well as the place it is grown.

Community Supported Agriculture (CSAs)—This is a system in which consumers commit to buy a share of a local farm's production each month. Consumers then receive a box of seasonal produce once a week. This is a good way to be exposed to unfamiliar produce and to get ideas of how to prepare it.

Health Food Stores and Co-ops—These stores will likely carry the widest variety of organic offerings, but not all their products will be organic. They also may be more expensive.

Supermarkets—Your local supermarket probably carries a wider variety of organic foods than ever before. O Organics is an example of a brand that is becoming increasingly available in grocery stores across the country.

Can You Afford to Eat Organic?

Organic food has a reputation for being more expensive than conventional food, and sometimes this is true. There are many strategies for eating organic and staying within your budget.

Prioritize—Decide which items are the most important for you. For example: If your children drink a lot of milk, it should probably top the list.

Know the Dirty Dozen—If you can't afford to buy all organic, try to focus on buying organic versions of the so-called "Dirty Dozen." These are the fruits and vegetables that tend to carry the most pesticide residues.

THE DIRTY DOZEN
most contaminated produce:

1. Peaches
2. Apples
3. Bell Peppers
4. Celery
5. Nectarines
6. Strawberries
7. Cherries
8. Kale
9. Lettuce
10. Grapes (Imported)
11. Carrots
12. Pears

Source: www.foodnews.org
by the Environmental Working Group

Eat Low on the Food Chain—Organic meats and poultry are more expensive than vegetables, fruits, and grains. You might want to eat more meatless meals or decrease your portions of meat.

Buy Local and in Season—Out-of-season fruits and vegetables that have been flown from a long distance tend to be more expensive and use more energy to transport.

Start an Organic Garden—You can start small with a simple clay pot of organic herbs and go from there.

Cook More—Instead of buying packaged food, buy fresh foods like grains, beans, and vegetables and cook them yourself. Freshly prepared food is usually better for you, too.

Shop Around—Find a trusted organic brand at a good price.

How Can I Learn More?

We've sprinkled this cookbook with interesting facts, tips, bits of history, and quotes so you can enjoy learning about organic food a little bit at a time.

ORGANIC QUOTE

"With some foods—meat, milk, spinach, strawberries, cherries, peaches, and apples, to name a few—going organic really can help avoid the potential health risks associated with pesticides and animal infections."

Source: Dr. Mehmet Oz, professor, surgeon, and frequent guest on *The Oprah Winfrey Show*

The information shared here is just the tip of the iceberg when it comes to what is available. And there is a wonderful community of very committed people who are eager to share their thoughts and feelings about what it means to embrace an organic lifestyle. If you want to know more about organic food or the community of impassioned people behind it, there are lots of great Web sites to explore.

ORGANIZATION	INFORMATION	WEB SITE
USDA NOP	Substances and practices allowed by law	www.ams.usda.gov (click on National Organic Program)
The Organic Center	Research on the benefits of organic foods	www.organiccenter.org
Organic Trade Association	Industry and consumer information	www.ota.com
Organic Farming Research Foundation	Organic farming research and applications	www.ofrf.org
Rodale Institute	Research on organic vs. conventional farming	www.rodaleinstitute.org
Environmental Working Group	Information on pesticides, including "The Dirty Dozen"	www.foodnews.org
Organic.org	Organic made easy (just as their tagline says)	www.organic.org

O Organics™

We always like to think that O Organics has the potential to make organic food appealing to anyone and everyone. So it's heartwarming to get comments like the one below. It also reminds us that we are not alone in our efforts. There are many who are eager to make eating organic food a way of life in our communities and, even closer to home, in our own families. We're excited to be a part of that growing momentum.

When we started developing the O Organics brand, we realized it wasn't that easy to buy organic food. We thought people should be able to buy a full range of products and do so in a

"**I** wanted to say thanks for creating the *O* Organics line. I am *sooo* pleased with it. Each item that I buy is better than the next. I even have my hubby eating organic food, and he likes it."

—STEPHANIE, CHESAPEAKE BEACH, MD

regular grocery store, without having to spend a lot of money.

And since kids are really important people and a strong motivation to start buying organic food, we wanted to have something for them at each stage of their development.

for baby

for toddler

"Feeding children organic foods is something simple and practical that parents can do right now to protect their children and help them build healthy bodies."

—Dr. Alan Greene, Pediatrician and Board Member of The Organic Center

We know from experience that, in time, eating organic food can become a family affair as everyone begins to join in. And the reasons for going organic become more complex as people appreciate that it isn't just a personal choice but one that affects other people, animals, and our planet.

"Remember when you were a kid and you wanted to help save the world? Well, I have that job. It doesn't get much better than that. You too can help save the world one bite at a time."

—Julie Shryne, O Organics™ Senior Brand Manager

for kids

O Organics™ Recipes

BY DOMENICA CATELLI

"I champion organics for three simple reasons: taste, health benefits, and the environment. As a mother, chef, and educator, I feel so much better about what I create and share as a result of these benefits. If we simply choose one new organic product a week, we can all make a difference."

O Organics' mission starts with making organic food easily accessible, but it truly comes to life when good food is shared through passionate cooking. Organic foods can be more flavorful, and we believe organic recipes should be the same. So we engaged an experienced chef and cookbook author who shares our same beliefs to develop organic recipes with our product line in mind.

As a professional chef who is an advocate for the use of organic foods, Domenica Catelli strives to make organic cooking both healthy and delicious. She comes with strong credentials, having served as executive chef for the organic restaurant Raven's at the Stanford Inn in Mendocino, California. She has also been the spokesperson for the Organic Trade Association's national campaign, "Go Organic! for Earth Day," a judge on *Iron Chef America*, and a guest speaker on *Oprah and Friends* with Dr. Mehmet Oz on XM radio. And she knows what it means to be a mom who has to balance preparing good food with convenience every day.

The 22 recipes in this section are designed to assist with shopping by calling out those products that O Organics produces. Since O Organics consists of more than 300 products across every aisle of the grocery store, it is our hope that you will find many opportunities to create delicious organic dishes.

We raise a glass (of some organic beverage) to good organic cooking shared with family and the best of friends.

French Toast Casserole

Making this casserole saves you the trouble of standing over a griddle flipping individual slices of French toast. O Organics seeds and grains bread is packed with organic sunflower seeds, sesame seeds, oats, and wheat flour. It is naturally low in fat and is cholesterol-free.

1 (22-ounce) loaf O Organics seeds and grains bread
Butter-flavored cooking spray
8 O Organics large egg whites
2 cups O Organics fat-free milk
1 cup O Organics 100% pure no pulp orange juice
1 tablespoon O Organics ground cinnamon
2 tablespoons O Organics maple syrup
1 tablespoon vanilla extract
1 teaspoon ground nutmeg
Dash salt
½ cup O Organics blueberries
1 cup O Organics maple syrup
Powdered sugar (optional)

1. Preheat oven to 350°.
2. Arrange bread slices in 2 overlapping rows in a 13 x 9–inch baking dish coated with cooking spray.

3. Place egg whites in a large bowl; stir well with a whisk. Add milk and next 6 ingredients, stirring well with a whisk. Pour egg mixture over bread, covering all surfaces. Let stand 10 minutes. Coat with cooking spray; sprinkle with blueberries.

4. Bake, uncovered, at 350° for 40 to 45 minutes or until top is golden. Cut into squares and serve with maple syrup and powdered sugar, if desired. **YIELD:** 8 servings (serving size: 1 French toast square and 2 tablespoons syrup).

CALORIES 364; FAT 3.8g (sat 0.1g, mono 0.1g, poly 0.1g); PROTEIN 12.9g; CARB 68g; FIBER 5.3g; CHOL 1mg; IRON 1.8mg; SODIUM 490mg; CALC 167mg

Asparagus and Tomato Pesto Pasta

Fast and fresh, this pasta is also great served with grilled chicken breasts. Use the extra pesto to make Turkey and Pesto Grilled Cheese Sandwiches (recipe on page 32). The pesto will keep in the refrigerator for up to two weeks.

  8 ounces uncooked spaghetti or O Organics™ whole
     wheat spaghetti
  1 tablespoon O Organics extravirgin olive oil
 ¼ teaspoon crushed red pepper
2½ cups (2-inch) sliced asparagus (about 12 ounces)
1½ cups O Organics grape tomatoes, halved
  2 O Organics garlic cloves, minced
 ½ teaspoon salt
 ¼ teaspoon freshly ground black pepper
  2 tablespoons Mixed Herb Pesto (recipe on page 21)
  2 tablespoons chopped O Organics fresh basil
 ¼ cup grated Parmesan cheese

1. Cook pasta according to package directions, omitting salt and fat. Drain pasta in a colander over a bowl, reserving ¼ cup cooking liquid.

2. Heat olive oil in a large nonstick skillet over medium-high heat. Add red pepper and asparagus; cook 5 minutes or until asparagus is crisp-tender. Add tomatoes and garlic; cook 1 minute. Add pasta, salt, and remaining ingredients; toss well. Cook 2 minutes or until thoroughly heated, adding reserved ¼ cup pasta water, if needed.

YIELD: 4 servings (serving size: about 1½ cups).

CALORIES 336; FAT 10.1g (sat 2.1g mono 5.9g poly 1.9g); PROTEIN 12.1g; CARB 50.5g; FIBER 3.8g; CHOL 5mg; IRON 4mg; SODIUM 417mg; CALC 105mg

Asparagus and Tomato
Pesto Pasta

MIXED HERB PESTO:

2   tablespoons pine nuts, toasted
2   *O* Organics garlic cloves
1½ cups *O* Organics fresh flat leaf parsley
1   cup *O* Organics fresh mixed herbs (such as mint,
    basil, dill, oregano, and thyme)
¼   cup grated Parmesan cheese
¼   teaspoon salt
⅓   cup *O* Organics extravirgin olive oil

1. With food processor on, drop pine nuts and garlic through food chute; process until minced. Add parsley and next 3 ingredients; process until herbs are finely minced. With processor on, slowly pour oil through food chute; process until well blended. Spoon pesto into a zip-top plastic bag; store in refrigerator. **YIELD:** ¾ cup.
NOTE: For the 1 cup *O* Organics fresh mixed herbs, we used a combination of ½ cup fresh basil, 1 tablespoon fresh mint, 1 tablespoon fresh dill, 1 tablespoon fresh oregano, and 1 tablespoon fresh thyme.

PER TABLESPOON: CALORIES 75; FAT 7.8g (sat 1.3g, mono 4.9g, poly 1.4g); PROTEIN 1.2g; CARB 1g; FIBER 0.4g; CHOL 1mg; IRON 0.7mg; SODIUM 78mg; CALC 36mg

ORGANIC HISTORY

The USDA organic logo came into being in 2002. Since then, the organic market has experienced double-digit growth for over five years.

Source: USDA National Organic Program

Spicy Rotini Caprese

Caprese refers to a simple Italian salad of fresh mozzarella, tomatoes, and basil. This version adds whole wheat pasta for a heartier salad and crushed red pepper for a spicy kick. *O* Organics whole wheat pasta is made with 100% organic whole grain durum wheat that's grown without the use of synthetic pesticides. The entire durum wheat kernel is milled to produce pastas that are high in fiber with a rich nutty flavor.

1   (16-ounce) package uncooked *O* Organics whole
    wheat rotini
2½ teaspoons kosher salt, divided
2   tablespoons *O* Organics extravirgin olive oil
3   *O* Organics garlic cloves, minced
1   teaspoon crushed red pepper
2   pints *O* Organics grape tomatoes, cut in half
    lengthwise
8   ounces fresh mozzarella or bocancini, cut into
    ½-inch pieces
¼   cup *O* Organics fresh basil leaves, cut into thin strips
¼   teaspoon *O* Organics black pepper

1. Cook pasta according to package directions, adding 2 teaspoons kosher salt to water.
2. While pasta cooks, heat oil in a large nonstick skillet over medium heat. Reduce heat to low; add garlic and red pepper; sauté 1 minute. Add tomato; increase heat to medium, and sauté 2 minutes.
3. Drain pasta, reserving ½ cup pasta water; add pasta to tomatoes. Stir in mozzarella, basil, remaining ½ teaspoon salt, and black pepper. Add desired amount of reserved pasta water to pasta mixture; toss well. **YIELD:** 6 servings (serving size: 1½ cups).

CALORIES 415; FAT 14.5g (sat 6.1g, mono 5.8g, poly 0.9g); PROTEIN 17.2g; CARB 62g; FIBER 9.3g; CHOL 30mg; IRON 1mg; SODIUM 593mg; CALC 225mg

Spinach, Olive, and Tomato Pizza

O ORGANICS™ FOUR CHEESE STONE BAKED PIZZA FROM ITALY

Don't slave over a homemade pizza crust. Don't even order out. Just dress up an award-winning frozen *O* Organics four cheese stone baked pizza from Italy with a few additions and you'll think you're eating "the special" from a gourmet pizzeria.

Spinach, Olive, and Tomato Pizza

This pizza is so amazing that it won top honors in a national taste testing in 2009 in which 100,000 consumers participated.

   1   (8.1-ounce) O Organics four cheese stone baked pizza
   ⅓   cup O Organics baby spinach
   ¼   cup O Organics pitted kalamata olives, coarsely chopped (9 olives)
   ⅓   cup chopped O Organics grape tomatoes
   1   tablespoon chopped O Organics fresh basil, divided

1. Preheat oven according to package directions on pizza.
2. Arrange spinach, olives, tomato, and half of basil over pizza.
3. Bake pizza directly on oven rack according to package directions. Remove pizza from oven and sprinkle with remaining basil. **YIELD:** 2 servings (serving size: half of pizza).

CALORIES 298; FAT 12.6g (sat 4g, mono 3.5g, poly 5.0g); PROTEIN 12.4g; CARB 41g; FIBER 2.6g; CHOL 25mg; IRON 1mg; SODIUM 963mg; CALC 208mg

Simple Veggie Curry with Jasmine Rice

This vegetable curry is not only easy to prepare, but is loaded with good-for-you foods. *O* Organics frozen California style vegetables is a unique mix of organic broccoli florets, cauliflower florets, and carrot sticks.

   1   tablespoon O Organics extravirgin olive oil
   1½ cups chopped O Organics yellow onion
   1   tablespoon curry powder
   1   tablespoon minced peeled fresh ginger
   2½ cups (½-inch) cubed O Organics yellow potato (2 medium)
   2   cups O Organics vegetable broth, divided
   3   O Organics carrots, cut into ½-inch pieces
   1   (16-ounce) bag O Organics frozen California style vegetables
   1   cup O Organics raisins
   ½   cup O Organics plain low-fat yogurt
   1   teaspoon salt
   4   cups hot cooked O Organics long-grain Thai jasmine rice

1. Heat oil in a Dutch oven over medium heat. Add onion to pan; cook 10 minutes or until tender, stirring occasionally.
2. Add curry powder and ginger to pan; cook, stirring constantly, 1 minute. Add potato and 1 cup broth. Cover and cook 10 minutes or until potato is tender.
3. Add remaining broth, carrot, and frozen vegetables. Cover and bring to a boil over high heat; reduce heat, and simmer 7 minutes or until vegetables are tender, stirring occasionally. Stir in raisins, yogurt, and salt. Serve over rice. **YIELD:** 6 servings (serving size: 1 cup vegetables and ⅔ cup rice).

CALORIES 390; FAT 3g (sat 0.6g, mono 1.8g, poly 0.4g); PROTEIN 7.9g; CARB 83.7g; FIBER 6.4g; CHOL 2mg; IRON 2.4mg; SODIUM 643mg; CALC 89mg

Soy-Ginger Stir-Fry with Tofu

(pictured on page 2)

This colorful and filling vegetarian entrée boasts a hefty nutritional profile. And on top of that, it just tastes great.

2 tablespoons low-sodium soy sauce, divided
1 tablespoon water
1 (14-ounce) package soft tofu, drained and cut into
   ½-inch cubes
2 tablespoons O Organics extravirgin olive oil,
   divided
½ medium O Organics yellow onion, vertically sliced
2 tablespoons grated fresh ginger
2 cups sliced mushrooms
2½ cups O Organics fresh or frozen petite broccoli
   florets, chopped
2 cups snow peas, trimmed
1½ cups broccoli coleslaw
1 O Organics celery rib, cut into ½-inch pieces

1. Combine 1 tablespoon soy sauce, water, and tofu in a medium bowl; toss to coat. Set aside.
2. Heat 1 tablespoon oil in a large nonstick skillet over medium-high heat. Add onion and ginger; sauté 3 minutes. Add mushrooms and sauté 6 minutes or until tender.
3. Add broccoli and next 3 ingredients to pan; sauté 6 minutes or until vegetables are tender. Remove pan from heat. Stir in remaining 1 tablespoon soy sauce. Remove vegetables from pan; keep warm.
4. Heat remaining 1 tablespoon oil in pan over medium-high heat. Add tofu and cook 6 minutes or until browned. Add vegetables and cook 1 minute, stirring gently, or until thoroughly heated. **YIELD:** 4 servings (serving size: 1½ cups).

CALORIES 208; FAT 11g (sat 1g, mono 7.5g, poly 1.7g); PROTEIN 13.5g; CARB 13.8g; FIBER 4.9g; CHOL 0mg; IRON 3.1mg; SODIUM 318mg; CALC 197mg

Chicken Skewers

Brewer's yeast is a rich source of B vitamins and is often used as a health supplement. Serve these kid-friendly chicken bites with Broccoli with Pan-Roasted Peppers (recipe on page 190).

2 O Organics chicken breasts, cut into 1-inch cubes
1 teaspoon O Organics garlic powder
2 tablespoons low-sodium soy sauce
1 tablespoon water
1 tablespoon brewer's yeast
4 (6-inch) bamboo skewers
O Organics cooking spray

1. Preheat broiler.
2. Place first 5 ingredients in a medium bowl; toss well.
3. Thread chicken onto 4 (6-inch) skewers. Place skewers on a broiler pan coated with cooking spray; broil 3 to 4 minutes on each side or until done. **YIELD:** 2 servings (serving size: 2 skewers).
NOTE: As with all wooden skewers, be sure to soak them in water 30 minutes before you start the recipe. This will prevent the skewers from burning while broiling.

CALORIES 212; FAT 2.2g (sat 0.6g, mono 0.5g, poly 0.5g); PROTEIN 41.9g; CARB 3.9g; FIBER 1.5g; CHOL 99mg; IRON 2.3mg; SODIUM 649mg; CALC 31mg

ORGANIC HISTORY

In the Spring of 2009, First Lady Michelle Obama planted an organic garden at the White House. The garden provides fresh produce for the Obama family and serves as a valuable educational tool for all.

Chicken Skewers

Rosemary and Balsamic Beef with Arugula and Blue Cheese

(pictured on page 8)

Fresh herbs help turn this everyday dish into a masterpiece. For the best results, store fresh herbs in a plastic bag in your refrigerator's crisper.

> 2 tablespoons O Organics extravirgin olive oil
> 2 tablespoons O Organics balsamic vinegar
> 1 tablespoon minced O Organics fresh rosemary
> 1 pound beef tenderloin steak
> ¼ teaspoon kosher salt
> ¼ teaspoon freshly ground black pepper
> 2 cups O Organics baby arugula
> ¼ cup O Organics blue cheese dressing
> 1 cup pomegranate seeds
> 1 tablespoon fresh Italian parsley, chopped

1. Combine first 3 ingredients in a small bowl, stirring well. Brush marinade over steak; sprinkle with salt and pepper. Cover and let stand 45 minutes.
2. Preheat oven to 450°.
3. Place a 10-inch cast-iron skillet over medium-high heat. Add steak; cook 3 minutes on each side or until browned, turning occasionally.
4. Place skillet in oven. Bake steak at 450° for 10 minutes or until desired degree of doneness. Transfer steak to a warm platter; cover loosely with foil, and let stand 5 minutes.
5. Place ½ cup arugula on each of 4 individual serving plates. Cut meat into thin slices; arrange slices evenly over arugula. Drizzle accumulated juices evenly over steak, and top each salad with 1 tablespoon dressing and ¼ cup pomegranate seeds. Sprinkle salads evenly with parsley. Serve immediately. **YIELD:** 4 servings.

CALORIES 312; FAT 21g (sat 4.7g, mono 7.6g, poly 7.1g); PROTEIN 22.9g; CARB 8.9g; FIBER 0.6g; CHOL 64mg; IRON 1.9mg; SODIUM 321mg; CALC 47mg

Easy Cilantro Beef with Avocado-Mango Salsa

The bright yellow mango, red tomato, and green avocado of the salsa add festive color to this easy grilled beef entrée.

> ¼ cup O Organics balsamic vinegar
> 2 tablespoons chopped fresh cilantro
> 2 tablespoons O Organics extravirgin olive oil
> 2 tablespoons low-sodium soy sauce
> 1 tablespoon freshly ground black pepper
> ½ teaspoon kosher salt
> 2 pounds flank steak, trimmed
> Avocado-Mango Salsa

1. Combine first 6 ingredients in a large zip-top plastic bag. Add steak; seal bag, and marinate in refrigerator 8 hours or overnight.
2. Prepare grill.
3. Remove steak from bag, discarding marinade. Place on grill rack, and grill 8 minutes on each side or until desired degree of doneness. Let steak stand 5 minutes. Cut steak diagonally across grain into thin slices. Serve steak with Avocado-Mango Salsa. **YIELD:** 8 servings (serving size: 3 ounces flank steak and about ¼ cup Avocado-Mango Salsa).

CALORIES 261; FAT 13.9g (sat 3.5g, mono 7.3g, poly 1.3g); PROTEIN 25.6g; CARB 9g; FIBER 1.9g; CHOL 37mg; IRON 2.4mg; SODIUM 352mg; CALC 43mg

AVOCADO-MANGO SALSA:

> 1 cup O Organics frozen mango, thawed
> 1 small avocado, peeled and chopped
> ½ cup O Organics grape tomatoes, quartered
> ¼ cup chopped fresh cilantro
> 2½ tablespoons minced shallot (about 1 small)
> 2 tablespoons fresh lime juice
> 1½ tablespoons minced seeded jalapeño pepper (about 1 medium)
> 1½ teaspoons ground cumin
> 1 teaspoon O Organics extravirgin olive oil
> ⅛ teaspoon salt

1. Combine all ingredients in a small bowl; stir gently to combine. **YIELD:** 9 servings (serving size: ¼ cup).

CALORIES 60; FAT 4.1g (sat 0.6g, mono 2.5g, poly 0.5g); PROTEIN 0.8g; CARB 6.3 g; FIBER 1.7g; CHOL 0mg; IRON 0.5mg; SODIUM 37mg; CALC 9mg

Easy Cilantro Beef with
Avocado-Mango Salsa

and broth; bring to a boil. Cover, reduce heat, and simmer 15 minutes. Stir in remaining ½ cup basil.

2. Place one-fourth of tomato mixture in a blender; process until smooth. Pour pureed mixture into a large bowl. Repeat procedure with remaining three-fourths of tomato mixture. Ladle soup into bowls. Top each serving with croutons, if desired. **YIELD:** 4 servings (serving size: ⅔ cup).

NOTE: Be sure to remove center piece of blender lid to allow steam from the hot soup to escape. Place a clean towel over opening in blender lid to avoid splatters.

CALORIES 83; FAT 2.4g (sat 0.4g, mono 1.7g, poly 0.4g); PROTEIN 3.6g; CARB 11.9g; FIBER 2.3g; CHOL 0mg; IRON 0.4mg; SODIUM 1,000mg; CALC 24mg

10-Minute Bean Soup

Canned beans allow you to prepare this soup in just over 10 minutes. While the soup simmers, assemble a garden salad or sandwich to round out your meal.

Tomato-Basil Soup

Tomato-Basil Soup

O Organics tomatoes come from the central valley of California, where the soil and climate are perfect for growing produce. The diced tomatoes are packed the same day they're harvested after they've been washed, steam-peeled, and diced.

  2 teaspoons O Organics extravirgin olive oil
  ¼ teaspoon crushed red pepper
  ½ cup chopped O Organics onion
  2 cloves O Organics garlic, minced
  1 cup coarsely chopped O Organics fresh basil leaves, divided
  1 (28-ounce) can O Organics diced tomatoes, undrained
  3 cups O Organics chicken broth
    O Organics seasoned croutons (optional)

1. Heat oil in a large Dutch oven over medium heat. Add crushed red pepper and onion; sauté 5 minutes. Add garlic and ½ cup basil; sauté 2 minutes. Add tomatoes

  1 tablespoon O Organics extravirgin olive oil
  2 garlic cloves, minced
  ½ teaspoon crushed red pepper
  6 cups O Organics chicken broth
  1 (28-ounce) can O Organics diced tomatoes
  1 (15-ounce) can O Organics kidney beans, rinsed and drained
  1 (15-ounce) can O Organics black beans, rinsed and drained
  1 (15-ounce) can O Organics pinto beans, rinsed and drained
    O Organics sour cream (optional)
    Minced fresh cilantro (optional)

1. Heat oil in a large Dutch oven over medium-high heat. Add garlic and crushed red pepper; sauté 30 seconds.

2. Add broth and next 4 ingredients. Cover and cook 10 minutes, stirring occasionally.

3. Ladle soup into bowls. Garnish with sour cream and cilantro, if desired. **YIELD:** 6 servings (serving size: 2 cups).

CALORIES 191; FAT 2.4g (sat 0.3g, mono 1.7g, poly 0.4g); PROTEIN 11.4g; CARB 30g; FIBER 8.4g; CHOL 0mg; IRON 2.2mg; SODIUM 1,028mg; CALC 44mg

Mediterranean Lentil Soup

Red lentils, also known as Egyptian lentils, are a great source of calcium, vitamin A, and iron. If you have trouble finding red lentils, you may substitute brown (European) lentils. Serve with whole wheat crackers, if desired.

1 tablespoon O Organics extravirgin olive oil
1 medium O Organics yellow onion, finely chopped
2 medium O Organics carrots, finely chopped
2 stalks O Organics celery, finely chopped
1 tablespoon O Organics dried dill
4 O Organics garlic cloves, minced
8 cups O Organics chicken or vegetable broth
1 (16-ounce) package dried small red lentils (about 2¼ cups)
1 (14.5-ounce) can O Organics diced tomatoes
1 (15-ounce) can O Organics chickpeas (garbanzo beans), rinsed and drained
¼ cup fresh lemon juice

1. Heat oil in a large Dutch oven over medium-high heat. Add onion, carrot, and celery; cook 6 minutes or until onion is translucent, stirring frequently. Add dill and garlic, and cook 1 minute or until tender, stirring constantly. Add broth, lentils, and tomatoes. Bring to a boil; cover, reduce heat, and simmer 15 minutes or until lentils are tender.

2. Add chickpeas to pan. Cook 1 minute or until thoroughly heated. Stir in lemon juice just before serving.

YIELD: 8 servings (serving size: about 1¾ cup).

CALORIES 292; FAT 3.5g (sat 0.3g, mono 1.5g, poly 1.3g); PROTFIN 20.5g; CARB 45.4g; FIBER 10.8g; CHOL 0mg; IRON 4.2mg; SODIUM 677mg; CALC 62mg

Lemony Chicken
and Greens Soup

Lemony Chicken and Greens Soup

Kale is a great addition to this hearty soup. It provides beneficial amounts of iron, calcium, and vitamins A and C.

   8 cups O Organics chicken broth
1½ cups uncooked orzo (rice-shaped pasta)
1½ cups chopped cooked O Organics chicken
   2 cups chopped fresh kale
   2 stalks celery, finely chopped
   3 O Organics carrots, finely chopped
   2 cups O Organics fresh baby spinach
   ¼ teaspoon freshly ground black pepper
   2 tablespoons chopped O Organics fresh dill
   2 tablespoons fresh lemon juice
   ½ cup grated fresh Parmesan cheese

1. Bring broth and orzo to a boil in a large Dutch oven; cook 7 minutes.
2. Add chicken, kale, celery, and carrot; cook 5 minutes. Stir in spinach, pepper, dill, and lemon juice. Ladle soup into bowls. Sprinkle each serving evenly with cheese. Serve immediately. **YIELD:** 8 servings (serving size: 1½ cups).

CALORIES 230; FAT 3.7g (sat 1.3g, mono 1g, poly 1g); PROTEIN 18g; CARB 29g; FIBER 2.6g; CHOL 27mg; IRON 0.9mg; SODIUM 757mg; CALC 143mg

ORGANIC QUOTE

"Organic farming has been shown to provide major benefits for wildlife and the wider environment. The best that can be said about genetically engineered crops is that they will now be monitored to see how much damage they cause."

—Prince Charles

Turkey and Chicken Sausage Chili

Serve this flavorful chili with classic condiments, such as sour cream, chopped green onions, and shredded Cheddar cheese. Not only do they add flavor, but they add festive color, too.

   2 tablespoons O Organics extravirgin olive oil
   1 pound lean ground turkey
   1 (12-ounce) package chicken sausage, cut into ¼-inch slices
   1 medium O Organics yellow onion, chopped
   1 tablespoon ground cumin
   ½ teaspoon crushed red pepper
   3 tablespoons fresh O Organics garlic, chopped
   1 tablespoon low-sodium soy sauce
   1 (14.5-ounce) can diced tomatoes with basil, garlic, and oregano
   1 (15-ounce) can O Organics black beans, undrained
   1 (15-ounce) can O Organics red kidney beans, undrained
   1 (15-ounce) can O Organics pinto beans, undrained
   1 cup O Organics chicken broth
   1 cup water
   ¾ cup O Organics sharp cheddar cheese
   O Organics chopped green onions (optional)
   Fat-free sour cream (optional)

1. Heat oil in a Dutch oven over medium heat. Add turkey and sausage; cook 6 minutes or until browned, stirring to crumble turkey. Remove from pan and keep warm.
2. Add onion, cumin, and crushed red pepper to pan; cook 5 minutes over medium heat or until onion is translucent. Add garlic; cook 30 seconds, stirring constantly.
3. Return turkey and sausage to pan. Add soy sauce and next 6 ingredients. Bring to a boil; cover, reduce heat, and simmer 15 minutes. Ladle chili into bowls, and sprinkle evenly with cheese. Serve with green onions and sour cream, if desired. **YIELD:** 9 servings (serving size: about 1 cup).

CALORIES 351; FAT 12.1g (sat 4g, mono 4.8g, poly 3.1g); PROTEIN 29g; CARB 32.8g; FIBER 9g; CHOL 68mg; IRON 6.9mg; SODIUM 813mg; CALC 162mg

Hummus, Tomato, and Cucumber Sandwiches

  6 tablespoons hummus
  8 slices O Organics seeds and grains bread
  4 small plum tomatoes, thinly sliced
24 thin slices English cucumber
  1 tablespoon O Organics balsamic vinegar
  4 slices red onion
  8 large O Organics basil leaves
  4 slices O Organics sharp Cheddar cheese

1. Spread hummus evenly on one side of each slice of bread.
2. Combine tomatoes, cucumber, and vinegar in a small bowl; divide evenly among 4 bread slices. Top each with 1 onion slice, 2 basil leaves, 1 cheese slice, and 1 bread slice. **YIELD:** 4 servings (serving size: 1 sandwich).

CALORIES 335; FAT 15.9g (sat 5.7g, mono 4.6g, poly 5.4g); PROTEIN 13.5g; CARB 35.5g; FIBER 6.1g; CHOL 25mg; IRON 1.6mg; SODIUM 574mg; CALC 221mg

HUMMUS:

  1 (15-ounce) can O Organics chickpeas (garbanzo beans), rinsed and drained
¼ cup fresh lemon juice
  1 tablespoon tahini (sesame-seed paste)
  2 O Organics garlic cloves
½ teaspoon ground cumin
½ teaspoon salt
⅓ cup O Organics extravirgin olive oil

1. Combine first 6 ingredients in a food processor; pulse until blended. With food processor on, slowly pour olive oil through food chute; process until smooth or to desired consistency. **YIELD:** 1¾ cups.

CALORIES 36; FAT 3.1g (sat 0.4g, mono 2g, poly 0.5g); PROTEIN 0.7g; CARB 2g; FIBER 0.3g; CHOL 0mg; IRON 0.2mg; SODIUM 51mg; CALC 5mg

Spicy Egg Salad Sandwiches

  2 tablespoons chopped O Organics fresh dill
  1 tablespoon O Organics extravirgin olive oil
  1 tablespoon dill pickle juice
  1 tablespoon mayonnaise
¼ teaspoon salt
⅛ teaspoon O Organics black pepper
¾ cup finely minced O Organics celery (2 stalks)
¼ cup minced O Organics yellow onion
  1 tablespoon minced seeded jalapeño pepper
  6 hard-cooked large O Organics eggs, coarsely chopped
  8 slices O Organics seeds and grains bread

1. Combine first 6 ingredients in a large bowl, stirring well. Add celery and next 3 ingredients; stir gently until combined.
2. Spoon about ½ cup egg salad onto each of 4 bread slices; top with remaining slices. **YIELD:** 4 servings (serving size: 1 sandwich).

CALORIES 339; FAT 17.3g (sat 3.3g, mono 6.8g, poly 5.8g); PROTEIN 15.7g; CARB 28.6g; FIBER 4.4g; CHOL 319mg; IRON 1.7mg; SODIUM 668mg; CALC 86mg

Turkey and Pesto Grilled Cheese Sandwich

Fresh pesto and roasted turkey add exceptional flavors to an everyday grilled cheese. You can store extra Mixed Herb Pesto in the refrigerator for up to two weeks. This recipe can easily be doubled to serve two or even quadrupled to serve four.

  2 teaspoons Mixed Herb Pesto (recipe on page 21)
  2 slices O Organics seeds and grains bread
  1 slice O Organics Havarti cheese
  2 (2-ounce) slices O Organics oven-roasted turkey breast
     Butter-flavored cooking spray

1. Spread 1 teaspoon pesto on each slice of bread; top each bread slice with cheese, turkey, and remaining bread slice. Lightly coat sandwich with cooking spray.
2. Heat a large nonstick skillet over medium heat. Cook sandwich 3 minutes on each side or until lightly toasted. **YIELD:** 1 serving (serving size: 1 sandwich).

CALORIES 448; FAT 18.9g (sat 6.8g, mono 4.7g, poly 4.4g); PROTEIN 38g; CARB 26.7g; FIBER 4.3g; CHOL 66.5mg; IRON 1.9mg; SODIUM 1,250mg; CALC 263mg

Spicy Egg Salad Sandwiches

Basil and Cheese–Stuffed Turkey Burgers

A traditional turkey burger gets a makeover when stuffed with basil and Cheddar. Serve with baked chips if you'd like.

- 1½   pounds ground turkey breast
- ½   teaspoon salt
- ½   teaspoon O Organics black pepper
- 2   teaspoons ground cumin
- ½   tablespoon O Organics garlic powder
- 1   tablespoon O Organics extravirgin olive oil
- 4   slices O Organics sharp Cheddar cheese
- 4   O Organics fresh basil leaves
- O Organics cooking spray
- 4   (1.8-ounce) white wheat hamburger buns
- O Organics tomato ketchup (optional)
- O Organics Dijon mustard (optional)

1. Prepare grill.
2. Combine first 6 ingredients in a medium bowl. Divide mixture into 8 equal portions, shaping each into a ½-inch-thick patty. Place 1 slice of cheese and 1 basil leaf in the center of 1 patty, tearing cheese slice to fit and leaving a ¼-inch border around edges. Top with 1 patty and press edges to seal. Press patty to ½-inch-thickness. Repeat procedure with remaining patties, cheese, and basil.
3. Place patties on grill rack coated with cooking spray. Grill 4 minutes on each side or until done. Top each bottom half of bun with 1 patty. Add ketchup and mustard, if desired. Top patties with remaining bread slices. **YIELD:** 4 servings (serving size: 1 burger).

CALORIES 413; FAT 16g (sat 6.8g, mono 4.7g, poly 3.8g); PROTEIN 50g; CARB 23g; FIBER 5.7g; CHOL 93mg; IRON 4.3mg; SODIUM 799mg; CALC 416mg

ORGANIC TIP
A simple way to think about the definition of organic food is to think in terms of the four no's: no synthetic pesticides, no genetic modification, no growth hormones, and no antibiotics.

Crunchy Asian Veggie Slaw

Agave nectar, also known as century plant, is a great alternative sweetener with a low glycemic index.

- 2   small radishes, halved
- ¼   cup chopped peeled jicama
- ¼   cup chopped O Organics carrots
- 2¼   cups thinly sliced cabbage
- ¼   cup O Organics frozen edamame, thawed
- ¼   cup O Organics frozen green peas, thawed
- ½   medium red bell pepper, cut into 2-inch strips
- ½   cup diced peeled avocado
- ½   cup chopped peeled cucumber
- 2   tablespoons rice vinegar
- ¼   teaspoon salt
- ¼   teaspoon O Organics black pepper
- 1   tablespoon agave nectar
- 1   tablespoons O Organics extravirgin olive oil
- 1½   teaspoons tamari
- 1   teaspoons dark sesame oil
- 2   tablespoons fresh lime juice
- 2   tablespoons chopped fresh cilantro
- 1   tablespoon chopped O Organics fresh mint
- 1½   teaspoons black sesame seeds

1. Combine first 3 ingredients in a food processor; process until finely chopped.
2. Combine radish mixture and cabbage in a large bowl. Add edamame and next 4 ingredients.
3. Combine vinegar and next 4 ingredients in a small bowl, stirring with a whisk. Add tamari, sesame oil, and lime juice; stir with a whisk to combine. Pour dressing over cabbage mixture, tossing well to coat. Add cilantro, mint, and sesame seeds; toss to coat. Serve immediately.
YIELD: 4 servings (serving size: ⅔ cup).

CALORIES 151; FAT 9.9g (sat 1.5g, mono 5.1g, poly 2.8g); PROTEIN 3.7g; CARB 14.6g; FIBER 4.6g; CHOL 0mg; IRON 1mg; SODIUM 308mg; CALC 40mg

Crunchy Asian Veggie Slaw

Apple, Fresh Herb, and Walnut Salad

2 tablespoons O Organics balsamic vinegar
1 tablespoon O Organics extravirgin olive oil
½ teaspoon kosher salt
½ teaspoon O Organics black pepper
1 (5-ounce) package O Organics herb salad mix
1 O Organics Granny Smith apple, cut into
    16 wedges
½ cup O Organics walnut pieces and halves, chopped

ORGANIC FACT
Organic apples are 25% higher in 11 key nutrients than non-organic apples. "It's the organic apple a day that keeps the doctor away."

Source: CCOF

1. Combine first 4 ingredients in a large bowl; stir well with a whisk. Add salad mix, apple, and walnuts; toss well. **YIELD:** 6 servings (serving size: about 1⅔ cups).

CALORIES 109; FAT 8.7g (sat 0.9g, mono 2.5g, poly 4.9g); PROTEIN 2.2g; CARB 7.9g; FIBER 1.9g; CHOL 0mg; IRON 1.5mg; SODIUM 178mg; CALC 36mg

Basil-Balsamic Bean Salad

O Organics beans are picked when perfectly ripe, removed from their shells, then very carefully cleaned and cooked.

1   (15-ounce) can O Organics kidney beans, rinsed and drained
1   (15-ounce) can O Organics black beans, rinsed and drained
1   (15-ounce) can O Organics chickpeas (garbanzo beans), rinsed and drained
¾   cup finely minced O Organics celery (2 stalks)
½   cup finely chopped red onion
⅓   cup chopped O Organics fresh basil leaves
3   tablespoons O Organics balsamic vinegar
2   teaspoons O Organics extravirgin olive oil
¼   teaspoon O Organics black pepper

1. Combine all ingredients in a large bowl, stirring well.
YIELD: 10 servings (serving size: ½ cup).

CALORIES 95; FAT 1.4g (sat 0.1g, mono 0.7g, poly 0.2g); PROTEIN 5g; CARB 16g; FIBER 3.5g; CHOL 0mg; IRON 1.4mg; SODIUM 55mg; CALC 34mg

Blueberry Smoothie Pops

Blueberry Smoothie Pops

Wild blueberries have a beautiful deep blue color and intense flavor not found in farmed berries. *O* Organics blueberries are grown in the mountains of Quebec.

1   cup O Organics frozen wild blueberries
1   ripe banana, frozen
2   cups O Organics blueberry juice
½   cup O Organics vanilla low-fat yogurt
2   tablespoons O Organics honey

1. Combine all ingredients in a blender; process until smooth, scraping sides. Pour mixture into popsicle molds and freeze 8 hours or until firm. **YIELD:** 12 servings (serving size: 1 pop).

NOTE: Peel the banana before freezing it so the stringy fibers won't stick to the fruit.

CALORIES 60; FAT 0.2g (sat 0.1g, mono 0g, poly 0g); PROTEIN 0.5g; CARB 14.7g; FIBER 0.6g; CHOL 1mg; IRON 0.2mg; SODIUM 10mg; CALC 14mg

APPETIZERS & BEVERAGES

Caramelized Black Bean "Butter", page 40;
and Mango Mojito, page 53

Toffee Dip with Apples

Crisp, tart apples are a perfect match for this sweet dip. Consider swapping out Fuji for the Red Delicious apples, if you prefer.

- ¾ cup packed brown sugar
- ½ cup powdered sugar
- 1 teaspoon vanilla extract
- 1 (8-ounce) block ⅓-less-fat cream cheese, softened
- ¾ cup toffee bits (about 4 ounces)
- 1 cup pineapple juice
- 6 Red Delicious apples, each cored and cut into 8 wedges
- 6 Granny Smith apples, each cored and cut into 8 wedges

1. Combine first 4 ingredients in a bowl; beat at medium speed of a mixer until smooth. Add toffee bits, and mix well. Cover and chill.

2. Combine juice and apples in a bowl; toss well. Drain apples; serve with dip. **YIELD:** 2 cups (serving size: 1 tablespoon dip and 3 apple wedges).

CALORIES 92 (28% from fat); FAT 2.9g (sat 1.8g, mono 0.8g, poly 0.2g); PROTEIN 0.8g; CARB 16.9g; FIBER 1.4g; CHOL 8mg; IRON 0.2mg; SODIUM 51mg; CALC 13mg

Caramelized Black Bean "Butter"

(pictured on page 38)

- 1 tablespoon olive oil
- 4 cups chopped onion
- 2 (15-ounce) cans black beans, rinsed and drained
- 1 tablespoon balsamic vinegar
- 2 teaspoons unsweetened cocoa
- ½ teaspoon salt
- ½ teaspoon paprika
- 1 tablespoon chopped fresh parsley

1. Heat oil in a large nonstick skillet over medium-high heat. Add onion; sauté 10 minutes or until golden. Place onion, beans, vinegar, cocoa, salt, and paprika in a food processor; process until smooth. Place bean mixture in a medium bowl. Sprinkle with parsley. **YIELD:** 3 cups (serving size: 1 tablespoon).

CALORIES 17 (2% from fat); FAT 0.4g (sat 0.1g, mono 0.2g, poly 0g); PROTEIN 0.7g; CARB 3.1g; FIBER 0.8g; CHOL 0mg; IRON 0.2mg; SODIUM 48mg; CALC 7mg

Lime-Spiked Black Bean Dip

This Tex-Mex dip is always a popular dish for casual gatherings.

- 2 (15-ounce) cans black beans, rinsed and drained
- 1 cup grated carrot
- ½ cup fresh lime juice (about 2 limes)
- ¼ cup finely chopped green onions
- ¼ cup chopped fresh cilantro
- 1 teaspoon minced garlic
- ¼ teaspoon salt
- ⅛ teaspoon ground red pepper

1. Place black beans in a food processor, and pulse until almost smooth. Combine beans, carrot, and remaining ingredients in a medium bowl, stirring until well blended. Let stand 30 minutes. **YIELD:** 5 cups (serving size: 2 tablespoons).

CALORIES 19 (5% from fat); FAT 0.1g (sat 0g, mono 0.1g, poly 0g); PROTEIN 1.2g; CARB 3.9g; FIBER 1.3g; CHOL 0mg; IRON 0.3mg; SODIUM 61mg; CALC 8mg

Field Pea Dip

A take on Middle Eastern hummus, this dip uses field peas instead of chickpeas.

- 2 cups fresh pink-eyed peas
- 2 (14½-ounce) cans fat-free, less-sodium chicken broth
- 6 tablespoons low-fat mayonnaise
- 2 tablespoons tahini (sesame-seed paste)
- 2 tablespoons hot pepper vinegar
- 1 tablespoon fresh lemon juice
- 2 teaspoons paprika
- 2 garlic cloves, minced
- Chopped fresh chives (optional)

1. Combine peas and broth in a large saucepan; bring to a boil. Reduce heat; simmer, partially covered, 30 minutes or until tender. Drain peas. Place peas in a food processor; pulse 10 times or until coarsely chopped.

2. Combine peas, mayonnaise, and next 5 ingredients in a bowl, stirring until blended. Garnish with chives, if desired. **YIELD:** 2 cups (serving size: 2 tablespoons).

CALORIES 109 (27% from fat); FAT 3.3g (sat 0.5g, mono 1.6g, poly 1g); PROTEIN 5.5g; CARB 15.2g; FIBER 2.5g; CHOL 2mg; IRON 1.9mg; SODIUM 53mg; CALC 28mg

Guacamole

Garlic and Sun-Dried Tomato Hummus

Sun-dried tomatoes replace tahini (sesame seed paste) to flavor this popular Middle Eastern dip. They also give the dish a warm coral-like color.

Cooking spray
2 (6-inch) pitas, each cut into 10 wedges
¼ cup water
2 tablespoons chopped oil-packed sun-dried tomato halves
½ teaspoon salt
¼ teaspoon freshly ground black pepper
2 garlic cloves
1 (15-ounce) can chickpeas (garbanzo beans), drained

1. Preheat oven to 425°.
2. Coat a baking sheet with cooking spray. Place pita wedges on pan; coat with cooking spray. Bake at 425° for 6 minutes or until golden.
3. Combine water, tomato, salt, pepper, garlic, and beans in a food processor; process until smooth. Serve with pita wedges. **YIELD:** 5 servings (serving size: ¼ cup hummus and 4 pita wedges).

CALORIES 175 (9% from fat); FAT 1.7g (sat 0.2g, mono 0.5g, poly 0.6g); PROTEIN 6.6g; CARB 33.7g; FIBER 4.5g; CHOL 0mg; IRON 1.9mg; SODIUM 623mg; CALC 52mg

Guacamole

Lime juice, onion, cilantro, and cumin lend lots of flavor. When storing, press plastic wrap against the surface to help keep the guacamole from turning brown.

1 cup finely chopped onion
¼ cup minced fresh cilantro
2 tablespoons fresh lime juice
½ teaspoon salt
¼ teaspoon ground cumin
¼ teaspoon freshly ground black pepper
2 ripe peeled avocados, seeded and coarsely mashed
12 ounces unsalted baked tortilla chips
Cilantro sprigs (optional)

1. Combine first 7 ingredients in a medium bowl, stirring well. Cover and chill. Serve with baked tortilla chips. Garnish with cilantro sprigs, if desired. **YIELD:** 16 servings (serving size: 2 tablespoons guacamole and about 10 chips).

CALORIES 122 (27% from fat); FAT 3.9g (sat 0.6g, mono 0g, poly 0g); PROTEIN 3g; CARB 21.1g; FIBER 3.6g; CHOL 0mg; IRON 0mg; SODIUM 74mg; CALC 3mg

Spinach and Artichoke Dip

Any potluck or open house will be complete with this lightened version of a popular restaurant appetizer.

  2 cups (8 ounces) shredded part-skim mozzarella cheese, divided
  ½ cup fat-free sour cream
  ¼ cup (1 ounce) grated fresh Parmesan cheese, divided
  ¼ teaspoon black pepper
  3 garlic cloves, crushed
  1 (14-ounce) can artichoke hearts, drained and chopped
  1 (8-ounce) block ⅓-less-fat cream cheese, softened
  1 (8-ounce) block fat-free cream cheese, softened
  ½ (10-ounce) package frozen chopped spinach, thawed, drained, and squeezed dry
  1 (13.5-ounce) package baked tortilla chips (about 16 cups)

1. Preheat oven to 350°.
2. Combine 1½ cups mozzarella, sour cream, 2 tablespoons Parmesan, and next 6 ingredients in a large bowl; stir until well blended. Spoon mixture into a 1½-quart baking dish. Sprinkle with remaining ½ cup mozzarella and remaining 2 tablespoons Parmesan. Bake at 350° for 30 minutes or until bubbly and golden brown. Serve with tortilla chips. **YIELD:** 5½ cups (serving size: ¼ cup dip and about 6 tortilla chips).

CALORIES 148 (30% from fat); FAT 5g (sat 2.9g, mono 1.5g, poly 0.5g); PROTEIN 7.7g; CARB 18.3g; FIBER 1.5g; CHOL 17mg; IRON 0.6mg; SODIUM 318mg; CALC 164mg

Warm Pumpkin Cheese Dip

The unusual combination of goat cheese and pumpkin was a surprise hit in our Test Kitchens. Serve the dip with crisp breadsticks, bagel chips, or toasted French or sourdough baguette slices.

  1¼ cups plain low-fat yogurt
  ½ teaspoon butter
  1 cup thinly sliced leek
  2 teaspoons chopped fresh or ½ teaspoon dried thyme
  1 teaspoon salt
  ¾ cup (3 ounces) goat cheese
  ⅓ cup evaporated fat-free milk
  1 (15-ounce) can pumpkin
  3 large egg whites

1. Preheat oven to 375°.
2. Spoon yogurt onto several layers of heavy-duty paper towels; spread to ½-inch thickness. Cover with additional paper towels; let stand 5 minutes. Scrape into a large bowl using a rubber spatula.
3. Melt butter in a skillet over medium-high heat. Add leek; sauté 5 minutes or until tender. Remove from heat, and stir in thyme and salt. Place strained yogurt, goat cheese, and remaining ingredients in a large bowl, and beat with a mixer at medium speed just until smooth. Stir in leek mixture. Spoon pumpkin mixture into a 1-quart baking dish. Bake at 375° for 25 minutes or until dip is bubbly and lightly browned. Serve warm. **YIELD:** 3½ cups (serving size: ¼ cup).

CALORIES 57 (36% from fat); FAT 2.3g (sat 1.6g, mono 0.5g, poly 0.1g); PROTEIN 3.9g; CARB 5.5g; FIBER 1g; CHOL 7mg; IRON 0.7mg; SODIUM 306mg; CALC 81mgg

Roasted Sweet Onion Dip

Serve this dip with pita chips or carrot sticks. Making the recipe a day ahead allows the flavors to meld.

  2 large Vidalia or other sweet onions, peeled and quartered
  1 tablespoon olive oil
  1 teaspoon salt, divided
  1 whole garlic head
  ⅓ cup low-fat sour cream
  ¼ cup chopped fresh parsley
  1 tablespoon fresh lemon juice

1. Preheat oven to 425°.

2. Place onion in a large bowl; drizzle with oil. Sprinkle with ½ teaspoon salt; toss to coat. Remove white papery skin from garlic head (do not peel or separate the cloves). Wrap in foil. Place onion and foil-wrapped garlic on a baking sheet. Bake at 425° for 1 hour; cool 10 minutes. Chop onion. Separate garlic cloves, and squeeze to extract garlic pulp. Discard skins. Combine onion, garlic, ½ teaspoon salt, sour cream, and remaining ingredients in a large bowl. Cover and chill 1 hour. **YIELD:** 8 servings (serving size: ¼ cup).

CALORIES 66 (34% from fat); FAT 2.5g (sat 0.8g, mono 1.3g, poly 0.2g); PROTEIN 1.7g; CARB 10.3g; FIBER 1.5g; CHOL 3.3mg; IRON 0.4mg; SODIUM 308mg; CALC 42mg

Spiced Red Lentil Dip with Pita Crisps

You can substitute green or brown lentils for the red, but the dip won't be as pretty.

DIP:
- 1 cup dried small red lentils
- 1 bay leaf
- 1 tablespoon olive oil
- 1 cup finely chopped onion
- 2 tablespoons pine nuts
- 1 tablespoon tomato paste
- 1 teaspoon fine sea salt
- 1 teaspoon ground coriander seeds
- ½ teaspoon ground cumin
- ½ teaspoon ground caraway seeds
- ⅛ teaspoon ground red pepper
- 3 garlic cloves, minced
- 3 tablespoons fresh lemon juice

PITA CRISPS:
- 4 (6-inch) pitas, each cut into 5 wedges
- Cooking spray
- ⅛ teaspoon fine sea salt
- ⅛ teaspoon freshly ground black pepper

1. Preheat oven to 350°.

2. To prepare dip, place lentils and bay leaf in a large saucepan; cover with water to 2 inches above lentils. Bring to a boil. Cover, reduce heat, and simmer 8 minutes or until tender. Drain well. Discard bay leaf.

3. Heat oil in a small nonstick skillet over medium-high heat. Add onion and nuts; saute 5 minutes or until nuts are lightly browned. Stir in tomato paste and next

6 ingredients; cook 5 minutes, stirring occasionally. Stir in juice. Combine lentils and onion mixture in a food processor; process until smooth.

4. To prepare pita crisps, coat 1 side of each pita wedge with cooking spray; sprinkle wedges evenly with ⅛ teaspoon salt and black pepper. Arrange wedges in a single layer on a baking sheet. Bake at 350° for 20 minutes or until golden. **YIELD:** 10 servings (serving size: about ¼ cup dip and 2 pita crisps).

CALORIES 159 (15% from fat); FAT 2.6g (sat 0.4g, mono 1.4g, poly 0.6g); PROTEIN 7.4g; CARB 27g; FIBER 3.9g; CHOL 0mg; IRON 2mg; SODIUM 395mg; CALC 46mg

Spiced Red Lentil Dip with Pita Crisps

Adobo Chips with Warm Goat Cheese and Cilantro Salsa

The salsa derives smoky heat from chipotle chiles, and adobo sauce adds a vinegary touch to the chips.

SALSA:
- 1 (7-ounce) can chipotle chiles in adobo sauce
- 2 cups chopped fresh cilantro (about 1 bunch)
- 1 cup finely chopped tomatillos (about 4)
- ¼ cup minced red onion
- ¼ cup fresh lime juice

CHIPS:
- 2½ teaspoons fresh lime juice
- 1 teaspoon canola oil
- 1 teaspoon adobo sauce
- ½ teaspoon paprika
- ¼ teaspoon cumin
- 8 (6-inch) white corn tortillas

CHEESE:
- ½ cup (4 ounces) block-style fat-free cream cheese, softened
- ¼ cup (2 ounces) goat cheese

1. To prepare salsa, remove 2 chipotle chiles from can, and finely chop chiles to measure 2 teaspoons. Remove 1 teaspoon adobo sauce from can, and set aside (reserve remaining chipotle chiles and adobo sauce for another use). Combine 2 teaspoons chiles, cilantro, tomatillos, red onion, and ¼ cup lime juice in a bowl; cover and chill 1 hour.

2. Preheat oven to 375°.

3. To prepare chips, combine 2½ teaspoons lime juice, canola oil, adobo sauce, paprika, and cumin in a small bowl, stirring with a whisk. Brush 1 tortilla with about ¼ teaspoon juice mixture, spreading to edge. Top with another tortilla; repeat procedure with juice mixture. Repeat procedure 6 more times (you will have 1 stack of 8 tortillas). Using a sharp knife, cut tortilla stack into 6 wedges. Place wedges in a single layer on baking sheets. Bake at 375° for 15 minutes; turn wedges. Bake an additional 10 minutes.

4. Reduce oven temperature to 350°.

5. To prepare cheese, combine cream cheese and goat cheese in a small bowl; stir until blended. Spread cheese mixture into a shallow 6-ounce ramekin or baking dish; cover with foil. Bake at 350° for 10 minutes or just until warm. **YIELD:** 8 servings (serving size: 6 chips, 1½ tablespoons cheese mixture, and about ¼ cup salsa).

CALORIES 95 (29% from fat); FAT 3.3g (sat 1.2g, mono 0.9g, poly 0.6g); PROTEIN 4.9g; CARB 13.4g; FIBER 1.8g; CHOL 4.4mg; IRON 0.5mg; SODIUM 131mg; CALC 60mg

Avocado-Mango Salsa with Roasted Corn Chips

12 (6-inch) corn tortillas, each cut into 6 wedges
Cooking spray
¼ teaspoon kosher salt, divided
1¼ cups chopped peeled avocado
1 cup chopped peeled mango
1 tablespoon finely chopped fresh cilantro
4 teaspoons fresh lime juice
Cilantro sprigs (optional)

1. Preheat oven to 425°.
2. Arrange tortilla wedges in a single layer on baking sheets coated with cooking spray. Coat wedges with cooking spray, and sprinkle ⅛ teaspoon salt evenly over wedges. Bake at 425° for 8 minutes or until crisp.
3. Combine remaining ⅛ teaspoon salt, avocado, mango, chopped cilantro, and juice, tossing gently. Garnish with cilantro sprigs, if desired. Let stand 10 minutes. Serve with chips. **YIELD:** 12 servings (serving size: about 3 table-spoons salsa and 6 chips).

CALORIES 92 (30% from fat); FAT 3.1g (sat 0.5g, mono 1.7g, poly 0.6g); PROTEIN 1.9g; CARB 15.8g; FIBER 2.4g; CHOL 0mg; IRON 0.6mg; SODIUM 83mg; CALC 49mg

ORGANIC TIP
Starting an organic herb garden can be an easy weekend project. Herb plants require low maintenance and save money. To start, try growing commonly used culinary herbs in a large clay pot.

Warm Olives with Fennel and Orange

It's amazing what changing the expected temperature of a dish can do. Gentle heat from the oven intensifies the richness of olives, fennel, and orange rind in this Mediterranean-accented appetizer. The multilayered flavors dazzle palates that expect lackluster olives straight from the jar. Buy pitted kalamata olives to speed up preparation.

1 tablespoon extravirgin olive oil
1½ teaspoons grated orange rind
1 teaspoon chopped fresh rosemary
½ teaspoon fennel seeds
1 small fennel bulb, cut into ¼-inch-thick wedges
12 kalamata olives, pitted
12 pimiento-stuffed olives
1 tablespoon balsamic vinegar

1. Heat oil in a large nonstick skillet over medium heat. Add rind, rosemary, fennel seeds, and fennel wedges; cook 5 minutes, stirring frequently. Add olives; cook 1 minute. Remove from heat; stir in vinegar. Place fennel mixture in an 8-inch square baking dish. Cover and let stand at least 2 hours.
2. Preheat oven to 250°.
3. Uncover olive mixture. Bake at 250° for 10 minutes or until heated, stirring once. **YIELD:** 6 servings (serving size: about ⅓ cup).

CALORIES 72 (71% from fat); FAT 5.7g (sat 0.3g, mono 4.7g, poly 0.7g); PROTEIN 0.5g; CARB 5.2g; FIBER 1.3g; CHOL 0mg; IRON 0.4mg; SODIUM 331mg; CALC 24mg

Vegetable and Tofu Lettuce Wraps with Miso Sambal

The creamy texture of both the avocado pieces and the tofu slices is a pleasant contrast to the crisp vegetables.

MISO SAMBAL:

- 2 tablespoons chile paste with garlic (such as sambal oelek)
- 2 tablespoons chopped peeled fresh ginger
- 2 tablespoons white miso (soybean paste)
- 2 tablespoons rice wine vinegar
- 1½ tablespoons sugar
- 1½ teaspoons dark sesame oil

WRAPS:

- 1 cup matchstick-cut English cucumber
- ½ cup cilantro sprigs
- 2 tablespoons chopped dry-roasted peanuts
- 1 (12.3-ounce) package reduced-fat firm tofu, drained and cut into ½-inch-thick strips
- ½ avocado, peeled and thinly sliced
- 12 large Boston lettuce leaves

1. To prepare miso sambal, combine first 6 ingredients in a blender; process until smooth.

2. To prepare wraps, divide cucumber, cilantro, peanuts, tofu, and avocado evenly among lettuce leaves. Drizzle each with about 1½ teaspoons sambal; roll up. **YIELD:** 6 servings (serving size: 2 wraps).

CALORIES 106 (51% from fat); FAT 6g (sat 0.9g, mono 2.9g, poly 1.5g); PROTEIN 5.5g; CARB 8.5g; FIBER 1.5g; CHOL 0mg; IRON 1.1mg; SODIUM 261mg; CALC 27mg

Chunky Cherry Tomatoes with Basil

This vibrant-colored mixture shouldn't stand for much longer than an hour before serving or the salt will draw all the juices from the tomatoes. Serve with slices of toasted country bread, or use as a topping for grilled fish or roasted asparagus.

   3 cups quartered cherry tomatoes
   1 cup loosely packed, thinly sliced fresh basil
   1 tablespoon extravirgin olive oil
   1 tablespoon red wine vinegar
   1 tablespoon balsamic vinegar
   ½ teaspoon salt
   ¼ teaspoon freshly ground black pepper
   1 large garlic clove, minced

1. Combine all ingredients in a medium bowl; let stand 1 hour. **YIELD:** 3 cups (serving size: ¼ cup).

CALORIES 20 (59% from fat); FAT 1.3g (sat 0.2g, mono 0.9g, poly 0.2g); PROTEIN 0.4g; CARB 2.3g; FIBER 0.6g; CHOL 0mg; IRON 0.3mg; SODIUM 101mg; CALC 9mg

Savory Yogurt Cheesecake with Caramelized Onions

FILLING:
   1 (32-ounce) carton plain low-fat yogurt
   ½ cup (4 ounces) block-style fat-free cream cheese, softened
   1 cup part-skim ricotta cheese
   ½ teaspoon salt
   ¼ teaspoon freshly ground black pepper
   1 large egg yolk
CRUST:
   ½ cup all-purpose flour (about 2¼ ounces)
   ½ cup yellow cornmeal
   1 teaspoon sugar
   ½ teaspoon salt
   Dash of freshly ground black pepper
   2½ tablespoons butter, chilled and cut into small pieces
   ¼ cup ice water
   Cooking spray
ONIONS:
   1 teaspoon butter
   8 cups sliced onion (about 1½ pounds)
   1 tablespoon sugar
   ½ teaspoon salt
   ¼ teaspoon freshly ground black pepper
   1 teaspoon dried thyme

1. To prepare filling, place colander in a 2-quart glass measure or medium bowl. Line colander with 4 layers of cheesecloth, allowing cheesecloth to extend over outside edges. Spoon yogurt into colander. Cover loosely with plastic wrap, and refrigerate 12 hours. Spoon 1¾ cups yogurt cheese into a bowl; discard liquid. Place cream cheese in a bowl; beat with a mixer at medium speed until smooth. Add yogurt cheese, ricotta cheese, ½ teaspoon salt, ¼ teaspoon pepper, and egg yolk. Beat at low speed just until blended.

2. Preheat oven to 350°.

3. To prepare crust, lightly spoon flour into a dry measuring cup; level with a knife. Place flour, cornmeal, 1 teaspoon sugar, ½ teaspoon salt, and dash of pepper in a food processor; pulse 3 times or until combined. Add 2½ tablespoons butter; pulse 4 times or until mixture resembles coarse meal. With processor on, add ice water through food chute, processing just until moist (do not form a ball). Press cornmeal mixture into bottom of an 8-inch springform pan coated with cooking spray. Bake at 350° for 15 minutes or until lightly browned. Cool on a wire rack.

4. To prepare onions, while crust bakes, melt 1 teaspoon butter in a large nonstick skillet over medium heat. Add onion; cook 15 minutes, stirring occasionally. Stir in 1 tablespoon sugar, ½ teaspoon salt, and ¼ teaspoon pepper. Cover and cook 25 minutes or until browned and tender, stirring occasionally. Stir in thyme.

5. Spread yogurt mixture into prepared crust. Bake at 350° for 35 minutes or until almost set. Cool on a wire rack. (Cheesecake will continue to set as it cools.) Serve at room temperature. Cut cheesecake into wedges, and top each serving with onions. **YIELD:** 10 servings (serving size: 1 cheesecake wedge and about 2 tablespoons onions).

CALORIES 198 (30% from fat); FAT 6.5g (sat 3.7g, mono 1.9g, poly 0.4g); PROTEIN 10.2g; CARB 25.6g; FIBER 2.5g; CHOL 37mg; IRON 1.1mg; SODIUM 454mg; CALC 240mg

---

ORGANIC FACT

Research indicates that organic tomatoes have significantly higher levels of flavonoids, lycopene, and vitamin C that act as antioxidants.

Source: The Organic Center

Hot Mulled Ginger-Spiced Cider

This party punch is prepared in a slow cooker, freeing up the stove top for other dishes on your menu.

  3 whole cloves
  2 (4 x 1-inch) strips orange rind
  2 whole allspice
  1 (3-inch) cinnamon stick
  1 (½-inch) piece peeled fresh ginger
12 cups apple cider
 ½ cup apple jelly
 ¼ teaspoon ground nutmeg

1. Place first 5 ingredients on a 5-inch-square double layer of cheesecloth. Gather edges of cheesecloth together; tie securely.
2. Place cheesecloth bag, cider, jelly, and nutmeg in an electric slow cooker. Cover and cook on HIGH 4 hours. Remove and discard cheesecloth bag. **YIELD:** 12 servings (serving size: 1 cup).

CALORIES 174 (0% from fat); FAT 0g; PROTEIN 1g; CARB 43.8g; FIBER 0g; CHOL 0mg; IRON 0mg; SODIUM 0mg; CALC 0mg

Iced Mint Tea

For a lighter minty flavor, remove the mint sprigs after they've steeped in the tea and before chilling. This tea is very sweet, but you can reduce the amount of sugar.

  8 cups boiling water
  1 tablespoon loose Chinese green tea
25 fresh mint sprigs (about 1½ ounces)
 ½ cup sugar

1. Combine 8 cups boiling water and tea in a medium bowl; cover with plastic wrap, and steep 2½ minutes. Remove plastic wrap, and strain tea mixture through a fine sieve into a large pitcher. Discard loose tea leaves. Add mint sprigs to tea, and steep 5 minutes. Add sugar; stir until sugar dissolves. Cool completely, and refrigerate. Serve over ice. **YIELD:** 8 cups (serving size: 1 cup).

CALORIES 52 (2% from fat); FAT 0.1g (sat 0g, mono 0g, poly 0.1g); PROTEIN 0.2g; CARB 13.3g; FIBER 0.4g; CHOL 0mg; IRON 0.3mg; SODIUM 9mg; CALC 18mg

Fresh Ginger Beer

If you like ginger ale, you'll enjoy preparing this popular tangy carbonated beverage at home. Add your favorite rum to create a memorable cocktail. If you can't find superfine sugar, place granulated sugar in a blender, and process until fine. You can find bottled ground fresh ginger in the produce section of the supermarket.

  2 cups cold water
  1 cup fresh lime juice (about 4 limes)
  4 teaspoons bottled ground fresh ginger
 ¾ cup superfine sugar
  3 cups sparkling water
Lime slices (optional)

1. Combine 2 cups water, juice, and ginger in a blender; process until blended.
2. Line a strainer with cheesecloth. Strain mixture over a pitcher; discard solids. Add sugar to pitcher; stir until dissolved.
3. Add sparkling water just before serving. Serve over ice. Garnish with lime slices, if desired. **YIELD:** 8 servings (serving size: 1 cup).

CALORIES 81 (0% from fat); FAT 0g; PROTEIN 0.1g; CARB 21.5g; FIBER 0.1g; CHOL 0mg; IRON 0mg; SODIUM 3mg; CALC 21mg

Fresh Ginger Beer

Watermelon Agua Fresca

4 cups cubed seeded watermelon, divided
4 cups water
2 tablespoons sugar
2 tablespoons fresh lime juice

1. Finely chop 2 cups watermelon; set aside.
2. Place remaining 2 cups watermelon in a blender; process until smooth. Strain pureed watermelon through a sieve into a pitcher; discard solids. Add 4 cups water, sugar, and juice; stir until sugar dissolves. Stir in chopped watermelon. Cover and chill at least 1 hour. **YIELD:** 6 servings (serving size: 1¼ cups).

CALORIES 72 (0% from fat); FAT 0g; PROTEIN 0.7g; CARB 22.9g; FIBER 1.4g; CHOL 0mg; IRON 0.5mg; SODIUM 6.8mg; CALC 14mg

Cantaloupe-Banana Slush

2 cups coarsely chopped cantaloupe
2 cups sliced ripe banana (about 2 medium)
2 cups pineapple-orange-banana juice
1 tablespoon sugar
1 tablespoon lime juice

1. Arrange cantaloupe and banana in a single layer on a baking sheet; freeze until firm. Place frozen fruit in a food processor; process until chunky. With processor on, slowly add juice and remaining ingredients; process until smooth. **YIELD:** 5 servings (serving size: 1 cup).

CALORIES 140 (3% from fat); FAT 0.5g (sat 0.2g, mono 0.1g, poly 0.1g); PROTEIN 2g; CARB 33.8g; FIBER 2.5g; CHOL 0mg; IRON 0.3mg; SODIUM 14mg; CALC 11mg

Wake-Up Shake

¾ cup prune juice, chilled
¾ cup 2% reduced-fat milk, chilled
½ cup vanilla low-fat yogurt
¾ teaspoon vanilla extract
8 bite-sized pitted dried plums
1 ripe banana, cut into chunks
Dash of ground allspice

1. Combine all ingredients in a blender; process until smooth. **YIELD:** 3 servings (serving size: 1 cup).

CALORIES 215 (11% from fat); FAT 2.6g (sat 1.1g, mono 1.1g, poly 0.3g); PROTEIN 4.9g; CARB 45.2g; FIBER 1.9g; CHOL 7mg; IRON 1.5mg; SODIUM 71mg; CALC 161mg

Banana-Berry Smoothie

Banana-Berry Smoothie

Sip this power breakfast—which takes less time to whip up in a blender than toasting a bagel—while getting ready for work or on your way there. A scoop of powdered milk boosts the calcium contributed by the yogurt and the fortified orange juice. Additional nutritional benefits come from the potassium-rich banana and antioxidant-rich berries. Frozen berries ensure a thick, creamy consistency, but other fruits, such as frozen sliced peaches or bottled sliced mangoes, work well, too.

1¼ cups calcium-fortified orange juice
1¼ cups frozen mixed berries
1 cup sliced ripe banana
½ cup vanilla fat-free yogurt
⅓ cup nonfat dry milk
1 tablespoon sugar

1. Combine all ingredients in a blender; process until smooth. **YIELD:** 3 servings (serving size: 1 cup).

CALORIES 204 (3% from fat); FAT 0.6g (sat 0.2g, mono 0.1g, poly 0.2g); PROTEIN 6.6g; CARB 45.6g; FIBER 3.3g; CHOL 2mg; IRON 0.6mg; SODIUM 71mg; CALC 327mg

Blueberry Blender

3 cups fresh orange juice, chilled
¼ cup honey
1 pint fresh blueberries (2 cups)
1 medium cucumber, quartered

1. Combine all ingredients in a blender; process until smooth. Cover and chill 8 hours or overnight, if desired. Line a sieve with cheesecloth. Strain mixture into a medium bowl, pressing solids with a wooden spoon or a rubber spatula to squeeze out juice; discard solids. **YIELD:** 4 servings (serving size: about 1 cup).

CALORIES 185 (3% from fat); FAT 0.7g (sat 0.1g, mono 0.1g, poly 0.2g); PROTEIN 2g; CARB 45.8g; FIBER 2.3g; CHOL 0mg; IRON 0.6mg; SODIUM 7mg; CALC 32mg

Chocolate–Peanut Butter Smoothie

Peel and slice bananas to freeze individually in zip-top bags for smoothies and shakes.

½ cup 1% low-fat milk
2 tablespoons chocolate syrup
2 tablespoons creamy peanut butter
1 frozen sliced ripe banana
1 (8-ounce) carton vanilla low-fat yogurt

1. Place all ingredients in a blender; process until smooth. **YIELD:** 2 servings (serving size: about 1 cup).

CALORIES 332 (29% from fat); FAT 10.8g (sat 3.2g, mono 4.5g, poly 2.3g); PROTEIN 12.7g; CARB 49.8g; FIBER 3.1g; CHOL 8mg; IRON 1mg; SODIUM 194mg; CALC 282mg

Pimm's Cup

This drink derives most of its flavor from Pimm's No. 1, a gin-based aperitif with fruit juices and spices.

¾ cup Pimm's No. 1
2 cups ginger ale, chilled
1⅓ cups sparkling water, chilled
4 lemon slices
1 medium cucumber, halved lengthwise and cut into 4 spears

1. Fill 4 tall (12-ounce) glasses with ice cubes.
2. Pour 3 tablespoons Pimm's into each glass. Pour ½ cup ginger ale and ⅓ cup sparkling water into each glass; stir

to combine. Garnish each serving with 1 lemon slice and 1 cucumber spear. Serve immediately. **YIELD:** 4 servings.

CALORIES 150 (0% from fat); FAT 0g; PROTEIN 0.8g; CARB 13.3g; FIBER 0.8g; CHOL 0mg; IRON 0.3mg; SODIUM 13mg; CALC 15mg

Sparkling Peach Splash

Juicy, ripe peaches create a fruity cocktail based on the popular Bellini.

2 cups chopped peeled peaches (about 3 peaches)
½ cup peach schnapps
2 tablespoons fresh lime juice
1 (750-milliliter) bottle Champagne or sparkling wine, chilled
8 peach slices (optional)

1. Combine first 3 ingredients in a blender; process until smooth. Freeze 1 hour.
2. Pour Champagne into a pitcher. Spoon peach mixture into pitcher; stir to combine. Garnish with peach slices, if desired. Serve immediately. **YIELD:** 8 servings (serving size: about ¾ cup).

CALORIES 133 (1% from fat); FAT 0.1g (sat 0g, mono 0g, poly 0.1g); PROTEIN 0.4g; CARB 12.1g; FIBER 0.9g; CHOL 0mg; IRON 0.4mg; SODIUM 6mg; CALC 11mg

Slushy Watermelon Mojito

Keep the limeade frozen so this beverage will be slushy.

5 cups cubed seeded watermelon
1 cup sparkling water, chilled
¾ cup white rum
¼ cup chopped fresh mint
1 (6-ounce) can frozen limeade concentrate, undiluted
Mint sprigs (optional)
Lime slices (optional)

1. Arrange watermelon in a single layer on a baking sheet; freeze 2 hours or until completely frozen.
2. Combine frozen watermelon, sparkling water, rum, mint, and limeade in a blender; process until smooth. Pour into 8 (6-ounce) stemmed glasses. Garnish with mint sprigs and lime slices, if desired. Serve immediately. **YIELD**: 8 servings (serving size: about ¾ cup).

CALORIES 119 (3% from fat); FAT 0.4g (sat 0.1g, mono 0.1g, poly 0.2g); PROTEIN 0.7g; CARB 17.5g; FIBER 0.6g; CHOL 0mg; IRON 0.3mg; SODIUM 2mg; CALC 11mg

Pimm's Cup, Sparkling Peach Splash,
and Slushy Watermelon Mojito

51

Lemon Drop
Liqueur

Grape Margarita Slush

¾ cup water
⅓ cup sugar
1 cup tequila
½ cup fresh lime juice (about 3 large limes)
⅓ cup Triple Sec (orange-flavored liqueur)
3 cups seedless green grapes
7 cups ice cubes

1. Combine ¾ cup water and sugar in a small saucepan over medium heat; cook 3 minutes or until sugar dissolves. Pour into a freezer-safe container; cool completely. Add tequila, juice, and Triple Sec to sugar mixture; stir to combine. Cover and freeze overnight. Place grapes in a large zip-top plastic bag; freeze overnight.
2. Place half of tequila mixture, 1½ cups grapes, and 3½ cups ice in a blender; process until desired consistency. Repeat with remaining tequila mixture, grapes, and ice. Serve immediately. **YIELD:** 10 cups (serving size: 1 cup).

CALORIES 149 (2% from fat); FAT 0.3g (sat 0.1g, mono 0g, poly 0.1g); PROTEIN 0.4g; CARB 19.6g; FIBER 0.5g; CHOL 0mg; IRON 0.2mg; SODIUM 2mg; CALC 6mg

Lemon Drop Liqueur

Pour over ice with two parts sparkling water for a cool, delicious lemon spritzer. To serve straight up, coat the rim of a chilled martini glass in lemon juice; then dip the rim in sugar. Garnish with a slice of lemon.

2 cups sugar
1 cup water
5 lemon rinds, cut into strips
3 cups vodka
¼ cup lemon juice

1. Combine sugar and water in a saucepan; cook over medium heat 5 minutes or until sugar dissolves, stirring constantly. Remove from heat; stir in lemon rinds. Cool completely. Stir in vodka and juice.
2. Sterilize 2 wide-mouthed, 1-quart jars according to manufacturer's directions. Divide vodka mixture between jars. Cover each jar with metal lid; screw on band. Store in a cool, dark place for 3 weeks, shaking jar every other day.
3. Line a fine-mesh sieve with a double layer of cheesecloth; strain mixture into a bowl. Discard solids. Return liqueur to jars or a clean decanter; store chilled in refrigerator or freezer. **YIELD:** 4¾ cups (serving size: ¼ cup).

Winter-Spiced Red Wine Sangría

1 cup apple juice
⅓ cup Triple Sec (orange-flavored liqueur)
¼ cup sugar
4 whole cloves
3 navel oranges, cut into ¼-inch slices
2 lemons, cut into ¼-inch slices
2 (3-inch) cinnamon sticks
1 Bartlett pear, cut into ½-inch cubes
1 (750-milliliter) bottle fruity red wine

1. Combine all ingredients in a large pitcher; stir until sugar dissolves. Cover and refrigerate for at least 4 hours or overnight. Discard cloves and cinnamon sticks before serving. **YIELD:** 10 servings (serving size: ¾ cup).

CALORIES 149 (0% from fat); FAT 0.1g (sat 0g, mono 0g, poly 0g); PROTEIN 0.5g; CARB 22g; FIBER 1.6g; CHOL 0mg; IRON 0.4mg; SODIUM 7mg; CALC 31mg

Easy Sangría

    1   (1.5-liter) bottle dry red wine, divided
    2   tablespoons brandy
    2   tablespoons Triple Sec (orange-flavored liqueur)
    ⅓   cup sugar
    ⅔   cup fresh orange juice
    2   tablespoons fresh lime juice
    2   tablespoons fresh lemon juice
    5   whole cloves
    3   whole allspice
    1   (3-inch) cinnamon stick
    2   cups sparkling water, chilled
    8   orange wedges
    5   lemon slices
    5   lime slices

1. Combine ½ cup wine, brandy, Triple Sec, and sugar in a 2-quart glass measure. Microwave at HIGH 1 minute or until mixture is warm; stir to dissolve sugar. Stir in remaining wine, juices, cloves, allspice, and cinnamon. Chill at least 2 hours.
2. Strain mixture through a sieve into a pitcher, and discard spices. Just before serving, stir in sparkling water and remaining ingredients. Serve over ice. **YIELD:** 8 servings (serving size: about ¾ cup).

CALORIES 199 (0% from fat); FAT 0.1g (sat 0g, mono 0g, poly 0.1g); PROTEIN 0.6g; CARB 15.8g; FIBER 0.1g; CHOL 0mg; IRON 0.9mg; SODIUM 10mg; CALC 18mg

Watermelon Margaritas

    2   cups diced seeded watermelon, frozen
    ¾   cup tequila
    ⅓   cup Triple Sec (orange-flavored liqueur)
    1   tablespoon sugar
    2   tablespoons lime juice
    2   cups crushed ice
Sugar (optional)
Lime slices (optional)
Orange slices (optional)

1. Place frozen watermelon, tequila, Triple Sec, 1 tablespoon sugar, and lime juice in a blender; process until smooth. Add ice, and process until smooth. Serve in glasses rimmed with sugar, and garnish with lime and orange slices, if desired. **YIELD:** 5 servings (serving size: 1 cup).

CALORIES 157 (2% from fat); FAT 0.2g (sat 0.2g, mono 0g, poly 0g); PROTEIN 0.2g; CARB 6g; FIBER 0.4g; CHOL 0mg; IRON 0.1mg; SODIUM 2mg; CALC 6mg

Frozen Strawberry Daiquiris

    3   cups sliced fresh strawberries
    1   cup white rum
    3   tablespoons fresh lime juice
    1   (12-ounce) can thawed limeade concentrate, undiluted
    1   cup crushed ice
    6   lime slices (optional)

1. Place first 4 ingredients in a blender; process until smooth. Add ice; process until smooth. Serve immediately; garnish with lime slices, if desired. **YIELD:** 6 servings (serving size: about 1 cup).

CALORIES 219 (2% from fat); FAT 0.4g (sat 0g, mono 0.1g, poly 0.2g); PROTEIN 0.7g; CARB 34.6g; FIBER 2.2g; CHOL 0mg; IRON 0.4mg; SODIUM 1mg; CALC 15mg

Mango Mojito

(pictured on page 38)

    2   lime wedges
    5   fresh mint leaves
    ¼   cup club soda
    3   tablespoons rum
    2   tablespoons Simple Syrup
    1   tablespoon mango nectar
Crushed ice

1. Squeeze lime wedges into a small glass; add wedges and mint to glass. Crush with the back of a spoon for 30 seconds. Add soda, rum, Simple Syrup, and nectar; stir gently. Serve over ice. **YIELD:** 1 serving (serving size: ½ cup).

(Totals include Simple Syrup) CALORIES 205 (0% from fat); FAT 0g; PROTEIN 0.1g; CARB 28.3g; FIBER 0.2g; CHOL 0mg; IRON 0.1mg; SODIUM 14mg; CALC 6mg

SIMPLE SYRUP:
    2   cups sugar
    1   cup water

1. Heat sugar and water in a small saucepan over medium-high heat until sugar dissolves (about 5 minutes), stirring constantly. **YIELD:** 2 cups (serving size: 2 tablespoons).

CALORIES 97 (0% from fat); FAT 0g; PROTEIN 0g; CARB 25g; FIBER 0g; CHOL 0mg; IRON 0mg; SODIUM 0mg; CALC 1mg

Lasagna Rolls with
Roasted Red Pepper Sauce,
page 66

VEGETARIAN ENTRÉES

Pain Perdu

Pain Perdu

Pain Perdu—literally "lost bread"—is a simple breakfast of day-old French bread dredged in beaten eggs and pan-fried in butter.

1½ cups fat-free milk
 2 large eggs
 2 large egg whites
 ¼ cup granulated sugar
 ½ teaspoon ground cinnamon
 ½ teaspoon ground nutmeg
1½ teaspoons vanilla extract
 ¼ teaspoon salt
16 (1-inch-thick) slices diagonally cut French bread baguette
 ¼ cup butter
 2 cups water
 ½ cup dry white wine
 ¼ cup granulated sugar
 1 tablespoon cornstarch
 2 cups fresh raspberries
 1 cup fresh blackberries
 1 cup fresh blueberries
 ½ cup halved fresh strawberries
 1 tablespoon powdered sugar

1. Combine first 8 ingredients, stirring well with a whisk. Arrange bread slices in a single layer in a large shallow dish. Pour milk mixture over bread slices, and let stand until milk is absorbed (about 2 minutes).
2. Melt 2 tablespoons butter in a large cast-iron skillet over medium heat. Arrange 8 bread slices in pan; cook 3 minutes on each side or until bread is golden brown. Remove from pan; keep warm. Repeat procedure with remaining 2 tablespoons butter and 8 bread slices.
3. Combine 2 cups water, wine, ¼ cup granulated sugar, and cornstarch in a large saucepan, stirring with a whisk. Bring to a boil; cook until reduced to 1 cup (about 5 minutes). Remove pan from heat. Add fruit to pan, stirring gently to coat. Serve sauce with bread slices. Sprinkle each serving with powdered sugar. **YIELD:** 8 servings (serving size: 2 bread slices and about ½ cup sauce).

CALORIES 377 (28% from fat); FAT 11.8g (sat 4.8g, mono 3.3g, poly 2.7g); PROTEIN 8.8g; CARB 58.2g; FIBER 6.3g; CHOL 69mg; IRON 1.6mg; SODIUM 424mg; CALC 89mg

Coconut French Toast with Grilled Pineapple and Tropical Salsa

This rich dish is best prepared with day-old bread. You can serve the pineapple slices raw, but the deep, caramelized flavors you get from grilling them are worth the extra effort.

SALSA:
 2 tablespoons flaked sweetened coconut
 2 teaspoons fresh lime juice
 2 cups chopped peeled ripe mangoes
 1 pint strawberries, chopped
FRENCH TOAST:
 2 large eggs
 4 large egg whites
 1 cup light coconut milk
 1 cup 1% low-fat milk
 ½ cup granulated sugar
 ½ teaspoon vanilla extract
 ¼ teaspoon salt
 2 large eggs
 1 (16-ounce) loaf French bread, cut into 16 slices
Cooking spray
REMAINING INGREDIENTS:
 1 medium pineapple, peeled, cored, and cut crosswise into 8 slices
Powdered sugar (optional)

1. To prepare salsa, combine first 4 ingredients; cover and chill.
2. Preheat oven to 400°.
3. To prepare French toast, combine 2 large eggs and next 7 ingredients in a large bowl, stirring well with a whisk. Place bread in egg mixture; press down with spatula to completely submerge bread in egg mixture. Let bread mixture stand 15 minutes.
4. Arrange soaked bread in a single layer on a jelly-roll pan coated with cooking spray. Bake at 400° for 12 minutes or until set. Remove from oven, and keep warm.
5. While bread bakes, heat a grill pan over medium-high heat. Coat pan with cooking spray. Arrange 4 pineapple slices in pan; cook 4 minutes on each side or until pineapple begins to brown. Remove from pan; keep warm. Repeat procedure with remaining pineapple and cooking spray. Arrange 2 French toast pieces on each of 8 plates; top each serving with 1 pineapple slice and ½ cup salsa. Sprinkle with powdered sugar, if desired. **YIELD:** 8 servings.

CALORIES 340 (16% from fat); FAT 6g (sat 3g, mono 1.3g, poly 0.9g); PROTEIN 13.9g; CARB 60.1g; FIBER 3.6g; CHOL 107mg; IRON 3.2mg; SODIUM 529mg; CALC 98mg

Frittata with Mushrooms, Linguine, and Basil

Break the pasta in half before cooking so it's easier to stir into the egg mixture. Add a small salad of gourmet greens for color on the plate.

   Cooking spray
   3 cups sliced cremini or button mushrooms
1¼ cups thinly sliced leek (about 2 large)
  ½ cup 1% low-fat milk
  2 teaspoons butter, melted
  ¾ teaspoon salt
  ⅛ teaspoon freshly ground black pepper
  4 large egg whites
  3 large eggs
  2 cups hot cooked linguine (about 4 ounces uncooked pasta)
  ⅓ cup chopped fresh basil
  ½ cup (2 ounces) shredded part-skim mozzarella cheese

1. Preheat oven to 450°.
2. Heat a large nonstick skillet over medium heat. Coat pan with cooking spray. Add mushrooms and sliced leek; cook 6 minutes or until leek is tender, stirring frequently.
3. Combine milk and next 5 ingredients in a large bowl, stirring with a whisk. Add leek mixture, pasta, and basil; toss gently to combine.
4. Heat pan over medium-low heat. Coat pan with cooking spray. Add egg mixture; cook until edges begin to set (about 4 minutes). Gently lift edge of egg mixture, tilting pan to allow some uncooked mixture to come in contact with pan. Cook 5 minutes or until almost set. Sprinkle with cheese; wrap handle of pan with foil. Bake at 450° for 7 minutes or until golden brown. Cut into 8 wedges. **YIELD:** 4 servings (serving size: 2 wedges).

CALORIES 269 (29% from fat); FAT 8.8g (sat 4.1g, mono 2.8g, poly 0.9g); PROTEIN 18.4g; CARB 28g; FIBER 2.8g; CHOL 174mg; IRON 2.6mg; SODIUM 661mg; CALC 177mg

Cheese Enchilada Casserole

  1 cup (4 ounces) reduced-fat shredded extrasharp Cheddar cheese
  1 cup chopped tomato
  1 cup fat-free cottage cheese
  ⅓ cup sliced green onions
  2 teaspoons chili powder
  2 garlic cloves, minced
  9 (6-inch) corn tortillas
  Cooking spray
  1 cup taco sauce
  ¼ cup (1 ounce) shredded Monterey Jack cheese
  2 tablespoons chopped green onions

1. Preheat oven to 375°.
2. Combine first 6 ingredients. Arrange 3 tortillas in a 1½-quart baking dish coated with cooking spray. Spread half of cheese mixture over tortillas. Repeat procedure with 3 tortillas and remaining cheese mixture; top with remaining tortillas.
3. Pour taco sauce over tortillas; sprinkle with Monterey Jack cheese. Bake at 375° for 20 minutes or until cheese melts. Sprinkle with 2 tablespoons green onions. **YIELD:** 4 servings (serving size: 1¼ cups).

CALORIES 299 (18% from fat); FAT 6g (sat 2.8g, mono 1.7g, poly 0.9g); PROTEIN 19.1g; CARB 42.3g; FIBER 4.3g; CHOL 15mg; IRON 1.4mg; SODIUM 1,029mg; CALC 332mg

Frittata with Mushrooms, Linguine, and Basil

Cheese Enchilada
Casserole

Huevos Rancheros with Queso Fresco

Queso fresco is a soft, crumbly, salty Mexican cheese. Look for it in cottage cheese–style tubs in the dairy section of large grocery stores and Hispanic markets. Substitute crumbled feta or goat cheese, if you prefer.

1 (10-ounce) can diced tomatoes and green chiles, undrained
1 (10-ounce) can red enchilada sauce
⅓ cup chopped fresh cilantro
1 tablespoon fresh lime juice
2 tablespoons water
1 (16-ounce) can pinto beans, rinsed and drained
Cooking spray
4 large eggs
4 (8-inch) fat-free flour tortillas
1 cup (4 ounces) crumbled queso fresco
Chopped cilantro (optional)

1. Combine tomatoes and enchilada sauce in a medium saucepan; bring to a boil. Reduce heat; simmer, uncovered, 5 minutes or until slightly thick. Remove from heat; stir in cilantro and juice, and set aside.

2. Place water and pinto beans in a microwave-safe bowl, and partially mash with a fork. Cover and microwave at HIGH 2 minutes or until hot.

3. Heat a large nonstick skillet over medium-high heat. Coat pan with cooking spray. Add eggs, and cook 1 minute on each side or until desired degree of doneness.

4. Warm tortillas according to package directions. Spread about ⅓ cup beans over each tortilla; top each tortilla with 1 egg. Spoon ½ cup sauce around each egg; sprinkle each serving with ¼ cup cheese and cilantro, if desired. **YIELD:** 4 servings (serving size: 1 topped tortilla).

CALORIES 340 (26% from fat); FAT 9.8g (sat 3.2g, mono 2.7g, poly 1g); PROTEIN 15.7g; CARB 37.8g; FIBER 6.1g; CHOL 222mg; IRON 2.1mg; SODIUM 970mg; CALC 153mg

Southwestern Bean Casserole

This Tex-Mex dish is perfect for a weeknight dinner with the family. Use medium-hot salsa to enhance the flavor.

  1 teaspoon canola oil
Cooking spray
  1 cup chopped onion
  2 garlic cloves, minced
  1 cup canned no-salt-added cream-style corn, divided
  ½ cup drained canned chopped green chiles, divided
  ½ cup bottled salsa
  ½ teaspoon salt
  ¼ teaspoon ground cumin
  ¼ teaspoon black pepper
  2 (16-ounce) cans pinto beans, drained
  1 (14.5-ounce) can no-salt-added stewed tomatoes, undrained
  1 cup (4 ounces) reduced-fat shredded Cheddar cheese, divided
  ¾ cup yellow cornmeal
  ¼ cup all-purpose flour (about 1 ounce)
  1 teaspoon sugar
  ¼ teaspoon salt
  ½ cup low-fat buttermilk
  ¼ cup canola oil
  2 egg whites, lightly beaten

1. Preheat oven to 375°.
2. Heat 1 teaspoon oil in a large saucepan coated with cooking spray over medium-high heat. Add onion and garlic, and sauté 3 minutes. Add ½ cup corn, ¼ cup chiles, salsa, and next 5 ingredients; bring to a boil. Reduce heat, and simmer 15 minutes. Pour mixture into a 13 x 9–inch baking dish coated with cooking spray. Sprinkle with ½ cup cheese; set aside.
3. Combine cornmeal, flour, sugar, and ¼ teaspoon salt in a medium bowl. Combine remaining ½ cup corn, remaining ¼ cup chiles, remaining ½ cup cheese, buttermilk, ¼ cup oil, and egg whites; add to cornmeal mixture, stirring just until moist. Spread corn bread batter evenly over bean mixture. Bake casserole at 375° for 25 minutes or until corn bread is lightly browned. Let stand 5 minutes. **YIELD:** 7 servings (serving size: 1 cup).

CALORIES 376 (30% from fat); FAT 12.5g (sat 3.5g, mono 2.7g, poly 4.5g); PROTEIN 16.5g; CARB 51.3g; FIBER 5.2g; CHOL 11mg; IRON 3.6mg; SODIUM 680mg; CALC 225mg

Cuban Beans and Rice

Dry beans lend themselves well to slow cooking because, unlike on the stove top, there is no risk of burning over the long simmering period. This meatless entrée reheats well the next day for lunch.

  1 pound dried black beans
  2 cups water
  2 cups vegetable broth
  2 cups chopped onion
  1½ cups chopped red bell pepper
  1 cup chopped green bell pepper
  2 tablespoons olive oil
  3 teaspoons salt
  2 teaspoons fennel seeds, crushed
  2 teaspoons ground coriander
  2 teaspoons ground cumin
  2 teaspoons dried oregano
  2 tablespoons sherry or red wine vinegar
  2 (10-ounce) cans diced tomatoes and green chiles, drained
  5 cups hot cooked rice
Hot sauce (optional)

1. Sort and wash beans; place in a large bowl. Cover with water to 2 inches above beans; cover and let stand 8 hours. Drain beans.
2. Combine beans, 2 cups water, and next 10 ingredients in an electric slow cooker. Cover and cook on HIGH 5 hours or until beans are tender. Stir in vinegar and tomatoes. Serve over rice. Sprinkle with hot sauce, if desired. **YIELD:** 10 servings (servings size: 1 cup bean mixture and ½ cup rice).

CALORIES 314 (9% from fat); FAT 3.3g (sat 0.4g, mono 2g, poly 0.5g); PROTEIN 12.1g; CARB 58.3g; FIBER 6g; CHOL 0mg; IRON 3.7mg; SODIUM 816mg; CALC 24mg

ECO TIP
There are a variety of reasons why someone might choose to take on a vegetarian diet. One might be because it has less impact on the environment, since the time and effort to raise animals is avoided. Also, the cost is lower, thus making it easier to buy organic.

Bell Pepper-and-Potato Tagine over Couscous

Harissa is a fiery-hot condiment available in Middle Eastern markets.

  2 teaspoons olive oil
1¾ cups diced onion
  2 tablespoons tomato paste
  1 tablespoon chopped fresh mint
  ½ teaspoon crushed red pepper
  6 garlic cloves, crushed
  2 baking potatoes, peeled and each cut into 6 wedges
     (about 1 pound)
  2 cups (1-inch) red bell pepper strips
  2 cups (1-inch) green bell pepper strips
  1 teaspoon salt
  1 (15½-ounce) can chickpeas, drained
  3 cups chopped seeded tomato
  3 cups water
  1 teaspoon harissa (optional)
  ¾ cup uncooked couscous
  3 tablespoons chopped fresh parsley

1. Heat oil in a Dutch oven over medium-high heat. Add onion and next 5 ingredients; cook 10 minutes, stirring occasionally. Add peppers, salt, and chickpeas; sauté 5 minutes. Stir in tomato and water. Bring to a boil; partially cover, reduce heat, and simmer 25 minutes or until potatoes are tender. Remove vegetables with a slotted spoon; set aside. Reserve 1 cup cooking liquid.
2. Bring reserved cooking liquid to a boil in a medium saucepan; stir in harissa, if desired. Gradually stir in couscous. Remove from heat; cover and let stand 5 minutes. Fluff with a fork. Serve with vegetables; sprinkle with chopped parsley. **YIELD:** 5 servings (serving size: about 1⅓ cups tagine and ½ cup couscous).

CALORIES 382 (11% from fat); FAT 4.6g (sat 0.7g, mono 1.9g, poly 1.5g); PROTEIN 13.6g; CARB 74.3g; FIBER 9g; CHOL 0mg; IRON 4.5mg; SODIUM 596mg; CALC 77mg

Spicy Yellow Soybean, Lentil, and Carrot Curry

A dollop of cool yogurt balances the heat and spiciness from the curry paste, red pepper, and cilantro.

  1 tablespoon olive oil
2⅓ cups finely chopped onion
  1 tablespoon red curry paste
  4 cups vegetable broth, divided
  2 cups finely chopped carrot
  2 tablespoons minced peeled fresh ginger
  ⅛ teaspoon ground red pepper
  3 garlic cloves, minced
  1 cup dried small red lentils
  1 (15-ounce) can yellow soybeans, rinsed and drained
  ⅓ cup minced fresh cilantro
  ¼ teaspoon salt
  ¼ teaspoon freshly ground black pepper
  6 tablespoons plain fat-free yogurt
Fresh cilantro sprigs (optional)

1. Heat oil in a large saucepan over medium-high heat. Add onion; sauté 3 minutes or until tender. Stir in curry paste; cook 1 minute. Add ½ cup broth, carrot, ginger, red pepper, and garlic; cook 6 minutes or until carrot is tender, stirring occasionally. Add 3½ cups broth, lentils, and soybeans; bring to a boil. Reduce heat; simmer 10 minutes or until lentils are tender. Stir in cilantro, salt, and black pepper. Divide evenly among 6 shallow bowls; dollop with yogurt. Garnish with cilantro sprigs, if desired. **YIELD:** 6 servings (serving size: 1 cup curry and 1 tablespoon yogurt).

CALORIES 314 (28% from fat); FAT 9.7g (sat 1.3g, mono 3.2g, poly 3.9g); PROTEIN 22.8g; CARB 39.5g; FIBER 11.8g; CHOL 0mg; IRON 6.2mg; SODIUM 937mg; CALC 163mg

ORGANIC RESOURCE

J.I. Rodale is credited with coining the term "organic farming" in 1943. The Rodale Institute was established in 1947 in Kutztown, Pennsylvania. It conducts the longest-running US study comparing organic and conventional farming techniques.

Source: The Rodale Institute

Spicy Yellow Soybean, Lentil,
and Carrot Curry

Spaghetti Squash
with Edamame-Cilantro Pesto

64

Spaghetti Squash with Edamame-Cilantro Pesto

2 (2½-pound) spaghetti squashes
Cooking spray
½ teaspoon salt, divided
1¼ cups chopped fresh cilantro
1 cup vegetable broth
1 tablespoon extravirgin olive oil
¼ teaspoon freshly ground black pepper
2 garlic cloves, minced
1 pound frozen shelled edamame (green soybeans),
   thawed
¼ cup (1 ounce) grated fresh Parmesan cheese

1. Preheat oven to 350°.
2. Cut each squash in half lengthwise; discard seeds.
Place squash halves, cut sides down, on a baking sheet
coated with cooking spray. Bake at 350° for 1 hour or
until tender. Cool slightly. Scrape inside of squash with
a fork to remove spaghetti-like strands to measure about
8 cups. Place in a large bowl. Sprinkle with ¼ teaspoon
salt; toss gently to combine. Cover and keep warm.
3. Place cilantro, broth, oil, pepper, remaining ¼ teaspoon
salt, garlic, and edamame in a food processor; pulse until
coarsely chopped. Serve edamame pesto over squash;
sprinkle with cheese. **YIELD:** 6 servings (serving size: 1½ cups
squash, ½ cup edamame pesto, and 2 teaspoons cheese).

CALORIES 233 (29% from fat); FAT 7.6g (sat 1.3g, mono 2.8g, poly 2.4g); PROTEIN 12.5g;
CARB 31.3g; FIBER 8.8g; CHOL 3mg; IRON 3mg; SODIUM 533mg; CALC 182mg

Vegetarian Stuffed Peppers

6 medium red bell peppers
1 teaspoon olive oil
¾ cup finely chopped shallots
4 cups chopped mushrooms
1 cup chopped fresh parsley
¼ cup slivered almonds, toasted
3 tablespoons dry sherry
1½ teaspoons ancho chile powder
2½ cups cooked brown rice
1 cup tomato juice
½ teaspoon freshly ground black pepper
½ teaspoon garlic powder
¼ teaspoon salt
6 tablespoons (1½ ounces) grated fresh Parmesan cheese

1. Preheat oven to 350°.
2. Cut tops off bell peppers; discard seeds and membranes. Cook peppers in boiling water 5 minutes; drain.
3. Heat oil in a large nonstick skillet over medium-high
heat. Add shallots; sauté 3 minutes or until tender. Add
mushrooms, and sauté 4 minutes or until tender. Add
parsley, almonds, sherry, and chile powder; sauté 3 minutes. Add rice, juice, black pepper, garlic powder, and salt;
sauté 3 minutes. Spoon ¾ cup rice mixture into each bell
pepper; top each with 1 tablespoon cheese. Place peppers
in a 13 x 9–inch baking dish; bake at 350° for 15 minutes.
YIELD: 6 servings (serving size: 1 stuffed pepper).

CALORIES 223 (25% from fat); FAT 6.3g (sat 1.5g, mono 2.3g, poly 1.2g); PROTEIN 9.5g;
CARB 35.1g; FIBER 5.5g; CHOL 5mg; IRON 2.4mg; SODIUM 336mg; CALC 155mg

Portobello Mushroom Fajitas

Portobello mushrooms and red onions make a meaty fajita
filling with satisfying, pungent flavors.

1 tablespoon olive oil
4 cups (½-inch-thick) slices portobello mushrooms
   (about 8 ounces)
1 cup vertically sliced red onion
1 cup (¼-inch-thick) green bell pepper strips
2 garlic cloves, minced
3 tablespoons chopped fresh cilantro
1 tablespoon fresh lime juice
¼ teaspoon salt
¼ teaspoon freshly ground black pepper
1 serrano chile, minced
12 (6-inch) flour tortillas
1 cup (4 ounces) crumbled queso fresco
¾ cup salsa verde

1. Heat oil in a large nonstick skillet over medium-high
heat. Add mushrooms; sauté 5 minutes. Add onion, bell
pepper, and garlic. Reduce heat to medium, and cook
4 minutes or until bell pepper is crisp-tender, stirring
frequently. Remove from heat; stir in cilantro and next
4 ingredients.
2. Warm tortillas according to package directions. Spoon
about ¼ cup of mushroom mixture down center of each
tortilla; top each tortilla with 4 teaspoons cheese and
1 tablespoon salsa. Roll up. **YIELD:** 4 servings (serving size:
3 fajitas).

CALORIES 437 (26% from fat); FAT 12.7g (sat 3.6g, mono 6.8g, poly 1.5g); PROTEIN 13.8g;
CARB 65.9g; FIBER 4.9g; CHOL 9mg; IRON 3.9mg; SODIUM 792mg; CALC 219mg

Zucchini, Olive, and Cheese Quesadillas

If you want a change of pace from the usual bean, cheese, and salsa quesadillas, this recipe is for you. Just add a mixed greens salad to round out your meal.

  1 teaspoon olive oil
Cooking spray
  ⅓ cup finely chopped onion
  ½ teaspoon bottled minced garlic
1¼ cups shredded zucchini
  ¼ teaspoon dried oregano
  ⅛ teaspoon salt
  ⅛ teaspoon black pepper
  4 (8-inch) fat-free flour tortillas
  ½ cup (2 ounces) preshredded part-skim mozzarella cheese
  ½ cup diced tomato
  ¼ cup chopped pitted kalamata olives
  ¼ cup (1 ounce) crumbled feta cheese

1. Heat oil in a large nonstick skillet coated with cooking spray over medium-high heat. Add onion and garlic; sauté 1 minute. Add zucchini; sauté 2 minutes or until lightly browned. Remove from heat; stir in oregano, salt, and pepper.
2. Wipe pan clean with paper towels, and coat with cooking spray. Heat pan over medium heat. Add 1 tortilla to pan, and sprinkle with ¼ cup mozzarella. Top with half of zucchini mixture, ¼ cup tomato, 2 tablespoons olives, 2 tablespoons feta, and 1 tortilla. Cook 3 minutes or until lightly browned on bottom. Carefully turn quesadilla; cook 2 minutes or until lightly browned. Place quesadilla on a cutting board; cut in half using a serrated knife. Repeat procedure with remaining tortillas, mozzarella, zucchini mixture, tomato, olives, and feta. Serve warm.
YIELD: 2 servings.

CALORIES 447 (32% from fat); FAT 15.8g (sat 6.6g, mono 7.4g, poly 1.1g); PROTEIN 17.4g; CARB 58.7g; FIBER 4g; CHOL 33mg; IRON 3.1mg; SODIUM 1,466mg; CALC 307mg

Lasagna Rolls with Roasted Red Pepper Sauce

(pictured on page 54)

These rolls require some assembly time but are a nice change of pace from layered pasta. They also make a pretty presentation on a plate.

LASAGNA:
  8 uncooked lasagna noodles
  4 teaspoons olive oil
  ½ cup finely chopped onion
  1 (8-ounce) package presliced mushrooms
  1 (6-ounce) package baby spinach
  3 garlic cloves, minced
  ½ cup (2 ounces) shredded mozzarella cheese
  ½ cup part-skim ricotta cheese
  ¼ cup minced fresh basil, divided
  ½ teaspoon salt
  ¼ teaspoon crushed red pepper
SAUCE:
  1 tablespoon red wine vinegar
  ¼ teaspoon salt
  ⅛ teaspoon black pepper
  2 garlic cloves, minced
  1 (14.5-ounce) can diced tomatoes
  1 (7-ounce) bottle roasted red bell peppers, undrained
  ⅛ teaspoon crushed red pepper

1. To prepare lasagna, cook noodles according to package directions, omitting salt and fat. Drain and rinse noodles under cold water. Drain.
2. Heat oil in a large nonstick skillet over medium-high heat. Add onion, mushrooms, spinach, and 3 garlic cloves; sauté 5 minutes or until onion and mushrooms are tender. Remove from heat; stir in cheeses, 2 tablespoons basil, ½ teaspoon salt, and ¼ teaspoon crushed red pepper.
3. To prepare sauce, place vinegar and next 6 ingredients in a blender; process until smooth.
4. Place cooked noodles on a flat surface; spread ¼ cup cheese mixture over each noodle. Roll up noodles, jelly-roll fashion, starting with short side. Place rolls, seam sides down, in a shallow 2-quart microwave-safe dish. Pour ¼ cup sauce over each roll, and cover with heavy-duty plastic wrap. Microwave at HIGH 5 minutes or until thoroughly heated. Sprinkle with remaining 2 tablespoons basil. **YIELD:** 4 servings (serving size: 2 rolls).

CALORIES 393 (27% from fat); FAT 11.7g (sat 4.3g, mono 3.6g, poly 1.5g); PROTEIN 19.3g; CARB 58.3g; FIBER 5.9g; CHOL 20mg; IRON 3.8mg; SODIUM 924mg; CALC 253mg

Penne with Tomatoes, Olives, and Capers

This simple dish depends on fresh basil, garlic, and tomatoes to deliver big flavor. You can use almost any small pasta, such as macaroni, farfalle, rotelle, or tubetti.

1 tablespoon olive oil
¼ teaspoon crushed red pepper
3 garlic cloves, finely chopped
3 cups chopped plum tomato (about 1¾ pounds)
½ cup chopped pitted kalamata olives
1½ tablespoons capers
¼ teaspoon salt
6 cups hot cooked penne (about 4 cups uncooked tube-shaped pasta)
¾ cup (3 ounces) grated fresh Parmesan cheese
3 tablespoons chopped fresh basil

1. Heat olive oil in a large nonstick skillet over medium-high heat. Add red pepper and chopped garlic, and sauté 30 seconds. Add tomato, olives, capers, and salt. Reduce heat, and simmer 8 minutes, stirring occasionally. Add pasta to pan, tossing gently to coat; cook 1 minute or until thoroughly heated. Remove from heat.

2. Spoon pasta mixture in a large bowl; top with cheese and basil, tossing gently. **YIELD:** 4 servings (serving size: about 1¾ cups).

CALORIES 484 (28% from fat); FAT 15.1g (sat 4.7g, mono 7.7g, poly 1.7g); PROTEIN 19.1g; CARB 67.8g; FIBER 4.3g; CHOL 14mg; IRON 3.9mg; SODIUM 870mg; CALC 287mg

Triple Mushroom Pizza

Triple Mushroom Pizza

1 teaspoon sugar

1 package quick-rise yeast (about 2¼ teaspoons)

½ cup warm water (100° to 110°)

1½ cups all-purpose flour (about 6¾ ounces), divided

½ teaspoon salt, divided

Cooking spray

2 teaspoons cornmeal

2 teaspoons olive oil

2 cups thinly sliced shiitake mushroom caps (about 4 ounces)

2 cups sliced cremini mushrooms (about 4 ounces)

1½ cups (¼-inch-thick) slices portobello mushrooms (about 4 ounces)

⅔ cup (about 2½ ounces) shredded sharp fontina cheese, divided

2 teaspoons chopped fresh thyme

¼ cup (1 ounce) grated fresh Parmesan cheese

¼ teaspoon sea salt

1. Dissolve sugar and yeast in warm water in a large bowl; let stand 5 minutes. Lightly spoon flour into dry measuring cups; level with a knife. Add 1¼ cups flour and ¼ teaspoon salt to yeast mixture; stir until a soft dough forms. Turn dough out onto a lightly floured surface. Knead until smooth and elastic (about 10 minutes); add enough of remaining flour, 1 tablespoon at a time, to prevent dough from sticking to hands (dough will feel tacky).

2. Place dough in a large bowl coated with cooking spray, turning to coat top. Cover and let rise in a warm place (85°), free from drafts, 30 minutes or until doubled in size. (Gently press two fingers into dough. If indentation remains, dough has risen enough.) Punch dough down; cover and let stand 5 minutes. Line a baking sheet with parchment paper; sprinkle with cornmeal. Roll dough into a 12-inch circle on a floured surface. Place dough on prepared baking sheet. Crimp edges of dough with fingers to form a rim; let rise 10 minutes.

3. Preheat oven to 475°.

4. While dough rises, heat 2 teaspoons olive oil in a large nonstick skillet over medium heat. Add ¼ teaspoon salt and mushrooms; cook 7 minutes or until mushrooms soften and moisture almost evaporates, stirring frequently.

5. Sprinkle ¼ cup fontina cheese evenly over dough, and arrange mushroom mixture evenly over fontina. Sprinkle with 2 teaspoons thyme. Sprinkle remaining fontina and Parmesan cheese evenly over top. Bake at 475° for 15 minutes or until crust is lightly browned. Remove to cutting board, and sprinkle with ¼ teaspoon sea salt. Cut into 8 slices. Serve immediately. **YIELD:** 4 servings (serving size: 2 slices).

CALORIES 335 (28% from fat); FAT 10.5g (sat 4.8g, mono 3.3g, poly 0.9g); PROTEIN 16g; CARB 43.3g; FIBER 3.2g; CHOL 26mg; IRON 3.6mg; SODIUM 724mg; CALC 211mg

Potato Gnocchi with Spinach and Yellow Squash

Look for gnocchi (Italian dumplings) in the dry pasta section of your supermarket.

1 (1-pound) package vacuum-packed potato gnocchi

1 tablespoon olive oil

1 yellow squash, quartered lengthwise and thinly sliced

1½ teaspoons bottled minced garlic

1 (10-ounce) package fresh spinach, torn

¼ cup fat-free milk

¼ teaspoon freshly ground black pepper

⅛ teaspoon salt

½ cup (2 ounces) shredded smoked Gouda cheese or grated sharp provolone cheese

1. Cook gnocchi in boiling water according to package directions.

2. While gnocchi cooks, heat oil in a large skillet over medium heat. Add squash; sauté 4 minutes or until crisp-tender. Add garlic; sauté 1 minute. Add spinach, and cover and cook 2 minutes or just until spinach wilts. Reduce heat to low; stir in milk, pepper, and salt. Add gnocchi and cheese; stir gently. Serve immediately.

YIELD: 4 servings (serving size: 1 cup).

CALORIES 234 (29% from fat); FAT 7.7g (sat 3g, mono 3.6g, poly 0.5g); PROTEIN 10.8g; CARB 44.5g; FIBER 5.7g; CHOL 16mg; IRON 3.7mg; SODIUM 655mg; CALC 203mg

Roasted Fresh Corn, Poblano, and Cheddar Pizza

Refrigerated dough tends to shrink when removed from the can. Be sure to let the dough rest a few minutes before you start to work with it so it will be more pliable.

2 poblano chiles
Cooking spray
2 cups fresh corn kernels (about 4 ears)
½ cup chopped green onions
1 garlic clove, minced
½ cup 1% low-fat milk
2 large egg whites
1 large egg
½ teaspoon salt
¼ teaspoon freshly ground black pepper
1 cup (4 ounces) shredded sharp Cheddar cheese
1 (13.8-ounce) can refrigerated pizza crust dough
2 tablespoons fat-free sour cream
2 tablespoons chopped fresh cilantro

1. Preheat broiler.
2. Place poblano chiles on a foil-lined baking sheet; broil 10 minutes or until blackened and charred, turning occasionally. Place in a zip-top plastic bag; seal. Let chiles stand 10 minutes. Peel and discard skins, seeds, and stems. Chop chiles.
3. Lower oven temperature to 425°.
4. Heat a large nonstick skillet over medium-high heat. Coat pan with cooking spray. Add corn, green onions, and garlic; sauté 2 minutes or until lightly browned. Stir in milk; cook over medium heat 2 minutes or until liquid almost evaporates. Cool slightly. Place egg whites, egg, salt, and black pepper in a bowl; stir with a whisk. Stir in poblano chiles, corn mixture, and cheese.
5. Line a baking sheet with parchment paper. Unroll dough onto parchment paper; pat dough to form a 13 x 8–inch rectangle. Spread corn mixture over dough, leaving a 1-inch border. Fold 1 inch of dough over corn mixture. Bake at 425° for 12 minutes or until set. Serve with sour cream; sprinkle with cilantro. **YIELD:** 6 servings (serving size: 1 piece, 1 teaspoon sour cream, and 1 teaspoon cilantro).

CALORIES 331 (28% from fat); FAT 10.3g (sat 4.4g, mono 2.2g, poly 0.3g); PROTEIN 15.8g; CARB 44.5g; FIBER 1.6g; CHOL 57mg; IRON 2.5mg; SODIUM 808mg; CALC 186mg

Grilled Salad Pizza

1 package dry yeast (about 2¼ teaspoons)
⅔ cup warm water (100° to 110°)
3½ teaspoons olive oil, divided
1⅔ cups all-purpose flour (about 7½ ounces)
1 teaspoon sugar
½ teaspoon salt
½ teaspoon dried oregano
¼ teaspoon dried thyme
Cooking spray
½ cup (2 ounces) shredded part-skim mozzarella cheese
¼ cup (1 ounce) grated fresh Parmesan cheese
2½ cups coarsely chopped trimmed arugula (about 4 ounces)
1½ cups chopped seeded tomato
¼ cup chopped fresh basil
2 teaspoons balsamic vinegar
1½ teaspoons Dijon mustard
1 (14-ounce) can artichoke hearts, drained and chopped

1. Dissolve yeast in ⅔ cup warm water in a large bowl, and let stand 5 minutes. Stir in 1½ teaspoons oil. Lightly spoon flour into dry measuring cups; level with a knife. Combine flour, sugar, salt, oregano, and thyme. Add to yeast mixture; stir well. Turn dough out onto a lightly floured surface. Knead until smooth and elastic (about 10 minutes).
2. Place dough in a large bowl coated with cooking spray, turning to coat top. Cover and let rise in a warm place (85°), free from drafts, 45 minutes or until doubled in size. (Press two fingers into dough. If indentation remains, dough has risen enough.) Punch dough down; cover and let rest 5 minutes. Divide in half. Roll each half into a 9-inch circle on a floured surface.
3. Heat a grill pan over medium heat. Coat pan with cooking spray. Place one dough portion on pan; cook 10 minutes. Turn dough over; sprinkle with ¼ cup mozzarella and 2 tablespoons Parmesan. Cook 10 minutes; remove from pan. Repeat procedure with remaining dough and cheeses.
4. Combine 2 teaspoons oil, arugula, and next 5 ingredients in a medium bowl. Spoon 2 cups salad onto each pizza crust using a slotted spoon. Cut each pizza into 4 wedges. Serve immediately. **YIELD:** 4 servings (serving size: ½ pizza).

CALORIES 357 (25% from fat); FAT 9.8g (sat 3.3g, mono 4.4g, poly 1.1g); PROTEIN 15.5g; CARB 53.5g; FIBER 3.8g; CHOL 13mg; IRON 4.2mg; SODIUM 572mg; CALC 269mg

Grilled Salad Pizza

Tofu Fried Rice

Using frozen peas and carrots plus bottled minced garlic and ginger is an easy way to speed up the preparation of this simple Chinese standby. You can keep any leftover sake tightly capped in the refrigerator for up to three weeks, or substitute one tablespoon of rice wine vinegar for the sake.

2   cups uncooked instant rice
2   tablespoons vegetable oil, divided
1   (14-ounce) package reduced-fat firm tofu, drained and cut into (½-inch) cubes
2   large eggs, lightly beaten
1   cup (½-inch) slices green onions
1   cup frozen peas and carrots, thawed
2   teaspoons bottled minced garlic
1   teaspoon bottled minced fresh ginger
2   tablespoons sake (rice wine)
3   tablespoons low-sodium soy sauce
1   tablespoon hoisin sauce
½   teaspoon dark sesame oil
Thinly sliced green onions (optional)

1. Cook rice according to package directions, omitting salt and fat.

2. While rice cooks, heat 1 tablespoon vegetable oil in a large nonstick skillet over medium-high heat. Add tofu; cook 4 minutes or until lightly browned, stirring occasionally. Remove from pan. Add eggs to pan; cook 1 minute or until done, breaking egg into small pieces. Remove from pan. Add 1 tablespoon vegetable oil to pan. Add 1 cup onions, peas and carrots, garlic, and ginger; sauté 2 minutes.

3. While vegetable mixture cooks, combine sake, soy sauce, hoisin sauce, and sesame oil. Add cooked rice to pan; cook 2 minutes, stirring constantly. Add tofu, egg, and soy sauce mixture; cook 30 seconds, stirring constantly. Garnish with sliced green onions, if desired.

YIELD: 4 servings (serving size: 1½ cups).

CALORIES 376 (26% from fat); FAT 11g (sat 2g, mono 3g, poly 5.1g); PROTEIN 15.8g; CARB 50.6g; FIBER 3.2g; CHOL 106mg; IRON 3.8mg; SODIUM 629mg; CALC 79mg

Kung Pao Tofu Rice

To save on cleanup, microwave the rice first and use the same container for combining the remaining ingredients. Packaged grilled tofu can be found in most supermarkets in the refrigerated case along with the other soy and organic products.

  1 cup water
  ½ cup instant brown rice
  ½ cup shredded carrot
  ½ cup thinly sliced bok choy
  ¼ cup chopped green onions
  2 tablespoons chopped fresh cilantro
  3 ounces packaged grilled tofu, cut into ½-inch cubes (such as Marjon, about ½ cup)
  1 tablespoon rice vinegar
1½ tablespoons creamy peanut butter
  2 teaspoons water
  2 teaspoons low-sodium soy sauce
  ½ teaspoon chili garlic sauce
  ⅛ teaspoon salt

1. Combine 1 cup water and brown rice in a medium microwave-safe bowl; cover. Microwave at HIGH 4 minutes. Microwave at MEDIUM 5 minutes. Fluff with a fork. Let cool to room temperature. Add carrot and next 4 ingredients; toss gently to combine.
2. Combine vinegar and next 5 ingredients, stirring with a whisk. Add to rice mixture; toss gently to combine.
YIELD: 2 servings (serving size: about 1 cup).

CALORIES 217 (37% from fat); FAT 9g (sat 1.5g, mono 2.3g, poly 2.8g); PROTEIN 10g; CARB 25.7g; FIBER 3.4g; CHOL 0mg; IRON 1.2mg; SODIUM 471mg; CALC 48mg

ORGANIC FACT
Research suggests that organic produce can taste better than non-organic, but finding the freshest produce available also has a big impact on taste.

Thai Summer Squash and Tofu with Fresh Corn

This dish is rich and soupy; the basmati rice makes a flavorful base. Fresh corn adds a natural sweetness.

  1 teaspoon canola oil
  1 cup diced yellow squash
  1 cup diced zucchini
  1 (12.3-ounce) package reduced-fat extra-firm tofu, drained and cut into ½-inch cubes
  ½ teaspoon salt, divided
  3 cups fresh corn kernels (about 6 ears)
  1 cup light coconut milk
  ¾ cup (½-inch) sliced green onions
  ⅓ cup water
  1 tablespoon chopped fresh basil
  1 tablespoon chopped fresh cilantro
  1 teaspoon low-sodium soy sauce
  ¼ teaspoon freshly ground black pepper
  1 jalapeño pepper, seeded and chopped
  2 cups hot cooked basmati rice
  2 tablespoons chopped unsalted cashews, toasted

1. Heat oil in a large nonstick skillet over medium-high heat. Add squash, zucchini, and tofu; sprinkle with ¼ teaspoon salt. Stir-fry 8 minutes or until lightly browned. Stir in remaining ¼ teaspoon salt, corn, and next 8 ingredients. Reduce heat, and simmer 8 minutes or until corn is tender. Serve with rice. Sprinkle with cashews. **YIELD:** 4 servings (serving size: 1¼ cups vegetables, ½ cup rice, and 1½ teaspoons nuts).

CALORIES 283 (28% from fat); FAT 8.7g (sat 3g, mono 2.4g, poly 2.1g); PROTEIN 12.9g; CARB 43.4g; FIBER 5.5g; CHOL 0mg; IRON 3.1mg; SODIUM 462mg; CALC 78mg

Curried Noodles with Tofu

Coconut milk gives this meatless dish a velvety richness. Look for green curry paste in the Asian-foods section of your supermarket. Use it conservatively, though—a little goes a long way.

 6 ounces uncooked rice sticks (rice-flour noodles), angel hair pasta, or vermicelli
 1 cup light coconut milk
 1 tablespoon sugar
 2 tablespoons low-sodium soy sauce
 1½ tablespoons grated peeled fresh ginger
 1 teaspoon green curry paste
 ½ teaspoon salt
 4 garlic cloves, minced
 Cooking spray
 1 (12.3-ounce) package extra-firm tofu, drained and cut into 1-inch cubes
 1 cup red bell pepper strips
 4 cups shredded napa (Chinese) cabbage
 1 cup chopped green onions
 3 tablespoons chopped fresh cilantro

1. Place noodles in a large bowl. Add hot water to cover; let stand 5 minutes. Drain.
2. Combine light coconut milk, sugar, soy sauce, fresh ginger, green curry paste, salt, and minced garlic in a small bowl.
3. Heat a large nonstick skillet over medium-high heat. Coat pan with cooking spray. Add tofu; sauté 10 minutes or until golden brown. Remove tofu from pan, and keep warm.
4. Add bell pepper to pan; sauté 1 minute or until crisp-tender. Add cabbage; sauté 30 seconds. Stir in noodles, coconut milk mixture, and tofu; cook 2 minutes or until noodles are tender. Stir in onions and fresh cilantro.
YIELD: 4 servings (serving size: 1¼ cups).

CALORIES 300 (15% from fat); FAT 4.9g (sat 2.3g, mono 0.4g, poly 1.1g); PROTEIN 11.5g; CARB 51.4g; FIBER 4.5g; CHOL 0mg; IRON 3.6mg; SODIUM 678mg; CALC 89mg

Rice Noodles with Tofu and Bok Choy

Look for water-packed tofu, which will hold its shape when cooked and tossed with the rice noodles. If rice noodles are unavailable, substitute angel hair pasta.

 1 (6-ounce) package rice noodles
 ¼ cup low-sodium soy sauce
 2 tablespoons rice vinegar
 1 teaspoon sugar
 1 teaspoon dark sesame oil
 ½ teaspoon crushed red pepper
 Cooking spray
 2 cups (¼-inch-thick) red bell pepper strips
 5 cups sliced bok choy
 ½ pound firm water-packed tofu, drained and cut into ½-inch cubes
 3 garlic cloves, minced
 ½ cup thinly sliced green onions
 3 tablespoons chopped fresh cilantro

1. Cook noodles in boiling water 6 minutes; drain. Combine soy sauce, vinegar, sugar, oil, and crushed red pepper, stirring well with a whisk.
2. Heat a large nonstick skillet over medium-high heat. Coat pan with cooking spray. Add bell pepper strips; sauté 2 minutes. Add bok choy; sauté 1 minute. Add tofu and garlic; sauté 2 minutes. Add noodles and soy sauce mixture; cook 2 minutes or until thoroughly heated, tossing well to coat. Sprinkle with onions and cilantro.
YIELD: 4 servings (serving size: 2 cups).

CALORIES 281 (17% from fat); FAT 5.2g (sat 0.8g, mono 0.9g, poly 2.3g); PROTEIN 12.9g; CARB 46.7g; FIBER 4.2g; CHOL 0mg; IRON 3.8mg; SODIUM 575mg; CALC 190mg

ORGANIC FACT

When refrigerated soy milk was first marketed, it was typically organic. That is not always true now, so it's important to check the labels to be sure you are getting an organic product. Look for the USDA organic logo for 95% or better organic content.

Rice Noodles with Tofu
and Bok Choy

Vegetarian Meat Loaf

Using heart-healthy meatless ground beef and fat-free crumbles instead of ground round saves about 10 grams of fat per serving and adds almost five grams of fiber. Serve with mashed potatoes and sautéed green beans for a hearty dinner.

1   cup chopped celery
1   cup sliced carrots
1   medium onion, peeled and quartered
3   garlic cloves, minced
1   tablespoon canola oil
¾   cup ketchup, divided
⅓   cup dry breadcrumbs
2   large eggs
1   (12-ounce) package meatless ground burger
1   (12-ounce) package meatless fat-free crumbles
Cooking spray

1. Preheat oven to 350°.
2. Combine first 4 ingredients in a food processor; process until finely chopped.
3. Heat oil in a large nonstick skillet over medium-high heat. Add onion mixture; sauté 5 minutes or until tender. Place onion mixture, ½ cup ketchup, breadcrumbs, eggs, ground burger, and crumbles in a large bowl; mix well.
4. Place mixture in a 9 x 5–inch loaf pan coated with cooking spray. Spread remaining ¼ cup ketchup over loaf. Bake at 350° for 35 minutes. Let stand 10 minutes. Cut loaf into 8 slices. **YIELD:** 8 servings.

CALORIES 197 (16% from fat); FAT 3.7g (sat 0.7g, mono 1g, poly 1.3g); PROTEIN 20.5g; CARB 22.3g; FIBER 5.9g; CHOL 53mg; IRON 3mg; SODIUM 667mg; CALC 41mg

Vegetarian Chicken–Green Chile Enchilada Casserole

This meatless version of a family favorite uses soy-based chicken strips and has the heartiness and flavor of its classic counterpart. Meatless alternatives are low in saturated fat and cholesterol and are often high in fiber. Incorporating them in recipes is a great way to get the heart-health benefits of soy.

```
1    teaspoon vegetable oil
1    cup chopped onion
3    garlic cloves, minced
1    (4.5-ounce) can chopped green chiles, undrained
2    (6-ounce) packages meatless fat-free chicken strips
     (such as Lightlife Smart Menu), chopped
½    teaspoon ground cumin
½    teaspoon chili powder
2    (10-ounce) cans green chile enchilada sauce
Cooking spray
14   (6-inch) corn tortillas, cut into quarters
1½   cups (6 ounces) preshredded reduced-fat Mexican
     blend cheese, divided
Chopped fresh cilantro (optional)
```

1. Preheat oven to 375°.

2. Heat oil in a large nonstick skillet over medium-high heat. Add onion and garlic; sauté 5 minutes or until onion is tender. Add chiles; cook 3 minutes, stirring constantly. Remove from heat; stir in chopped chicken strips.

3. Combine ½ teaspoon cumin, ½ teaspoon chili powder, and enchilada sauce. Pour one-third of sauce mixture into an 11 x 7–inch baking dish coated with cooking spray. Arrange half of tortilla quarters over sauce mixture; top with onion mixture. Sprinkle with ¾ cup Mexican blend cheese; top with one-third of sauce mixture. Top with remaining tortillas and sauce mixture. Bake at 375° for 15 minutes. Sprinkle with remaining ¾ cup cheese; bake an additional 10 minutes. Sprinkle with cilantro, if desired. **YIELD:** 8 servings.

CALORIES 218 (29% from fat); FAT 7.3g (sat 2.3g, mono 1.4g, poly 1g); PROTEIN 17.8g; CARB 22.9g; FIBER 5.5g; CHOL 15mg; IRON 0.1mg; SODIUM 889mg; CALC 145mg

Biscuits and Vegetarian Sausage Gravy

Vegetarian sausage has a firmer texture than pork sausage. Crumbling the sausage helps distribute it evenly throughout the gravy.

```
1    (16.3-ounce) can reduced-fat refrigerated biscuit
     dough
1    tablespoon vegetable oil
½    (14-ounce) package meatless fat-free sausage
¼    cup all-purpose flour (about 1 ounce)
3    cups 1% low-fat milk
½    teaspoon salt
¼    teaspoon freshly ground black pepper
```

1. Prepare biscuits according to package directions.

2. Heat oil in a large nonstick skillet over medium-high heat. Add sausage; cook 3 minutes or until browned, stirring to crumble. Remove from heat; cool slightly. Crumble sausage into ½-inch pieces; return to pan.

3. Lightly spoon flour into a dry measuring cup; level with a knife. Combine flour and milk, stirring with a whisk until smooth. Add milk mixture, salt, and pepper to pan; bring to a boil over medium-high heat. Cover, reduce heat, and simmer 3 minutes or until thick. Split biscuits in half. Place 2 biscuit halves on each of 8 plates; top each serving with about ⅓ cup gravy. Serve immediately. **YIELD:** 8 servings.

CALORIES 268 (29% from fat); FAT 8.7g (sat 2.4g, mono 4g, poly 1g); PROTEIN 11.4g; CARB 36.9g; FIBER 0.6g; CHOL 4mg; IRON 1mg; SODIUM 910mg; CALC 131mg

ORGANIC FACT

Organic milk comes from cows that are not treated with growth hormones or antibiotics, which is good for consumers. In addition, organic standards require that cows have access to open pasture, which is good for the cows.

Source: USDA National Organic Program

MEATS

Fresh Herb–Coated Beef Tenderloin Steaks
with Mushroom Gravy, page 95

Meat Loaf

The meat loaf is easy to lift out of the slow cooker with the foil "hammock" that holds it.

1½ pounds extralean ground beef
¾ cup finely chopped onion
½ cup seasoned breadcrumbs
¼ cup finely chopped green bell pepper
¼ cup ketchup
2 tablespoons prepared mustard
1 teaspoon garlic powder
1 teaspoon dried oregano
¼ teaspoon salt
¼ teaspoon freshly ground black pepper
1 large egg white
Cooking spray
2 tablespoons ketchup

1. Combine first 11 ingredients in a large bowl; mix well. Form mixture into an 8½ x 4½–inch loaf.
2. Fold a 12-inch-long piece of foil in half lengthwise. Spray foil with cooking spray. Place meat loaf on foil, leaving a 2- to 3-inch border at each end of foil. Lift foil, and place in an electric slow cooker. Spread 2 table-spoons ketchup over top of meat loaf. Cook on HIGH 4 hours or until a thermometer registers 170°. Using foil, carefully lift meat loaf out of cooker. Let stand 10 minutes; cut into 6 slices. **YIELD:** 6 servings (serving size: 1 slice).

CALORIES 263 (38% from fat); FAT 11g (sat 4.3g, mono 4.7g, poly 0.7g); PROTEIN 26.1g; CARB 13.9g; FIBER 1.3g; CHOL 41mg; IRON 3.3mg; SODIUM 590mg; CALC 44mg

ORGANIC FACT

Organic ketchup has benefits that go far beyond taste. A USDA test revealed that, on average, organic brands have 57% higher levels of the anti-oxidant lycopene than the non-organic brands.

Source: The Organic Center

Moroccan Meatballs in Spicy Tomato Sauce

Sweet and savory seasoned meatballs simmer in an aromatic tomato sauce for a Mediterranean-style dinner. Use kitchen shears to coarsely chop the tomatoes while they are still in the can. You can shape the meatballs in advance and store them in the freezer to save time. The rest of the recipe is best prepared and cooked the same day.

MEATBALLS:
½ cup dry breadcrumbs
¼ cup dried currants
¼ cup finely chopped onion
½ teaspoon salt
½ teaspoon ground cumin
½ teaspoon dried oregano
¼ teaspoon ground cinnamon
1½ pounds lean ground beef
1 large egg white
Cooking spray

SAUCE:
¼ cup tomato paste
1 teaspoon fennel seeds
1 teaspoon grated orange rind
½ teaspoon ground cumin
¼ teaspoon ground cinnamon
¼ teaspoon salt
¼ teaspoon ground red pepper
1 (28-ounce) can whole tomatoes, coarsely chopped

REMAINING INGREDIENTS:
3 cups hot cooked couscous
Chopped fresh parsley (optional)

1. To prepare meatballs, combine first 9 ingredients in a bowl; shape meat mixture into 30 meatballs. Heat a large nonstick skillet over medium-high heat. Coat pan with cooking spray. Add half of meatballs to pan; cook 3 minutes or until browned, stirring frequently. Place browned meatballs in an electric slow cooker. Coat pan with cooking spray; repeat procedure with remaining 15 meatballs.
2. To prepare sauce, combine tomato paste and next 7 ingredients. Add to slow cooker; stir gently to coat. Cover and cook on LOW 6 hours. Serve over couscous. Garnish with parsley, if desired. **YIELD:** 6 servings (serving size: 5 meatballs, 1 cup sauce, and ½ cup couscous).

CALORIES 312 (17% from fat); FAT 6g (sat 2.2g, mono 2.2g, poly 0.9g); PROTEIN 28.7g; CARB 37.8g; FIBER 4.2g; CHOL 60mg; IRON 4.6mg; SODIUM 696mg; CALC 85mg

Moroccan Meatballs in Spicy Tomato Sauce

Stuffed Peppers

Precooking the peppers and bringing the sauce to a boil before adding it to the dish cuts down on the baking time.

1 (3½-ounce) bag boil-in-bag long-grain rice
4 medium red bell peppers
¾ pound ground sirloin
1 cup chopped onion
½ cup chopped fresh parsley
1 teaspoon paprika
½ teaspoon salt
⅛ teaspoon ground allspice
2 cups bottled tomato-and-basil pasta sauce, divided
½ cup (2 ounces) grated fresh Parmesan cheese
½ cup dry red wine
Cooking spray

1. Preheat oven to 450°.
2. Cook rice according to package directions, omitting salt and fat.
3. While rice cooks, cut tops off bell peppers; reserve tops. Discard seeds and membranes. Place peppers, cut sides down, in an 8-inch square baking dish; cover with plastic wrap. Microwave at HIGH 2 minutes or until peppers are crisp-tender. Cool.
4. Heat a large nonstick skillet over medium-high heat. Add beef and next 5 ingredients; cook 4 minutes or until beef is lightly browned, stirring to crumble. Remove from heat. Add cooked rice, ½ cup pasta sauce, and cheese to beef mixture, stirring to combine.
5. While beef cooks, combine 1½ cups pasta sauce and wine in a small saucepan; bring to a boil.
6. Spoon about ¾ cup beef mixture into each pepper. Place peppers in a 2-quart baking dish coated with cooking spray, and add wine mixture to pan. Cover with foil.
7. Bake at 450° for 20 minutes. Uncover; bake an additional 5 minutes or until lightly browned. Serve peppers with sauce. Garnish with pepper tops. **YIELD:** 4 servings (serving size: 1 stuffed pepper and ⅓ cup sauce).

CALORIES 347 (20% from fat); FAT 7.9g (sat 3.9g, mono 2.6g, poly 0.7g); PROTEIN 26.6g; CARB 39.9g; FIBER 4.6g; CHOL 55mg; IRON 4.1mg; SODIUM 747mg; CALC 284mg

Skillet Stuffed Peppers

Use any color bell pepper in this 20-minute recipe. Save time with packaged refrigerated mashed potatoes.

 2 large green bell peppers, halved lengthwise and
   seeded
Cooking spray
 ¾ pound ground round
 ½ cup water
 1 (1.25-ounce) package taco seasoning
 1 (20-ounce) package refrigerated mashed potatoes
 ¼ cup (1 ounce) reduced-fat shredded Cheddar
   cheese
Cracked black pepper (optional)

1. Place bell pepper halves, cut sides down, on a microwave-safe dish; cover with plastic wrap. Microwave at HIGH 3 minutes and 30 seconds or until pepper halves are crisp-tender. Let stand, covered, 3 minutes (peppers will soften).
2. Heat a large nonstick skillet over medium-high heat. Coat pan with cooking spray. Add beef to pan; cook 3 minutes, stirring to crumble. Add ½ cup water and seasoning; stir to combine. Cover, reduce heat, and cook 5 minutes or until done.
3. While beef cooks and peppers stand, cook potatoes in microwave according to package directions, omitting salt and fat.
4. Spoon ½ cup beef mixture into each pepper half; top each with ⅔ cup potatoes. Sprinkle each pepper half with 1 tablespoon cheese. Garnish with black pepper, if desired. **YIELD:** 4 servings (serving size: 1 stuffed pepper half).

CALORIES 338 (36% from fat); FAT 13.4g (sat 5.3g, mono 5.7g, poly 0.4g); PROTEIN 20.1g; CARB 29.3g; FIBER 5.1g; CHOL 59mg; IRON 2.4mg; SODIUM 663mg; CALC 48mg

ORGANIC FACT
Maintaining the quality of the Earth's water supplies is a challenge. Organic agricultural production helps prevent further damage to our precious water resources by using techniques such as rainwater catchments or drip-irrigation.

Beef-Taco Rice with Refried Beans

This is an easy dish to serve a crowd. Using instant rice, taco seasoning, canned refried beans, and preshredded cheese makes it quick to assemble. You can even find chopped onion and bell pepper in many produce sections.

 4 cups water
 1 cup chopped onion
 1 cup chopped green bell pepper
 ¼ teaspoon salt
 ¼ teaspoon black pepper
 1 (1.25-ounce) package taco seasoning, divided
 4 cups uncooked instant rice
 2 (8-ounce) cans no-salt-added tomato sauce
 1 pound ground round
Cooking spray
 1 (16-ounce) can fat-free refried beans
 1 (8-ounce) package preshredded reduced-fat
   Mexican blend or Cheddar cheese

1. Preheat oven to 350°.
2. Combine first 5 ingredients in a large saucepan; add half of taco seasoning. Bring to a boil. Remove from heat. Stir in rice; cover and let stand 5 minutes. Stir in tomato sauce.
3. Cook meat in a large nonstick skillet over medium-high heat until browned, stirring to crumble. Drain; return meat to pan. Stir in remaining taco seasoning.
4. Spread half of rice mixture in a 13 x 9–inch baking dish coated with cooking spray. Spread beans evenly over rice mixture; top with beef mixture and half of cheese. Spread remaining rice mixture over cheese; top with remaining cheese. Bake at 350° for 10 minutes or until cheese melts. **YIELD:** 10 servings (serving size: about 1¼ cups).

CALORIES 371 (18% from fat); FAT 7.5g (sat 3.6g, mono 2.5g, poly 0.4g); PROTEIN 23.7g; CARB 51.2g; FIBER 3.8g; CHOL 42mg; IRON 4.4mg; SODIUM 696mg; CALC 221mg

Spaghetti with Meat Sauce

A few additions to this bottled spaghetti sauce render customized flavor from a convenience product.

    12 ounces uncooked spaghetti
    ¾   pound ground sirloin
    1   cup chopped onion
    1½ teaspoons bottled minced garlic
    ¾   cup dry red wine
    1   (26-ounce) jar low-fat spaghetti sauce
    ⅔   cup 2% reduced-fat milk
    ½   teaspoon salt
    ¼   teaspoon black pepper

1. Cook pasta according to package directions, omitting salt and fat.
2. While pasta cooks, heat a large nonstick skillet over medium-high heat. Add beef; cook until browned, stirring to crumble. Drain beef; set aside.
3. Add onion and garlic to pan; sauté 3 minutes. Add wine; cook 3 minutes or until liquid almost evaporates.
4. Stir in beef and spaghetti sauce; bring to a boil. Reduce heat, and simmer 5 minutes, stirring occasionally. Stir in milk, salt, and pepper; cook 3 minutes, stirring occasionally. Serve sauce over pasta. **YIELD:** 6 servings (serving size: about 1 cup pasta and ⅔ cup sauce).

CALORIES 401 (15% from fat); FAT 6.9g (sat 1.8g, mono 2.9g, poly 1.1g); PROTEIN 22.8g; CARB 60.1g; FIBER 4.9g; CHOL 37mg; IRON 4.7mg; SODIUM 544mg; CALC 77mg

ORGANIC FACT
The USDA's National Organic Program does not allow cloned animals to be sold as organic.

Source: USDA National Organic Program

Make-Ahead Cheese-and-Hamburger Casserole

The penne doesn't have to be cooked beforehand because it absorbs the liquid when the dish is refrigerated overnight. If you want to make it the same day, cook the pasta before adding it to the other ingredients.

    1   pound ground round
    1   cup chopped onion
    3   garlic cloves, crushed
    1   (8-ounce) package presliced mushrooms
    6   tablespoons tomato paste
    1   teaspoon sugar
    1   teaspoon dried thyme
    1   teaspoon dried oregano
    ¼   teaspoon pepper
    1   (28-ounce) can whole tomatoes, undrained and
        chopped
    ⅓   cup all-purpose flour (about 1½ ounces)
    2½ cups 2% reduced-fat milk
    1   cup (4 ounces) crumbled feta cheese
    ¾   cup (3 ounces) shredded part-skim mozzarella cheese
    4   cups uncooked penne (tube-shaped pasta) or whole
        wheat penne
    1   tablespoon chopped fresh parsley (optional)

1. Combine first 3 ingredients in a large nonstick skillet, and cook over medium-high heat until browned, stirring to crumble. Add mushrooms; cook 5 minutes or until tender. Add tomato paste and next 5 ingredients; stir well. Bring to a boil; reduce heat, and simmer, uncovered, 20 minutes. Remove from heat.
2. Lightly spoon flour into a dry measuring cup; level with a knife. Place flour in a medium saucepan. Gradually add milk, stirring with a whisk until blended. Place over medium heat; cook 10 minutes or until thick, stirring constantly. Stir in cheeses; cook 3 minutes or until cheeses melt, stirring constantly. Reserve ½ cup cheese sauce; set aside. Pour remaining cheese sauce, beef mixture, and pasta in a 13 x 9–inch baking dish; stir gently. Drizzle reserved cheese sauce over pasta mixture. Cover and refrigerate 24 hours.
3. Preheat oven to 350°.
4. Bake at 350°, covered, for 1 hour and 10 minutes or until thoroughly heated. Sprinkle with fresh parsley, if desired. **YIELD:** 8 servings (serving size: about 1½ cups).

CALORIES 412 (23% from fat); FAT 10.8g (sat 5.5g, mono 3.2g, poly 0.9g); PROTEIN 27.5g; CARB 51.1g; FIBER 3.2g; CHOL 60mg; IRON 4.9mg; SODIUM 448mg; CALC 286mg

Mini Meat Loaves

A tangy mixture of ketchup and Dijon mustard not only flavors the meat loaves but also acts as a glaze that helps them brown nicely as they cook. Serve with mashed potatoes.

½   cup ketchup
1½ tablespoons Dijon mustard
1   pound ground sirloin
¾   cup finely chopped onion
¼   cup seasoned breadcrumbs
½   teaspoon salt
½   teaspoon dried oregano
⅛   teaspoon black pepper
1   large egg, lightly beaten
Cooking spray

1. Preheat oven to 400°.

2. Combine ketchup and mustard, stirring well with a whisk. Reserve 2½ tablespoons ketchup mixture. Combine remaining ketchup mixture, beef, and next 6 ingredients in a large bowl, stirring to combine.

3. Divide beef mixture into 4 equal portions. Shape each portion into a 4 x 2½–inch loaf; place loaves on a jelly-roll pan coated with cooking spray.

4. Spread about 2 teaspoons reserved ketchup mixture evenly over each meat loaf. Bake at 400° for 25 minutes or until done. **YIELD:** 4 servings (serving size: 1 meat loaf).

CALORIES 255 (28% from fat); FAT 7.9g (sat 2.8g, mono 3.2g, poly 0.4g); PROTEIN 27.4g; CARB 15.7g; FIBER 0.9g; CHOL 120mg; IRON 2.7mg; SODIUM 944mg; CALC 31mg

Cape Malay Curry

Curries from South Africa's Cape Malay are known for their complex combination of flavors and often feature sweet spices like cinnamon and ginger, dried fruit (especially apricots), and savory seasonings. This beef stew is great over rice, mashed potatoes, or egg noodles.

  1½ teaspoons ground turmeric
  1½ teaspoons ground cumin
  1½ teaspoons ground coriander
  1½ teaspoons chili powder
  ¾   teaspoon ground cinnamon
  ½   teaspoon salt
  2   teaspoons canola oil
  2   cups chopped onion
  1½ tablespoons minced peeled fresh ginger
  2   bay leaves
  1   garlic clove, minced
  1   pound beef stew meat, cut into bite-sized pieces
  1¼ cups less-sodium beef broth
  1   cup water
  1   cup chopped green bell pepper (about 1 medium)
  ⅓   cup chopped dried apricots
  ⅓   cup apricot spread
  2   teaspoons red wine vinegar
  ¼   cup low-fat buttermilk

1. Combine first 6 ingredients in a small bowl.
2. Heat oil in a Dutch oven over medium-high heat. Add spice mixture; cook 15 seconds, stirring constantly. Add onion; sauté 2 minutes. Add ginger, bay leaves, and garlic; sauté 15 seconds. Add beef; sauté 3 minutes. Add broth and next 5 ingredients; bring to a boil. Cover, reduce heat, and simmer 1½ hours. Uncover; discard bay leaves. Simmer 30 minutes or until beef is very tender. Remove from heat; stir in buttermilk. **YIELD:** 4 servings (serving size: 1¼ cups).

CALORIES 349 (30% from fat); FAT 11.5g (sat 3.4g, mono 5.1g, poly 1.2g); PROTEIN 25.7g; CARB 35.3g; FIBER 3.9g; CHOL 71mg; IRON 4.3mg; SODIUM 396mg; CALC 77mg

Beef Burgundy with Egg Noodles

This entrée actually tastes better when made a day in advance, which makes it a great choice for entertaining. Cook the egg noodles while you reheat the stew.

  ⅓   cup all-purpose flour (about 1½ ounces)
  2   teaspoons salt, divided
  ¾   teaspoon freshly ground black pepper, divided
  2¼ pounds beef stew meat
  3   bacon slices, chopped and divided
  1   cup chopped onion
  1   cup sliced carrot
  4   garlic cloves, minced
  1½ cups dry red wine
  1   (14-ounce) can less-sodium beef broth
  8   cups halved mushrooms (about 1½ pounds)
  2   tablespoons tomato paste
  2   teaspoons chopped fresh thyme
  2   bay leaves
  1   (16-ounce) package frozen pearl onions
  7   cups hot cooked medium egg noodles
      (about 6 cups uncooked noodles)
  3   tablespoons chopped fresh flat-leaf parsley

1. Lightly spoon flour into a dry measuring cup; level with a knife. Combine flour, 1 teaspoon salt, and ¼ teaspoon pepper in a large zip-top plastic bag. Add beef; seal and shake to coat.
2. Cook half of bacon in a large Dutch oven over medium-high heat until crisp. Remove bacon from pan with a slotted spoon; set aside. Add half of beef mixture to drippings in pan; cook 5 minutes, browning on all sides. Remove beef from pan; cover and keep warm. Repeat procedure with remaining bacon and beef mixture. Remove beef from pan; cover and keep warm.
3. Add chopped onion, carrot, and garlic to pan; sauté 5 minutes. Stir in wine and beef broth, scraping pan to loosen browned bits. Add bacon, beef, remaining 1 teaspoon salt, remaining ½ teaspoon black pepper, mushrooms, tomato paste, thyme, bay leaves, and pearl onions; bring to a boil. Cover, reduce heat, and simmer 45 minutes. Uncover and cook 1 hour or until beef is tender. Discard bay leaves. Serve beef mixture over noodles, and sprinkle with parsley. **YIELD:** 9 servings (serving size: about 1 cup beef mixture, ¾ cup noodles, and 1 teaspoon parsley).

CALORIES 447 (29% from fat); FAT 14.6g (sat 5.1g, mono 6.1g, poly 1.5g); PROTEIN 32.7g; CARB 45.7g; FIBER 3.9g; CHOL 117mg; IRON 6mg; SODIUM 677mg; CALC 47mg

Beef Burgundy with
Egg Noodles

Tequila-Marinated Beef-and-Pepper Fajitas

The convenience of using a stove-top grill pan is that it gives meat and vegetables the appearance and taste of food cooked outside without having to wait for the grill to preheat. These fajitas are a great weeknight supper, but you can also serve them with salsa and a dollop of light sour cream as an appetizer. Add a pitcher of sangría and you have all you need for a festive Tex-Mex menu.

```
¼    cup tequila
2    tablespoons chopped fresh cilantro
2    tablespoons fresh lime juice
1    tablespoon Worcestershire sauce
1    teaspoon ground cumin
½    teaspoon canola oil
¼    teaspoon ground red pepper
2    garlic cloves, minced
1    (1-pound) flank steak, trimmed
1    green bell pepper, cut into 4 wedges
1    red bell pepper, cut into 4 wedges
4    (¼-inch-thick) slices red onion
¼    teaspoon salt
¼    teaspoon black pepper
Cooking spray
4    (8-inch) fat-free flour tortillas
```

1. Combine first 8 ingredients in a large zip-top plastic bag; stir with a whisk. Add steak; seal bag, and marinate in refrigerator 1 hour. Remove steak from bag; discard marinade.
2. Sprinkle bell pepper wedges and onion slices with salt and pepper.
3. Heat a large grill pan over medium-high heat. Coat pan with cooking spray. Add bell pepper wedges to pan; cook 5 minutes. Turn bell pepper wedges over; add onion slices to pan. Cook 5 minutes, turning onion slices once. Remove bell pepper wedges and onion slices from pan; set aside, and keep warm. Add steak to pan; cook about 5 minutes on each side or until desired degree of doneness. Cut steak diagonally across grain into thin slices.
4. Warm tortillas according to package directions. Arrange about 3 ounces steak, 2 bell pepper wedges, and 1 onion slice down center of each tortilla; fold tortillas in half. **YIELD:** 4 servings.

CALORIES 346 (30% from fat); FAT 11.7g (sat 4.6g, mono 4.5g, poly 0.7g); PROTEIN 26.1g; CARB 28.4g; FIBER 2g; CHOL 58mg; IRON 4mg; SODIUM 577mg; CALC 19mg

Cajun Flank Steak

```
1    tablespoon garlic powder
1    tablespoon onion powder
2    teaspoons sugar
2    teaspoons paprika
1    teaspoon chili powder
¾    teaspoon salt
½    teaspoon black pepper
¼    teaspoon ground red pepper
1    (1-pound) flank steak, trimmed
Cooking spray
```

1. Combine first 8 ingredients in a small bowl. Rub spice mixture over both sides of flank steak.
2. Heat a nonstick grill pan over medium-high heat. Coat pan with cooking spray. Add steak; cook 5 minutes on each side. Cut steak diagonally across grain into thin slices. **YIELD:** 4 servings (serving size: 3 ounces).

CALORIES 195 (42% from fat); FAT 9g (sat 3.6g, mono 3.3g, poly 0.5g); PROTEIN 22.7g; CARB 6.1g; FIBER 0.9g; CHOL 54mg; IRON 2.6mg; SODIUM 512mg; CALC 19mg

Pepper Steak

```
Cooking spray
2    tablespoons all-purpose flour
2    tablespoons bottled minced garlic (about 6 cloves)
1    tablespoon minced peeled fresh ginger
¼    teaspoon salt
⅛    teaspoon black pepper
1    (1-pound) sirloin steak, trimmed and cut across
     grain into ¼-inch-thick strips
1    cup red bell pepper strips
½    cup beef consommé
1    teaspoon low-sodium soy sauce
1    teaspoon dark sesame oil
```

1. Heat a large nonstick skillet over medium-high heat. Coat pan with cooking spray. Combine flour and next 5 ingredients, tossing to coat. Add beef mixture to pan; sauté 3 minutes. Add bell pepper and remaining ingredients to pan; cover and cook 7 minutes or until peppers are crisp-tender, stirring occasionally. **YIELD:** 4 servings (serving size: 1 cup).

CALORIES 197 (28% from fat); FAT 6.2g (sat 1.9g, mono 2.5g, poly 0.8g); PROTEIN 26.5g; CARB 7.7g; FIBER 0.9g; CHOL 69mg; IRON 3.7mg; SODIUM 419mg; CALC 22mg

Pepper Steak

Sirloin Steak with Tarragon-Garlic Sour Cream

The tangy sauce dresses up a steak house favorite. Packaged potato wedges round out the dish.

⅓ cup sour cream
¼ cup low-fat mayonnaise
2 tablespoons whole-grain Dijon mustard
1 teaspoon dried tarragon
1 teaspoon bottled minced garlic
½ teaspoon salt, divided
¼ teaspoon black pepper, divided
Cooking spray
1 (1-pound) boneless sirloin steak, trimmed
1 (20-ounce) package refrigerated red potato wedges

1. Combine first 5 ingredients in a small bowl; stir in ¼ teaspoon salt and ⅛ teaspoon pepper. Set aside.
2. Heat a large nonstick skillet over medium-high heat.

Coat the pan with cooking spray. Sprinkle both sides of steak with remaining ¼ teaspoon salt and remaining ⅛ teaspoon pepper; add steak to pan. Cook 5 minutes on each side or until desired degree of doneness. Remove from pan; let stand 5 minutes. Cut into ¼-inch-thick slices. Keep warm.
3. Wipe pan with a paper towel; return to heat. Recoat pan with cooking spray. Add the potatoes; sauté 15 minutes or until browned and thoroughly heated, stirring occasionally. Serve with steak and sauce. **YIELD:** 4 servings (serving size: 3 ounces steak, ⅔ cup potatoes, and 3 tablespoons sauce).

CALORIES 307 (32% from fat); FAT 11g (sat 4.8g, mono 3.6g, poly 0.4g); PROTEIN 26.4g; CARB 22.9g; FIBER 3.7g; CHOL 53mg; IRON 2.1mg; SODIUM 732mg; CALC 44mg

Shepherd's Pie Peppers

Shepherd's Pie assumes a new identity when stuffed into pepper shells.

  2 large green bell peppers (about 1 pound)
Cooking spray
  6 ounces lean boneless sirloin steak, cut into
     ¾-inch cubes
  ¾ cup fat-free beef broth
  ⅔ cup frozen peas and carrots
  ⅓ cup chopped onion
  2 tablespoons tomato paste
  1 teaspoon Worcestershire sauce
  ¼ teaspoon black pepper
  ⅛ teaspoon salt
  1 tablespoon cornstarch
  1 tablespoon water
  1 cup frozen mashed potatoes
  ½ cup fat-free milk
  2 teaspoons grated Parmesan cheese
Dash of paprika

1. Preheat oven to 400°.
2. Cut tops off bell peppers; discard tops, seeds, and membranes. Cook peppers in boiling water 5 minutes; drain and set aside.
3. Heat a large nonstick skillet over medium-high heat. Coat pan with cooking spray. Add beef; cook 6 minutes or until browned, stirring frequently. Drain and pat dry with paper towels. Wipe drippings from pan with a paper towel.
4. Return meat to pan; add beef broth and next 6 ingredients. Bring to a boil; cover, reduce heat, and simmer 10 minutes. Combine cornstarch and 1 tablespoon water, stirring well with a whisk. Add to meat mixture; bring to a boil. Cook 1 minute, stirring constantly. Divide meat mixture evenly between peppers. Place stuffed peppers in an 8-inch square baking dish.
5. Combine potatoes and milk in a microwave-safe bowl, stirring well. Microwave at HIGH 2 minutes, stirring after 1 minute. Let stand 2 minutes. Spoon warm potato mixture evenly over tops of stuffed peppers; lightly coat potato mixture with cooking spray. Combine Parmesan cheese and dash of paprika; sprinkle over potato mixture.
6. Bake at 400° for 20 minutes or until potatoes are golden. **YIELD:** 2 servings (serving size: 1 pepper).

CALORIES 386 (21% from fat); FAT 9g (sat 3.3g, mono 3.4g, poly 1.1g); PROTEIN 30.1g; CARB 43.3g; FIBER 6.2g; CHOL 66mg; IRON 3.7mg; SODIUM 991mg; CALC 173mg

Beef, Okra, and Potato Kebabs

This recipe features unusual, delicious grilled okra. Grilling infuses the okra pods with a smoky flavor, and it allows them to maintain their firm texture.

  8 fingerling potatoes, each cut in half lengthwise
  2 tablespoons chopped fresh parsley
  1½ tablespoons prepared horseradish
  1½ tablespoons whole-grain Dijon mustard
  1 tablespoon Worcestershire sauce
  1½ teaspoons sugar
  2 teaspoons olive oil
  ¼ teaspoon freshly ground black pepper
  ½ teaspoon salt, divided
  1 cup (1-inch-square) cut red bell pepper
 16 small okra pods
  8 shallots, peeled and halved
  1 (1-pound) boneless sirloin steak, trimmed and cut
     into 1-inch cubes
  1 medium yellow squash, halved lengthwise and cut
     into ½-inch slices (about 2 cups)
Cooking spray

1. Place potatoes in a saucepan; cover with water. Bring to a boil. Reduce heat, and simmer 15 minutes or until tender; drain. Cool.
2. Combine parsley, horseradish, Dijon mustard, Worcestershire sauce, sugar, olive oil, and ¼ teaspoon black pepper in a large bowl, stirring well. Stir in ¼ teaspoon salt. Add potatoes, bell pepper, okra, shallots, beef, and squash; toss well to coat. Cover and chill 1 hour.
3. Prepare grill.
4. Thread vegetables and beef alternately onto each of 8 (10-inch) skewers. Sprinkle kebabs evenly with remaining ¼ teaspoon salt. Place kebabs on grill rack coated with cooking spray, and grill 10 minutes or until desired degree of doneness, turning occasionally. **YIELD:** 4 servings (serving size: 2 kebabs).

CALORIES 338 (30% from fat); FAT 11.3g (sat 3.7g, mono 5.3g, poly 0.7g); PROTEIN 30.6g; CARB 30.4g; FIBER 3.9g; CHOL 76mg; IRON 4.8mg; SODIUM 564mg; CALC 76mg

Brandy and Mustard-Glazed Tenderloin Steaks

Brandy and Mustard-Glazed Tenderloin Steaks

Serve with mashed potatoes drizzled with olive oil. Place fresh broccoli florets in a bowl with a small amount of water. Microwave three minutes or until crisp-tender; garnish with grated lemon rind, if desired.

    4   (4-ounce) beef tenderloin steaks
    ¼   teaspoon salt
    ⅛   teaspoon black pepper
    2   teaspoons butter
    ¼   cup minced shallots
    ½   cup fat-free, less-sodium beef broth
    1   tablespoon Dijon mustard
    2   tablespoons brandy

1. Heat a large nonstick skillet over medium heat. Sprinkle both sides of steaks evenly with salt and pepper. Add steaks to pan; cook 3 minutes on each side or until browned. Remove steaks from pan; keep warm.
2. Melt butter in pan. Add shallots to pan, and cook 2 minutes, stirring occasionally. Add broth and mustard to pan; cook 1 minute or until sauce thickens, stirring occasionally. Stir in brandy. Return steaks to pan, and cook 1 minute on each side or until desired degree of doneness. Serve sauce with steaks. **YIELD:** 4 servings (serving size: 1 steak and 4 teaspoons sauce).

CALORIES 218 (38% from fat); FAT 9.3g (sat 3.9g, mono 3.5g, poly 0.4g); PROTEIN 25.7g; CARB 2.7g; FIBER 0.2g; CHOL 81mg; IRON 2.1mg; SODIUM 371mg; CALC 34mg

Steak Diane

This recipe will impress your family and guests with very little effort. For an easy side of roasted potatoes, start with precut potato wedges from the refrigerated section of the grocery store.

    ½   teaspoon salt, divided
    ¼   teaspoon black pepper
    6   (4-ounce) beef tenderloin steaks, trimmed
         (about 1 inch thick)
    1   teaspoon butter
    ½   cup finely chopped shallots
    ⅓   cup water
    2   tablespoons Worcestershire sauce
    1½   tablespoons fresh lemon juice
    1½   tablespoons dry sherry
    2   tablespoons chopped fresh parsley

1. Heat a large, heavy skillet over medium-high heat. Sprinkle ¼ teaspoon salt and black pepper evenly over steaks. Add steaks to pan; cook 4 minutes on each side or until desired degree of doneness. Remove from pan; cover and keep warm.
2. Melt butter in pan over medium heat. Add shallots; cook 2 minutes or until tender, stirring occasionally. Add water, Worcestershire sauce, lemon juice, and sherry, stirring with a whisk. Reduce heat; simmer 1 minute. Stir in remaining ¼ teaspoon salt. Spoon sauce over steaks; sprinkle with parsley. **YIELD:** 6 servings (serving size: 1 steak and 1½ tablespoons sauce).

CALORIES 197 (40% from fat); FAT 8.7g (sat 3.3g, mono 3.3g, poly 0.3g); PROTEIN 24.2g; CARB 3.8g; FIBER 0.1g; CHOL 73mg; IRON 3.5mg; SODIUM 312mg; CALC 18mg

ORGANIC RESOURCE
The Organic Center's mission is to generate credible, peer-reviewed scientific information and communicate the verifiable benefits of organic farming and products to society. See www.organic-center.org to learn about the latest organic research.

Source: The Organic Center

Vietnamese Grilled Steak with Portobellos and Mint-Cilantro Mojo

Vietnamese Grilled Steak with Portobellos and Mint-Cilantro Mojo

A hint of nutmeg in the sauce reflects the French influence in Vietnamese cooking. Combining mint with cilantro adds a refreshing element to the mojo, a Caribbean condiment consisting of garlic, citrus juice, and oil. Mojo is also good with grilled or roasted lamb. Steamed green beans make a colorful side on the plate.

SAUCE:
- ¼ cup chopped green onions
- ¼ cup low-sodium soy sauce
- 1½ tablespoons chopped peeled fresh ginger
- 1 tablespoon brown sugar
- 1 tablespoon dark sesame oil
- 1 tablespoon honey
- ⅛ teaspoon ground nutmeg
- 1 garlic clove

MOJO:
- ½ cup cilantro leaves
- ½ cup mint leaves
- 3 tablespoons water
- 1 tablespoon olive oil
- 1 tablespoon fresh lemon juice
- 1 garlic clove

REMAINING INGREDIENTS:
- 2 portobello mushroom caps (about 4 ounces)
- 1 pound green beans, trimmed
- Cooking spray
- 1 (1-pound) boneless beef shoulder steak

1. To prepare sauce, combine first 8 ingredients in a food processor; process until smooth. Place in a small bowl.
2. To prepare mojo, combine cilantro and next 5 ingredients in a food processor; process until smooth. Place in a small bowl.
3. Remove brown gills from undersides of portobello mushrooms using a spoon; discard gills. Cut each mushroom into 6 slices; set aside.
4. Steam green beans 3 minutes or until tender; keep warm.
5. Heat a nonstick grill pan over medium-high heat. Coat pan with cooking spray. Add steak, and cook 2 minutes on each side or until browned. Remove from pan; cut steak diagonally across grain into thin slices. Toss mushrooms with half of sauce; add to pan. Stir-fry 1 minute; remove from pan. Return steak to pan; cook 2 minutes or until desired degree of doneness. Drizzle steak with remaining sauce. Arrange steak, mushrooms, and green beans on serving plates. Serve with mojo. **YIELD:** 4 servings (serving size: 3 ounces steak, 3 mushroom slices, 1 cup green beans, and about 1 tablespoon mojo).

CALORIES 364 (41% from fat); FAT 16.6g (sat 4.9g, mono 7.6g, poly 2.2g); PROTEIN 35.6g; CARB 18.9g; FIBER 4.5g; CHOL 62mg; IRON 4.2mg; SODIUM 608mg; CALC 84mg

Fresh Herb–Coated Beef Tenderloin Steaks with Mushroom Gravy

(pictured on page 78)

BEEF:
- 1 teaspoon salt
- 1 teaspoon chopped fresh thyme
- 1 teaspoon chopped fresh rosemary
- ½ teaspoon freshly ground black pepper
- 4 garlic cloves, minced
- 4 (4-ounce) beef tenderloin steaks, trimmed (1 inch thick)
- Cooking spray

GRAVY:
- 1 teaspoon olive oil
- ½ teaspoon chopped fresh thyme
- 1 (8-ounce) package presliced cremini mushrooms
- 4 garlic cloves, minced
- ½ cup fat-free, less-sodium chicken broth
- ½ cup white wine
- 1 tablespoon water
- 1 teaspoon cornstarch

1. Preheat oven to 450°.
2. Combine first 5 ingredients. Coat both sides of steaks with cooking spray; rub steaks evenly with thyme mixture. Place steaks on rack of a broiler or roasting pan coated with cooking spray; bake at 450° for 8 minutes on each side or until desired degree of doneness. Remove from oven; keep warm.
3. To prepare gravy, heat oil in a large nonstick skillet over medium-high heat. Add ½ teaspoon thyme, mushrooms, and 4 garlic cloves; cook 5 minutes or until mushrooms are tender. Add broth and wine; bring to a boil. Cook until reduced by half (about 4 minutes).
4. Combine water and cornstarch in a small bowl, stirring with a whisk. Add cornstarch mixture to mushroom mixture in pan; bring to a boil. Cook 1 minute or until slightly thick, stirring constantly. Serve with steaks.
YIELD: 4 servings (serving size: 1 steak and ¼ cup gravy).

CALORIES 202 (29% from fat); FAT 6.5g (sat 2.2g, mono 2.9g, poly 0.4g); PROTEIN 24.5g; CARB 6.3g; FIBER 0.7g; CHOL 52mg; IRON 2mg; SODIUM 692mg; CALC 44mg

Beef Tenderloin Steaks with Creole Spice Rub

The steaks need to stand for a few minutes after cooking to allow their juices to reabsorb. Try this sassy side dish: Sauté chopped bell peppers, onion, garlic, and ground red pepper, and then add frozen corn. Make a quick dessert by slicing strawberries and tossing them with sour cream and brown sugar.

1	teaspoon dry mustard
1	teaspoon garlic powder
1	teaspoon ground sage
1	teaspoon dried thyme
¾	teaspoon salt
½	teaspoon ground cumin
½	teaspoon ground red pepper
½	teaspoon freshly ground black pepper
4	(4-ounce) beef tenderloin steaks, trimmed (1 inch thick)

Cooking spray

1. Combine first 8 ingredients; rub mixture evenly over steaks.

2. Heat a large nonstick skillet over medium-high heat. Coat pan with cooking spray. Add steaks to pan; cook 4 minutes on each side or until desired degree of doneness. Remove from heat; let stand 5 minutes. **YIELD:** 4 servings (serving size: 1 steak).

CALORIES 155 (35% from fat); FAT 6g (sat 2g, mono 2.2g, poly 0.4g); PROTEIN 22.8g; CARB 1.4g; FIBER 0.5g; CHOL 52mg; IRON 2.1mg; SODIUM 490mg; CALC 31mg

Pepper-Crusted Filet Mignon with Horseradish Cream

Horseradish and sour cream make a cooling yet spicy sauce for the peppery steaks.

> 2 (4-ounce) beef tenderloin steaks, trimmed (about ¾ inch thick)
> ½ teaspoon sea salt
> ¼ teaspoon freshly ground black pepper
> 1 teaspoon butter
> Cooking spray
> 1 garlic clove, minced
> ¼ cup fat-free sour cream
> ½ teaspoon prepared horseradish

1. Sprinkle steaks with salt and pepper.
2. Melt butter in a nonstick skillet coated with cooking spray over medium heat. Add steaks; cook 3 minutes on each side or until desired degree of doneness. Sprinkle steaks evenly with garlic; cook 1 minute on each side over medium-low heat.
3. Combine sour cream and horseradish; serve with steaks.
YIELD: 2 servings (serving size: 1 steak and 2 tablespoons horseradish cream).

CALORIES 231 (44% from fat); FAT 11.3g (sat 4.8g, mono 4g, poly 0.5g); PROTEIN 25.2g; CARB 5.6g; FIBER 0.1g; CHOL 78mg; IRON 3.3mg; SODIUM 684mg; CALC 58mg

ORGANIC FACT
To be certified as organic livestock, the animals' health needs and natural behaviors must be met. Thus, organic livestock are given access to the outdoors, fresh air, water, sunshine, grass and pasture, and are fed 100% organic feed.

Source: USDA National Organic Program

Balsamic-Glazed Filet Mignon

Pair this steak with classic sides like mashed potatoes and steamed green beans. The menu comes together easily enough for a weeknight meal, but it's sophisticated enough to share with guests.

> 4 (4-ounce) beef tenderloin steaks
> ¼ teaspoon salt
> ¼ teaspoon freshly ground black pepper
> Cooking spray
> 2 teaspoons bottled minced garlic
> ⅛ teaspoon crushed red pepper
> 3 tablespoons dry sherry
> 2 tablespoons low-sodium soy sauce
> 1 tablespoon balsamic vinegar
> 2 teaspoons honey

1. Sprinkle both sides of steaks evenly with salt and black pepper. Heat a large nonstick skillet over medium-high heat. Coat pan with cooking spray. Add steaks to pan; cook 3 minutes on each side or until desired degree of doneness. Remove steaks from pan; keep warm.
2. Add garlic and red pepper to pan; sauté 30 seconds. Add sherry to pan; bring to a boil. Cook 30 seconds. Add soy sauce and remaining ingredients; bring to a boil, stirring occasionally. Reduce heat, and cook 1 minute. Serve with steaks. **YIELD:** 4 servings (serving size: 1 steak and about 1 tablespoon sauce).

CALORIES 215 (39% from fat); FAT 9.2g (sat 3.4g, mono 3.5g, poly 0.7g); PROTEIN 24g; CARB 4.7g; FIBER 0.1g; CHOL 70mg; IRON 3.3mg; SODIUM 406mg; CALC 9.7mg

Pan-Seared Pork Cutlets with Nectarine Salsa

The rub gives a boost to a potentially bland cut of meat. The contrast of hot and sweet is sure to make this a family favorite. You can substitute peaches for the nectarines if you prefer.

 2 teaspoons chili powder
 1 teaspoon ground coriander
 ½ teaspoon ground cumin
 ½ teaspoon paprika
 ¼ teaspoon salt
 ¼ teaspoon freshly ground black pepper
 8 (2-ounce) pork loin cutlets
 1 teaspoon olive oil
Cooking spray
 ½ cup bottled salsa
 ¼ cup apricot preserves
 4 cups sliced peeled nectarines (about 3 pounds)
 ¼ cup chopped fresh cilantro
 2 tablespoons chopped fresh oregano

1. Combine first 6 ingredients; rub mixture over both sides of pork. Heat oil in a large nonstick skillet coated with cooking spray over medium-high heat. Add pork; sauté 2 minutes on each side or until done. Remove from pan; keep warm.

2. Add salsa and preserves to pan; bring to a boil. Cook 1 minute. Stir in nectarines, cilantro, and oregano; cook mixture 1 minute or until thoroughly heated. Serve salsa with pork. **YIELD:** 4 servings (serving size: 2 cutlets and 1 cup salsa).

CALORIES 322 (31% from fat); FAT 11g (sat 1.6g, mono 4.1g, poly 1.1g); PROTEIN 25.5g; CARB 32.6g; FIBER 4.7g; CHOL 68mg; IRON 2.7mg; SODIUM 327mg; CALC 60mg

Bourbon-Glazed Pork Chops and Peaches

The bourbon-and-honey marinade also yields a sauce for the dish. Be sure the marinade comes to a full boil, a step that is necessary for food safety and is a recommended practice whenever a meat marinade is later used as a sauce.

 ⅓ cup bourbon
 ¼ cup honey
 3 tablespoons low-sodium soy sauce
 1 tablespoon canola oil
 ½ teaspoon ground ginger
 ¼ teaspoon crushed red pepper
 ¼ teaspoon freshly ground black pepper
 4 (4-ounce) boneless center-cut loin pork chops (about ¾ inch thick)
 2 peaches, halved and pitted
Cooking spray

1. Combine bourbon, honey, soy sauce, canola oil, ginger, red pepper, and ¼ teaspoon black pepper in a large bowl. Add pork and peaches; toss well to coat.

2. Heat a nonstick grill pan over medium-high heat. Coat pan with cooking spray. Remove pork and peaches from bowl, reserving marinade. Place pork and peaches on grill pan; cook 4 minutes on each side or until pork is done.

3. While pork cooks, place marinade in a microwave-safe bowl; microwave at HIGH 2 minutes. Spoon over pork and peaches. **YIELD:** 4 servings (serving size: 1 chop, 1 peach half, and 2 tablespoons sauce).

CALORIES 285 (29% from fat); FAT 9.3g (sat 3.1g, mono 4.3g, poly 1.1g); PROTEIN 26.4g; CARB 24.3g; FIBER 1.2g; CHOL 73mg; IRON 1.4mg; SODIUM 489mg; CALC 27mg

Bourbon-Glazed Pork Chops
and Peaches

Buttermilk-Brined Pork Chops

Though these pork chops require overnight brining, they make dinner the next night a breeze. Brine the chops up to two days beforehand. Just remove them from the brine after an overnight soak, discarding the brine; cover the chops in plastic wrap, and refrigerate until ready to cook. Add roasted butternut squash and steamed green beans.

    2   cups fat-free buttermilk
    2   tablespoons kosher salt
    2   tablespoons sugar
    1   tablespoon grated lemon rind
    1   teaspoon chopped fresh rosemary
    1   teaspoon chopped fresh sage
    4   (6-ounce) bone-in center-cut pork chops (about
        ½ inch thick)
    2   teaspoons freshly ground black pepper
  Cooking spray

1. Combine first 6 ingredients in a large zip-top plastic bag; shake well to dissolve salt and sugar. Add pork to bag; seal and refrigerate at least 8 hours or overnight, turning bag occasionally.
2. Remove pork from bag; discard buttermilk mixture. Pat pork dry with a paper towel. Sprinkle pork with pepper.
3. Heat a large nonstick grill pan over medium-high heat. Coat pan with cooking spray. Add pork chops; cook about 3½ minutes on each side or until desired degree of doneness. **YIELD:** 4 servings (serving size: 1 chop).

CALORIES 183 (35% from fat); FAT 7.2g (sat 2.5g, mono 3.2g, poly 0.6g); PROTEIN 26g; CARB 2g; FIBER 0.3g; CHOL 69mg; IRON 0.8mg; SODIUM 345mg; CALC 43mg

ORGANIC FACT
Organic practices prohibit the use of growth hormones, antibiotics, or other animal drugs in animal feed for the purpose of stimulating the growth or production of livestock.

Source: USDA National Organic Program

Pork Loin Chops with Cinnamon Apples

Tart Granny Smiths balance the caramel sweetness of brown sugar. Braeburn apples work well, too.

    1   teaspoon dried rubbed sage
    ½   teaspoon salt
    ¼   teaspoon freshly ground black pepper
    4   (4-ounce) boneless center-cut loin pork chops
        (about ½ inch thick)
    ½   teaspoon vegetable oil
  Cooking spray
    1   teaspoon butter
    4   cups (½-inch) slices peeled Granny Smith apples
        (about 4 medium)
    1   tablespoon brown sugar
    1   teaspoon fresh lemon juice
    ½   teaspoon ground cinnamon
  Dash of salt

1. Combine dried sage, ½ teaspoon salt, and black pepper; sprinkle over pork. Heat oil in a large nonstick skillet coated with cooking spray over medium heat. Add pork; cook 3 minutes on each side or until done. Remove pork from pan; cover and keep warm.
2. Melt butter in pan over medium heat. Add apples and next 4 ingredients; cook 5 minutes or until tender, stirring frequently. Serve apple mixture with pork chops.
YIELD: 4 servings (serving size: 1 pork chop and ¾ cup apple mixture).

CALORIES 251 (30% from fat); FAT 8.3g (sat 3.1g, mono 3.3g, poly 0.9g); PROTEIN 24.1g; CARB 20.2g; FIBER 2.3g; CHOL 67mg; IRON 0.9mg; SODIUM 388mg; CALC 38mg

Pork Loin Chops with
Cinnamon Apples

Ginger-Curry Pork and Rice

If you don't have dried apricots on hand, you can substitute golden raisins instead. Coat your knife with cooking spray for chopping the dried fruit. Fresh ginger livens up this dish and gives it a mild, peppery heat. The sauce is also good with skinless, boneless chicken thighs.

  2 (4-ounce) boneless center-cut loin pork chops
  ⅛ teaspoon black pepper
Dash of salt
  1 tablespoon canola oil, divided
  ½ teaspoon grated lime rind
  1 tablespoon fresh lime juice
1½ teaspoons grated peeled fresh ginger
  ½ cup chopped onion
  ½ teaspoon red curry paste
  1 cup fat-free, less-sodium chicken broth
  2 tablespoons chopped dried apricots
  1 teaspoon honey
  1 garlic clove, minced
1½ cups cooked basmati rice
  2 tablespoons thinly sliced green onions

1. Sprinkle pork with pepper and salt. Heat 2 teaspoons oil in a medium nonstick skillet over medium-high heat. Add pork; cook 2½ minutes on each side or until browned. Remove from heat. Combine rind, juice, and ginger in a shallow dish; add pork, turning to coat.

2. Add remaining 1 teaspoon oil to pan, and place over medium heat. Add ½ cup onion and curry paste; cook 2 minutes or until onion is tender, stirring frequently. Add pork mixture, broth, apricots, honey, and garlic; bring to a boil. Cover, reduce heat, and simmer 10 minutes or until pork is done. Remove pork from pan. Increase heat to medium-high. Add rice; cook 2 minutes or until thoroughly heated, stirring frequently. Serve rice with pork; top each serving with 1 tablespoon green onions. **YIELD:** 2 servings (serving size: 1 pork chop and 1 cup rice mixture).

CALORIES 486 (26% from fat); FAT 14.3g (sat 3.3g, mono 4.8g, poly 5.1g); PROTEIN 33.5g; CARB 53.7g; FIBER 4.8g; CHOL 62mg; IRON 2mg; SODIUM 965mg; CALC 56mg

Pan-Seared Pork Chops with Molasses-Plum Sauce

Aside from seasoning the meat, salt also brings the sweet-savory flavors of the sauce into balance. If you prefer, you can easily substitute dried cherries or cranberries for the blueberries and still get a great-tasting dish. Serve these saucy pork chops alongside rice or couscous.

2 teaspoons olive oil
½ cup chopped onion
¾ cup fat-free, less-sodium chicken broth
¼ cup dried blueberries
3 tablespoons cider vinegar
2 tablespoons molasses
½ teaspoon salt, divided
½ teaspoon freshly ground black pepper, divided
⅛ teaspoon ground coriander
3 plums, pitted, peeled, and coarsely chopped
   (about 1¾ cups)
Cooking spray
4 (6-ounce) bone-in center-cut pork chops
   (about 1 inch thick)
Fresh parsley sprigs (optional)

1. Heat oil in a medium saucepan over medium heat. Add onion; cook 3 minutes or until tender, stirring frequently. Stir in chicken broth, blueberries, vinegar, molasses, ¼ teaspoon salt, ¼ teaspoon black pepper, coriander, and plums; bring to a boil. Reduce heat, and simmer 20 minutes or until plums are tender and mixture is thick.

2. Heat a large nonstick skillet over medium-high heat. Coat pan with cooking spray. Sprinkle remaining ¼ teaspoon salt and ¼ teaspoon pepper over chops. Add chops to pan; cook 2 minutes on each side or until browned. Reduce heat to medium; cook 4 minutes or until done. Remove chops from pan; cover and keep warm. Add plum mixture to pan, and bring to a simmer. Cook 2 minutes, scraping pan to loosen browned bits. Spoon plum mixture over pork. Garnish with parsley, if desired. **YIELD:** 4 servings (serving size: 1 pork chop and ¼ cup sauce).

CALORIES 299 (29% from fat); FAT 9.6g (sat 2.9g, mono 5g, poly 0.8g); PROTEIN 27.1g; CARB 26.6g; FIBER 1.9g; CHOL 69mg; IRON 1.7mg; SODIUM 434mg; CALC 61mg

Shredded Pork Tacos

104

Shredded Pork Tacos

Since pork tenderloin is already a lean cut of meat, it literally falls apart after eight hours. Use two forks to shred the meat while the mixture is still in the slow cooker. You can also serve the pork mixture on sandwich buns. Serve with a fruit salad of kiwi, oranges, honeydew melon, and grapes.

½ cup chopped onion
½ cup beer or water
2 tablespoons tomato paste
1 (1-pound) pork tenderloin, trimmed and cut into 1-inch pieces
1 (1.25-ounce) package 40%-less-sodium taco seasoning
1 jalapeño pepper, seeded and chopped
2 tablespoons chopped fresh cilantro
8 (6-inch) corn tortillas
2 cups shredded lettuce
½ cup (2 ounces) reduced-fat shredded sharp Cheddar cheese
¼ cup finely chopped onion
¼ cup reduced-fat sour cream

1. Combine first 6 ingredients in an electric slow cooker. Cover and cook on LOW 6 hours. Stir in cilantro.
2. Warm tortillas according to package directions. Spoon ¼ cup pork mixture onto each tortilla, and top each tortilla with ¼ cup lettuce, 1½ teaspoons finely chopped onion, 1 tablespoon cheese, and 1½ teaspoons sour cream. Fold tacos in half. **YIELD:** 4 servings (serving size: 2 tacos).

CALORIES 379 (28% from fat); FAT 11.6g (sat 4.8g, mono 2.9g, poly 1.2g); PROTEIN 42g; CARB 28.1g; FIBER 3.2g; CHOL 119mg; IRON 2.1mg; SODIUM 343mg; CALC 142mg

Rosemary and Pepper–Crusted Pork Tenderloin

Use a mortar and pestle to crush the fennel and celery seeds. Or place them in a zip-top plastic bag, and crush with a rolling pin.

2 teaspoons cracked black pepper
1 teaspoon dried rosemary, crushed
½ teaspoon kosher salt
½ teaspoon fennel seeds, crushed
½ teaspoon celery seeds, crushed
½ teaspoon dry mustard
1 (1-pound) pork tenderloin, trimmed
Cooking spray
2 tablespoons chopped fresh flat-leaf parsley

1. Preheat oven to 425°.
2. Combine first 6 ingredients; rub over pork. Place pork in a shallow roasting pan coated with cooking spray. Bake at 425° for 30 minutes or until a thermometer registers 160° (slightly pink). Let stand 5 minutes; cut into thin slices. Sprinkle with parsley. **YIELD:** 4 servings (serving size: 3 ounces).

CALORIES 158 (31% from fat); FAT 5.4g (sat 1.8g, mono 2.2g, poly 0.5g); PROTEIN 24.7g; CARB 1.3g; FIBER 0.6g; CHOL 75mg; IRON 1.8mg; SODIUM 289mg; CALC 23mg

ORGANIC FACT
It takes approximately 3,000 years for nature to produce six inches of topsoil. Organic bio-intensive farming can produce six inches of topsoil in as little as 50 years—60 times faster than the rate in nature.

Source: The Organic Center

Pork Tenderloin with Olive-Mustard Tapenade

This quick entrée is great served with orzo and a tossed Greek salad with feta cheese. To quickly flatten pork, press with the heel of your hand. A little of this tapenade adds a lot of flavor.

  1   (1-pound) pork tenderloin, trimmed and cut cross-wise into 8 pieces
  ½   teaspoon salt
  ¼   teaspoon black pepper
  ¼   teaspoon ground fennel
Cooking spray
  ¼   cup chopped pitted kalamata olives
  ¼   cup chopped pitted green olives or onion-stuffed green olives
  1   tablespoon chopped fresh parsley
  1   tablespoon Dijon mustard
  2   teaspoons balsamic vinegar
  1   garlic clove, minced, or ½ teaspoon bottled minced garlic

1. Heat a large nonstick skillet over medium-high heat. Press pork pieces into ½-inch-thick medallions. Combine salt, pepper, and fennel; rub evenly over pork. Lightly coat pork with cooking spray. Add pork to pan; cook 4 minutes on each side or until done.
2. While pork cooks, combine olives and next 4 ingredients. Serve olive mixture over pork. **YIELD:** 4 servings (serving size: 2 pork medallions and 2 tablespoons olive mixture).

CALORIES 163 (33% from fat); FAT 6g (sat 1.6g, mono 3.2g, poly 0.7g); PROTEIN 24.3g; CARB 2.2g; FIBER 0.7g; CHOL 74mg; IRON 2.2mg; SODIUM 590mg; CALC 31mg

Caribbean Pork and Plantain Hash

Use semiripe yellow plantains—not green or soft, ripe black ones. The plantains brown better if not stirred too much as they cook. Serve with a tomato and hearts of palm salad and mango slices drizzled with lime juice for an authentic island meal.

  1   tablespoon low-sodium soy sauce
  ¾   teaspoon salt, divided
  ¾   teaspoon dried thyme
  ¼   teaspoon ground ginger
  ¼   teaspoon ground red pepper
  ⅛   teaspoon ground allspice
  1   (1-pound) pork tenderloin, trimmed and cut into ½-inch pieces
  1½   tablespoons vegetable oil, divided
  1   tablespoon butter
  1½   cups coarsely chopped onion
  1   cup chopped green bell pepper
  2   large yellow plantains, chopped (about 3 cups)
  ½   teaspoon black pepper
  4   garlic cloves, minced
  1   teaspoon habanero hot pepper sauce
  2   tablespoons chopped fresh cilantro

1. Combine soy sauce, ¼ teaspoon salt, thyme, and next 4 ingredients; toss well to coat. Heat 1½ teaspoons oil in a large nonstick skillet over medium-high heat. Add pork mixture; sauté 4 minutes or until done. Remove from pan. Add 1 tablespoon oil and butter to pan. Add onion, bell pepper, plantains, ½ teaspoon salt, and black pepper; cook 6 minutes, stirring occasionally. Stir in garlic; sauté 2 minutes or until plantains are tender. Drizzle with hot sauce, and stir well. Sprinkle with cilantro. **YIELD:** 4 servings (serving size: about 1½ cups).

CALORIES 384 (29% from fat); FAT 12.5g (sat 4g, mono 3.8g, poly 3.7g); PROTEIN 26.8g; CARB 44.9g; FIBER 4.7g; CHOL 81mg; IRON 2.8mg; SODIUM 674mg; CALC 38mg

Caribbean Pork and Plantain Hash

Roasted Pork Tenderloin Medallions
with Dried Cranberry Sauce

Roasted Pork Tenderloin Medallions with Dried Cranberry Sauce

A tablespoon of grape jelly helps thicken the tangy-sweet sauce. Tenderloin is lean and juicy when it's properly prepared. Use a meat thermometer to avoid overcooking. Add broccoli and whole wheat couscous to round out the meal.

PORK:
1 teaspoon dried sage
1 teaspoon dried thyme
¾ teaspoon salt
½ teaspoon freshly ground black pepper
1 (1-pound) pork tenderloin, trimmed
Cooking spray
SAUCE:
1 cup fat-free, less-sodium chicken broth
1 cup dried cranberries
½ cup cranberry cocktail juice
1 tablespoon grape jelly

1. Preheat oven to 400°.
2. To prepare pork, combine first 4 ingredients; rub evenly over pork.
3. Heat a large ovenproof nonstick skillet over medium-high heat. Coat pan with cooking spray. Add pork; cook 4 minutes on each side or until browned. Place pan in oven; cook pork at 400° for 12 minutes or until a meat thermometer registers 160° (slightly pink). Place pork on a cutting board; keep warm.
4. To prepare sauce, add broth, dried cranberries, and juice to pan; bring to a boil, scraping pan to loosen browned bits. Stir in jelly; cook 8 minutes or until mixture is slightly thick, stirring occasionally. Cut pork into (½-inch) slices. Serve with sauce. **YIELD:** 4 servings (serving size: about 3 ounces pork and ¼ cup sauce).

CALORIES 282 (20% from fat); FAT 6.3g (sat 2.2g, mono 2.8g, poly 0.7g); PROTEIN 24g; CARB 33.6g; FIBER 2.1g; CHOL 75mg; IRON 2.1mg; SODIUM 596mg; CALC 21mg

Pork with Apricots, Dried Plums, and Sauerkraut

Sauerkraut balances the sweetness of the apricot preserves and orange juice. Slow cooking nicely tenderizes the pork and dried fruit.

1 (2-pound) pork tenderloin, trimmed
1 cup chopped onion
¾ cup apricot preserves
½ cup dried apricots
½ cup pitted dried plums
¼ cup fat-free, less-sodium chicken broth
¼ cup orange juice
2 tablespoons cornstarch
1 teaspoon salt
½ teaspoon dried thyme
¼ teaspoon freshly ground black pepper
1 (10-ounce) package refrigerated sauerkraut

1. Place pork in an electric slow cooker. Combine onion and next 10 ingredients in a large bowl; pour sauerkraut mixture over pork. Cover and cook on LOW 7 hours. Remove pork from slow cooker, and let pork stand 10 minutes. Cut pork into ¼-inch-thick slices; serve with sauerkraut mixture. **YIELD:** 8 servings (serving size: 3 ounces pork and about ½ cup sauerkraut mixture).

CALORIES 313 (19% from fat); FAT 6.6g (sat 2.2g, mono 3g, poly 0.7g); PROTEIN 25.4g; CARB 38.3g; FIBER 2.5g; CHOL 67mg; IRON 1.7mg; SODIUM 41mg; CALC 594mg

ORGANIC FACT

While "natural" is typically not defined in the food industry, it is for meat. The USDA defines natural meat as meat that is minimally processed and without artificial ingredients. USDA-certified organic meat has a higher standard and is produced without growth hormones and antibiotics, plus the animals are given organic feed and allowed access to pasture.

Source: USDA

Pork Tenderloin with Fresh Mango Salsa

Look for mangoes that gently yield to pressure and smell fruity.

2   (1-pound) pork tenderloins, trimmed
1   teaspoon salt
½   teaspoon freshly ground black pepper
1½ cups diced peeled mango (about 2 large)
1   teaspoon grated orange rind
3   tablespoons diagonally sliced green onions
2   teaspoons grated peeled fresh ginger
3   tablespoons fresh orange juice
½   teaspoon ground coriander
¼   teaspoon ground cardamom
1   tablespoon olive oil

1. Cut each tenderloin crosswise into 8 pieces. Place plastic wrap over pork; pound to an even thickness using a meat mallet or rolling pin. Sprinkle evenly with salt and pepper.
2. Combine mango and next 6 ingredients. Heat oil in a large nonstick skillet over medium-high heat. Add half of pork; cook 3 minutes on each side or until done. Remove from pan; repeat procedure with remaining pork. Serve with mango salsa. **YIELD:** 8 servings (serving size: 2 pork medallions and about 3 tablespoons salsa).

CALORIES 195 (22% from fat); FAT 4.7g (sat 1.3g, mono 2.6g, poly 0.5g); PROTEIN 27.5g; CARB 9.9g; FIBER 1.2g; CHOL 67mg; IRON 1.6mg; SODIUM 349mg; CALC 15mg

Honey-Hoisin Pork Tenderloin

Look for hoisin sauce in the Asian section of your market. Serve this pork dish with a salad and mashed potatoes.

2   tablespoons sliced green onions
2   tablespoons hoisin sauce
2   tablespoons low-sodium soy sauce
2   tablespoons honey
1   tablespoon hot water
2   garlic cloves, minced
1   (1-pound) pork tenderloin, trimmed
¼   teaspoon salt
Cooking spray
½   teaspoon sesame seeds

1. Preheat oven to 400°.
2. Combine first 6 ingredients in a small bowl. Pour ¼ cup honey mixture into a large zip-top plastic bag; reserve remaining honey mixture. Add pork to bag; seal and marinate in refrigerator 30 minutes, turning bag occasionally.
3. Remove pork from bag; discard marinade. Sprinkle pork with salt. Heat a large ovenproof skillet over medium-high heat. Coat pan with cooking spray. Add pork; cook 2 minutes, browning on all sides. Brush 1 tablespoon reserved honey mixture over pork; sprinkle with sesame seeds. Place pan in oven. Bake at 400° for 20 minutes or until a thermometer registers 160° (slightly pink) or until desired degree of doneness.
4. Place pork on a platter; let stand 5 minutes. Cut pork diagonally across grain into thin slices. Drizzle with remaining honey mixture. **YIELD:** 4 servings (serving size: 3 ounces pork).

CALORIES 195 (20% from fat); FAT 4.3g (sat 1.4g, mono 1.9g, poly 0.6g); PROTEIN 24.7g; CARB 13.6g; FIBER 0.5g; CHOL 74mg; IRON 1.7mg; SODIUM 633mg; CALC 12mg

Honey-Hoisin Pork Tenderloin

Ham and Cheese Hash Browns

Ham and Cheese Hash Browns

This recipe is a great way to use leftover ham. Though it resembles a skillet potato hash, it's more easily prepared in the microwave.

   3   cups frozen hash brown potatoes with onions and peppers
   ⅓   cup fat-free, less-sodium chicken broth
   ½   cup drained canned quartered artichoke hearts, chopped
   ¼   cup chopped green onions
   ⅛   teaspoon black pepper
   3   ounces smoked ham, cut into bite-sized pieces
   ½   cup (about 2 ounces) shredded Monterey Jack cheese

1. Combine potatoes and chicken broth in a 1-quart microwave-safe casserole. Cover with lid, and microwave at HIGH 12 minutes, stirring after 6 minutes.
2. Uncover dish. Stir in artichoke hearts, green onions, pepper, and ham. Sprinkle with shredded cheese. Microwave, uncovered, at HIGH 1 minute. **YIELD:** 2 servings (serving size: 1¾ cups).

CALORIES 378 (30% from fat); FAT 12.5g (sat 6.2g, mono 2.7g, poly 1.4g); PROTEIN 20g; CARB 41.8g; FIBER 6.1g; CHOL 55mg; IRON 1.3mg; SODIUM 817mg; CALC 204mg

ORGANIC FACT
Organic food can be identified with the help of the USDA organic logo on the package. Eggs that are certified organic carry this logo and should not be confused with "natural" or "cage-free" eggs, which do not suggest organic.

Potato, Ham, and Spinach Gratin

   2   teaspoons olive oil
   ½   cup thinly sliced shallots
   2   garlic cloves, minced
   1   cup chopped reduced-fat ham (about 4 ounces)
   1   teaspoon salt, divided
   ¾   teaspoon freshly ground black pepper, divided
   ⅛   teaspoon grated whole nutmeg
   1   (10-ounce) package frozen chopped spinach, thawed, drained, and squeezed dry
   ⅓   cup all-purpose flour (about 1½ ounces)
   2   cups 1% low-fat milk
   7   cups (⅛-inch-thick) Yukon gold potato slices (about 2½ pounds)
Cooking spray
   ¾   cup (3 ounces) shredded Gruyère or Swiss cheese

1. Preheat oven to 375°.
2. Heat oil in a small nonstick skillet over medium-high heat. Add shallots and garlic; sauté 2 minutes or until tender. Remove from heat; stir in ham, ¼ teaspoon salt, ¼ teaspoon pepper, nutmeg, and spinach.
3. Lightly spoon flour into a dry measuring cup; level with a knife. Combine flour, milk, remaining ½ teaspoon pepper, and ¼ teaspoon salt, stirring with a whisk.
4. Arrange half of potato slices in an 8-inch square baking pan coated with cooking spray; sprinkle potato with ¼ teaspoon salt. Spread spinach mixture over potato. Arrange remaining potato over spinach mixture; top with milk mixture. Sprinkle with remaining ¼ teaspoon salt. Cover with foil coated with cooking spray. Bake at 375° for 1 hour and 15 minutes or until potato is tender. Uncover and sprinkle with cheese; bake an additional 15 minutes.
5. Preheat broiler.
6. Broil 2 minutes or until cheese is lightly browned.
YIELD: 8 servings.

CALORIES 240 (24% from fat); FAT 6.3g (sat 2.9g, mono 2.5g, poly 0.5g); PROTEIN 12.8g; CARB 34g; FIBER 3g; CHOL 22mg; IRON 1.7mg; SODIUM 581mg; CALC 235mg

Ham and Asparagus Frittata

Here, we extended whole eggs by mixing them with egg whites to make a healthier entrée. Serve the frittata with fruit and toasted English muffins for a light supper.

⅔ cup chopped 33%-less-sodium ham
   (about 3 ounces)
½ cup (2 ounces) shredded low-fat Jarlsberg cheese
¼ teaspoon black pepper
⅛ teaspoon salt
3 large egg whites
2 large eggs
Cooking spray
½ cup finely chopped onion
½ cup finely chopped bell pepper
½ cup (1-inch) slices asparagus
¼ teaspoon dried Italian seasoning

1. Preheat broiler.
2. Combine first 6 ingredients in a medium bowl, stirring well with a whisk.
3. Heat a 9-inch skillet over medium-high heat. Coat pan with cooking spray. Add onion, bell pepper, and asparagus; sauté 3 minutes. Add egg mixture; reduce heat to medium. Cover and cook 3 minutes or until almost set. Sprinkle with Italian seasoning. Wrap handle of pan with foil; broil 3 minutes or until egg is set. Cut into 4 wedges. **YIELD:** 2 servings (serving size: 2 wedges).

CALORIES 251 (33% from fat); FAT 9.2g (sat 3.4g, mono 3.5g, poly 1.1g); PROTEIN 31.3g; CARB 9.6g; FIBER 2g; CHOL 247mg; IRON 2.1mg; SODIUM 791mg; CALC 373mg

ORGANIC TIP

People often make milk one of their first organic purchases for obvious reasons—including no use of growth hormones or antibiotics. Organic cheese is a good choice for the same reasons.

Corn, Bacon, and Green Onion Tart

Refrigerated pizza dough tends to draw up when it's first removed from the can. Let the dough rest a few minutes before you begin to work with it so it will be more pliable.

2 slices applewood-smoked bacon, chopped
2 cups fresh corn kernels (about 4 ears)
½ cup chopped green onions
1 cup 2% reduced-fat milk
¼ cup (1 ounce) grated fresh Parmesan cheese,
   divided
½ teaspoon kosher salt
½ teaspoon freshly ground black pepper
2 large egg whites, lightly beaten
1 large egg, lightly beaten
Cooking spray
1 (13.8-ounce) can refrigerated pizza crust dough

1. Preheat oven to 375°.
2. Cook bacon in a large nonstick skillet over medium-high heat 3 minutes or until lightly browned. Add corn and green onions; sauté 3 minutes. Place corn mixture in a large bowl. Add milk, 2 tablespoons cheese, salt, pepper, egg whites, and egg; stir until well blended.
3. Coat a 10½-inch round removable-bottom tart pan lightly with cooking spray. Unroll dough onto a lightly floured surface; let rest 5 minutes. Pat dough into bottom and up sides of prepared pan. Place pan on a baking sheet. Pour bacon mixture into dough; sprinkle with remaining 2 tablespoons cheese. Bake at 375° for 25 minutes or until set. Cool in pan 10 minutes on a wire rack. **YIELD:** 4 servings.

CALORIES 419 (22% from fat); FAT 10.1g (sat 3.8g, mono 1.5g, poly 0.7g); PROTEIN 19.1g; CARB 66.1g; FIBER 2.6g; CHOL 67mg; IRON 3.5mg; SODIUM 1,221mg; CALC 150mg

Corn, Bacon, and Green Onion Tart

Oven-Fried Chicken, page 137

POULTRY

Pilaf with Chicken, Spinach, and Walnuts

Pilaf has many variations. This Turkish version gains flavor from popcorn-scented basmati rice and fresh dill. Don't stir the rice as it simmers; doing so makes it gummy. Use leftover meat from a roasted chicken, or pick up a rotisserie chicken from your supermarket.

1½ tablespoons olive oil, divided
1 cup chopped onion
1½ cups uncooked basmati rice
1 cup diced plum tomato
½ teaspoon salt
1 (14-ounce) can fat-free, less-sodium chicken broth
1 (3-inch) cinnamon stick
1 (6-ounce) package fresh baby spinach
2 cups chopped roasted skinless, boneless chicken breasts (about 2 breasts)
½ cup coarsely chopped walnuts, toasted
1 tablespoon finely chopped fresh dill

1. Heat 1 tablespoon oil in a large nonstick skillet over medium-high heat. Add onion; sauté 10 minutes or until lightly browned. Stir in rice; cook 1 minute, stirring constantly. Stir in 1½ teaspoons oil, tomato, salt, broth, and cinnamon stick; bring to a boil. Cover, reduce heat, and simmer 15 minutes or until liquid is absorbed.
2. Stir in spinach; cook 2 minutes or until spinach wilts. Stir in chicken. Sprinkle evenly with walnuts and dill. Discard cinnamon stick. **YIELD:** 6 servings (serving size: 1⅓ cups).

CALORIES 368 (29% from fat); FAT 11.9g (sat 1.8g, mono 4g, poly 5.6g); PROTEIN 19.8g; CARB 47.5g; FIBER 2.1g; CHOL 33mg; IRON 1.5mg; SODIUM 616mg; CALC 58mg

Spicy Chicken Pasta

 1 (9-ounce) package fresh angel hair pasta
Cooking spray
 1 cup vertically sliced onion
 1 tablespoon dried basil
 1½ teaspoons bottled minced garlic
 ½ teaspoon crushed red pepper
 1 cup half-and-half
 ¼ cup reduced-fat sour cream
 1 teaspoon all-purpose flour
 ¼ teaspoon salt
 ⅛ teaspoon black pepper
 1 (6-ounce) package honey-roasted chicken breast cuts
 1 (10-ounce) package frozen chopped spinach, thawed, drained, and squeezed dry
 1 tablespoon grated fresh Parmesan cheese

1. Cook pasta according to package directions, omitting salt and fat. Drain in a colander over a bowl, reserving ¼ cup cooking liquid; set aside.
2. While pasta cooks, heat a large nonstick skillet over medium-high heat. Coat pan with cooking spray. Add onion; sauté 2 minutes. Add basil, garlic, and red pepper; sauté 1 minute. Combine half-and-half, sour cream, and flour, stirring with a whisk. Add reserved ¼ cup pasta cooking liquid and half-and-half mixture to pan; bring to a boil. Stir in salt, black pepper, chicken, and spinach; bring to a boil. Stir in cooked pasta; cook 1 minute or until thoroughly heated. Sprinkle with Parmesan. **YIELD:** 4 servings (serving size: about 1¾ cups).

CALORIES 383 (29% from fat); FAT 12.4g (sat 6.2g, mono 3.8g, poly 1.2g); PROTEIN 20.5g; CARB 46.1g; FIBER 6g; CHOL 108mg; IRON 5.3mg; SODIUM 784mg; CALC 253mg

Baked Chiles Rellenos

 5 large poblano chiles
Cooking spray
 2½ cups thinly sliced zucchini
 1 teaspoon minced garlic
 1 teaspoon ground cumin, divided
 2 jalapeño peppers
 1 (14.5-ounce) can diced tomatoes, drained
 1 (8-ounce) can tomato sauce
 1½ cups (6 ounces) preshredded part-skim mozzarella cheese
 1 cup shredded cooked chicken breast
 ½ teaspoon salt

1. Preheat broiler.
2. Place chiles on a foil-lined baking sheet; broil 3 inches from heat 8 minutes or until blackened, turning after 6 minutes. Place in a zip-top plastic bag; seal. Let stand 15 minutes. Peel and discard skins. Cut a lengthwise slit in each chile; discard seeds, leaving stems intact.
3. Heat a saucepan over medium-high heat. Coat pan with cooking spray. Add zucchini and garlic; cook 4 minutes or until crisp-tender. Stir in ½ teaspoon cumin, jalapeño, tomatoes, and sauce; bring to a boil. Reduce heat; simmer 15 minutes. Discard jalapeño.
4. Preheat oven to 350°.
5. Combine ½ teaspoon cumin, cheese, chicken, and salt in a bowl; toss. Spoon about ½ cup cheese mixture into each chile; secure with a wooden pick. Place stuffed chiles in an 11 x 7–inch baking dish coated with cooking spray; pour tomato mixture over chiles. Cover; bake at 350° for 20 minutes. Uncover; bake an additional 10 minutes.
YIELD: 5 servings (serving size: 1 stuffed chile and about ⅔ cup tomato mixture).

CALORIES 201 (33% from fat); FAT 7.7g (sat 3.8g, mono 2.2g, poly 0.8g); PROTEIN 20g; CARB 15.4g; FIBER 3.9g; CHOL 43mg; IRON 2mg; SODIUM 795mg; CALC 267mg

Roast Chicken Chimichangas

 2½ cups shredded roasted skinless, boneless chicken breasts
 1 cup (4 ounces) crumbled queso fresco cheese
 ¼ cup chopped green onions
 1 teaspoon dried oregano
 ¼ teaspoon ground cumin
 1 garlic clove, minced
 1 (4.5-ounce) can chopped green chiles, drained
 1 (16-ounce) can fat-free refried beans
 6 (8-inch) flour tortillas
Cooking spray
 ½ cup bottled green salsa

1. Preheat oven to 500°.
2. Combine first 7 ingredients in a large bowl; toss well.
3. Spread ¼ cup beans down center of each tortilla. Top each tortilla with ⅔ cup chicken mixture; roll up. Place rolls, seam sides down, on a large baking sheet coated with cooking spray. Coat tops with cooking spray. Bake at 500° for 7 minutes. Serve with salsa. **YIELD:** 6 servings (serving size: 1 chimichanga and about 4 teaspoons salsa).

CALORIES 380 (23% from fat); FAT 9.7g (sat 3.1g, mono 4.1g, poly 1.6g); PROTEIN 28.8g; CARB 42.5g; FIBER 6.5g; CHOL 55mg; IRON 3.8mg; SODIUM 728mg; CALC 157mg

Cilantro-Serrano Pesto with Grilled Chicken and Penne

Cotija is an aged Mexican cheese available in many super-markets and Latin grocery stores. Substitute Parmesan cheese if you can't find cotija. If the sauce is too thick, loosen it by adding a little hot cooking water from the pasta.

1½ cups fresh cilantro
½ cup fresh mint
½ cup cotija cheese
3 tablespoons toasted pecan halves
1 teaspoon kosher salt
2 garlic cloves
1 serrano chile, seeded and sliced
2 tablespoons extravirgin olive oil
2 teaspoons sherry vinegar
⅛ teaspoon freshly ground black pepper
¾ pound skinless, boneless chicken breast halves
Cooking spray
6 cups hot cooked penne pasta (about 3 ounces uncooked)
2 cups cherry tomatoes, halved

1. Place first 7 ingredients in a food processor, and process until well blended. With processor on, slowly pour olive oil through food chute; process until well blended. Place pesto in a large bowl; stir in sherry vinegar and black pepper.
2. Heat a grill pan over medium-high heat. Coat chicken with cooking spray. Add chicken to pan; cook 5 minutes on each side or until done. Cut chicken into bite-sized pieces. Add chicken, pasta, and tomatoes to pesto; toss to combine. **YIELD:** 6 servings (serving size: 1 cup).

CALORIES 429 (29% from fat); FAT 13.8g (sat 3.5g, mono 6.5g, poly 1.9g); PROTEIN 28.2g; CARB 47.1g; FIBER 2.4g; CHOL 60mg; IRON 11.5mg; SODIUM 492mg; CALC 104mg

ORGANIC FACT

In order to be certified with the USDA organic label, organic farmers give their chickens organic feed and access to outdoor areas. Furthermore, the farmers do not use any growth hormones or antibiotics.

Source: USDA National Organic Program

Chicken and Broccoli Casserole

For crispier broccoli, remove it from the boiling water after three minutes. Serve with a simple salad of mixed greens.

3 quarts water
1 (12-ounce) package broccoli florets
4 (6-ounce) skinless, boneless chicken breast halves
1 (12-ounce) can evaporated fat-free milk
¼ cup all-purpose flour (about 1 ounce)
¼ teaspoon salt
¼ teaspoon freshly ground black pepper
Dash of nutmeg
1 cup fat-free mayonnaise
½ cup fat-free sour cream
¼ cup dry sherry
1 teaspoon Worcestershire sauce
1 (10.75-ounce) can condensed 30% reduced-sodium, 98% fat-free cream of mushroom soup, undiluted
1 cup (4 ounces) grated fresh Parmesan cheese, divided
Cooking spray

1. Preheat oven to 400°.
2. Bring water to a boil in a large Dutch oven over medium-high heat. Add broccoli; cook 5 minutes or until crisp-tender. Transfer broccoli to a large bowl with a slotted spoon. Add chicken to boiling water; reduce heat, and simmer 15 minutes or until done. Transfer chicken to a cutting board; cool slightly. Cut chicken into bite-sized pieces; add chicken to bowl with broccoli.
3. Combine evaporated milk, flour, salt, pepper, and nutmeg in a saucepan, stirring with a whisk until smooth. Bring to a boil over medium-high heat; cook 1 minute, stirring constantly. Remove from heat. Add mayonnaise, next 4 ingredients, and ½ cup cheese, stirring until well combined. Add mayonnaise mixture to broccoli mixture; stir gently until combined.
4. Spoon mixture into a 13 x 9–inch baking dish coated with cooking spray. Sprinkle with remaining ½ cup cheese. Bake at 400° for 50 minutes or until mixture bubbles at edges and cheese begins to brown. Remove from oven; let cool on a wire rack 5 minutes. **YIELD:** 8 servings (serving size: about 1 cup).

CALORIES 276 (25% from fat); FAT 7.8g (sat 3.5g, mono 1.8g, poly 1.1g); PROTEIN 31.1g; CARB 18.9g; FIBER 2.1g; CHOL 66mg; IRON 1.6mg; SODIUM 696mg; CALC 365mg

Chicken and Broccoli Casserole

Tarragon Chicken-in-a-Pot Pies

Tarragon Chicken-in-a-Pot Pies

Popular in French cooking, tarragon adds anise flavor to the creamy chicken mixture. Hollowed-out rolls serve as edible, individual bowls that soak up the sauce.

    2   tablespoons all-purpose flour
    1   cup 1% low-fat milk
    ½   cup fat-free, less-sodium chicken broth
    ½   cup dry white wine
    1   tablespoon olive oil
    ⅔   cup chopped sweet onion
    1   pound skinless, boneless chicken breast, cut into
        bite-sized pieces
    1   cup sliced carrot
    1   cup (⅛-inch-thick) slices zucchini
    ½   teaspoon salt
    ½   teaspoon dried tarragon
    ½   teaspoon black pepper
    4   (4.5-ounce) country or peasant rolls

1. Place flour in a small bowl; slowly add milk, stirring with a whisk to form a slurry. Add broth and white wine.
2. Heat oil in a large saucepan over medium-high heat; add onion and chicken. Sauté 2 minutes; stir in carrot and next 4 ingredients. Cover, reduce heat, and cook 4 minutes. Stir slurry into chicken mixture, and bring to a boil. Cover, reduce heat, and simmer 10 minutes or until thick, stirring occasionally.
3. Cut rolls horizontally 1 inch from tops. Hollow out bottoms of rolls, leaving ¼-inch-thick shells; reserve torn bread and bread tops for another use. Spoon 1¼ cups chicken mixture into each bread shell. **YIELD:** 4 servings.

CALORIES 413 (17% from fat); FAT 7.8g (sat 2.7g, mono 3g, poly 0.7g); PROTEIN 35.7g; CARB 48.8g; FIBER 3.5g; CHOL 68mg; IRON 4.2mg; SODIUM 865mg; CALC 199mg

Salsa Chicken

Personalize this easy recipe by using your favorite tomato-based salsa. Or try a fruit salsa, such as peach, cranberry, or pineapple. Serve over hot cooked rice.

    1   pound skinless, boneless chicken breast, cut into
        bite-sized pieces
    2   teaspoons taco seasoning
        Cooking spray
    ⅔   cup salsa
    ⅔   cup (about 2½ ounces) reduced-fat shredded
        Cheddar cheese
    1   (4-ounce) can whole green chiles, drained and
        thinly sliced
    ¼   cup fat-free sour cream
    2   tablespoons sliced ripe olives

1. Preheat oven to 475°.
2. Combine chicken and seasoning in a medium bowl, tossing to coat. Heat a large nonstick skillet over medium-high heat. Coat pan with cooking spray. Add chicken; cook 4 minutes or until browned, stirring occasionally. Arrange chicken in an 8-inch square baking dish coated with cooking spray; top with salsa, cheese, and chiles. Bake at 475° for 8 minutes or until chicken is done and cheese melts. Top each serving with 1 tablespoon sour cream and 1½ teaspoons olives. **YIELD:** 4 servings.

CALORIES 207 (15% from fat); FAT 3.5g (sat 1.4g, mono 1.1g, poly 0.5g); PROTEIN 33.4g; CARB 9.5g; FIBER 2.1g; CHOL 71mg; IRON 1.5mg; SODIUM 587mg; CALC 130mg

ORGANIC TIP
Very few people have an all-organic diet. Initially, most people buy organic produce, dairy items, and meat, as these appear to have the most obvious health benefits.

Lemon Chicken and Rice with Artichokes

This one-dish meal is ready in less than half an hour. If you want another vegetable side dish, add steamed carrots tossed with a little butter and parsley.

Cooking spray
1 pound skinless, boneless chicken breast, cut into ½-inch strips
2¼ cups chopped onion
1 cup chopped red bell pepper
2 cups instant rice
¼ cup fresh lemon juice
¼ teaspoon salt
¼ teaspoon black pepper
1 (14-ounce) can fat-free, less-sodium chicken broth
1 (14-ounce) can quartered artichoke hearts, drained
2 tablespoons grated Romano or Parmesan cheese

1. Heat a Dutch oven over medium-high heat. Coat pan with cooking spray. Add chicken, onion, and bell pepper; sauté 5 minutes. Stir in rice, lemon juice, salt, black pepper, and broth; bring to a boil. Cover, reduce heat, and simmer 15 minutes or until rice is tender. Stir in artichokes; cook 1 minute or until thoroughly heated. Sprinkle with cheese. **YIELD:** 4 servings (serving size: 2 cups).

CALORIES 324 (8% from fat); FAT 2.8g (sat 1g, mono 0.7g, poly 0.5g); PROTEIN 35g; CARB 40.7g; FIBER 8.3g; CHOL 69mg; IRON 3.1mg; SODIUM 773mg; CALC 120mg

Rum-Glazed Pineapple, Mango, and Chicken Kebabs

Taste a bit of the Caribbean in every bite of this quick and easy summer barbecue treat. Serve with grilled corn on the cob and basmati or jasmine rice tossed with toasted coconut on the side.

¾ cup pineapple juice
¼ cup sugar
¼ cup dark rum
2 tablespoons finely chopped seeded jalapeño pepper
1 tablespoon cider vinegar
2 teaspoons cornstarch
2 tablespoons chopped fresh cilantro
1½ teaspoons grated lime rind
1½ pounds skinless, boneless chicken breast, cut into 30 cubes
2 mangoes, peeled and each cut into 9 (1-inch) cubes
18 (1-inch) cubes fresh pineapple
1½ tablespoons canola oil
1 teaspoon salt
Cooking spray

1. Prepare grill.
2. Combine first 4 ingredients in a medium saucepan; bring to a boil. Reduce heat; simmer 5 minutes. Combine vinegar and cornstarch in a small bowl. Add cornstarch mixture to pan; bring to a boil. Cook 1 minute, stirring constantly. Let stand 5 minutes. Stir in cilantro and rind.
3. Thread 5 chicken cubes, 3 mango cubes, and 3 pineapple cubes alternately onto each of 6 (12-inch) skewers. Brush kebabs with oil; sprinkle with salt. Place kebabs on grill rack coated with cooking spray; grill 4 minutes. Turn kebabs; brush with half of glaze, and grill 4 minutes. Turn kebabs; brush with remaining glaze. Grill 2 minutes, turning once. **YIELD:** 6 servings (serving size: 1 kebab).
NOTE: If using wooden skewers, soak them in water 30 minutes beforehand.

CALORIES 313 (30% from fat); FAT 10.4g (sat 2.4g, mono 3.5g, poly 3.5g); PROTEIN 26g; CARB 30g; FIBER 1.8g; CHOL 71mg; IRON 1.3mg; SODIUM 450mg; CALC 28mg

Chicken Pasanda

This traditional Pakistani dish also includes fresh pineapple cubes and pita wedges served on the side to dip into creamy cashew sauce.

½ cup roasted cashews
2 cups plain low-fat yogurt
1 cup coarsely chopped onion
¼ cup fresh lemon juice
2 tablespoons chopped peeled fresh ginger
2 jalapeño peppers, seeded
2½ teaspoons ground coriander seeds
¾ teaspoon ground cardamom
¾ teaspoon ground cinnamon
½ teaspoon black pepper
¼ teaspoon ground cloves
1 teaspoon salt, divided
4 (6-ounce) skinless, boneless chicken breast halves, each cut into 4 pieces
2 teaspoons canola oil
1 cup cubed fresh pineapple
2 tablespoons chopped cashews, roasted
2 tablespoons chopped fresh cilantro
4 (6-inch) pitas, each cut into 6 wedges

1. Place ½ cup roasted cashews in a food processor; process until smooth (about 2 minutes), scraping sides of bowl once. Add yogurt; process until well blended. Remove from processor; set aside.
2. Combine onion, lemon juice, ginger, and jalapeño in food processor or blender; process until finely chopped.
3. Combine coriander seeds and next 4 ingredients in a large zip-top plastic bag; add ½ teaspoon salt and chicken pieces. Seal bag, and shake to coat.
4. Heat oil in a large nonstick skillet over medium-high heat; add chicken pieces. Cook 4 minutes on each side or until done. Remove chicken from pan; keep warm.
5. Add onion mixture to pan. Reduce heat to medium; cook 3 minutes or until liquid evaporates, stirring frequently. Add remaining ½ teaspoon salt and yogurt mixture to pan; cook 3 minutes, stirring frequently.
6. Spoon ½ cup yogurt mixture onto each of 6 plates. Top each serving with 4 chicken pieces. Sprinkle each serving with about 2½ tablespoons pineapple, 1 teaspoon chopped cashews, and 1 teaspoon cilantro. Arrange 4 pita wedges on each plate. **YIELD:** 6 servings.

CALORIES 368 (27% from fat); FAT 11g (sat 2.5g, mono 4.5g, poly 2.5g); PROTEIN 27.7g; CARB 40.3g; FIBER 2.9g; CHOL 51mg; IRON 3.2mg; SODIUM 708mg; CALC 206mg

Chicken, Mushroom, and Cheese Quesadillas

Using preshredded cheese and presliced mushrooms makes preparation a snap.

  1 teaspoon olive oil
  1 teaspoon ground cumin
  ¼ teaspoon salt, divided
  ¼ teaspoon black pepper, divided
 12 ounces skinless, boneless chicken breasts, cut into ¼-inch-thick slices
  ¾ cup chopped onion
  1 (8-ounce) package presliced mushrooms
  1 garlic clove, minced
  1 jalapeño pepper, seeded and chopped
  4 (8-inch) flour tortillas
 1½ cups (6 ounces) preshredded light Mexican cheese blend, divided

1. Heat olive oil in a large nonstick skillet over medium-high heat. Combine cumin, ⅛ teaspoon salt, and ⅛ teaspoon pepper; sprinkle over chicken. Add chicken to pan; sauté 5 minutes or until browned. Remove chicken from pan; set aside. Add onion, mushrooms, garlic, jalapeño, ⅛ teaspoon salt, and ⅛ teaspoon pepper to pan; sauté 5 minutes. Remove from pan; let stand 5 minutes. Wipe pan with paper towels.
2. Heat pan over medium heat. Sprinkle each tortilla with about ⅓ cup cheese. Arrange ½ cup mushroom mixture over one half of each tortilla. Arrange chicken evenly over mushroom mixture. Carefully fold each tortilla in half. Add 2 quesadillas to pan; cook 2 minutes on each side or until lightly browned and cheese melts. Repeat procedure with remaining quesadillas. Serve immediately. **YIELD:** 4 servings (serving size: 1 quesadilla).

CALORIES 388 (29% from fat); FAT 12.5g (sat 5.7g, mono 2.5g, poly 0.9g); PROTEIN 38.5g; CARB 31.3g; FIBER 1.7g; CHOL 65mg; IRON 2.8mg; SODIUM 759mg; CALC 429mg

Chicken Scaloppine with Broccoli Rabe

If you can't find cutlets, pound chicken breast halves between heavy-duty plastic wrap to ¼-inch thickness. Broccoli florets can be substituted for the broccoli rabe; the cooking time may be a little longer, though. Add a side of roasted potato wedges and carrots, if desired.

  1 tablespoon olive oil
  ⅓ cup Italian-seasoned breadcrumbs
  ¼ teaspoon black pepper
  4 (6-ounce) skinless, boneless chicken breast cutlets
  ½ cup dry white wine
  ½ cup fat-free, less-sodium chicken broth
  3 tablespoons fresh lemon juice
  1 teaspoon butter
  1 pound broccoli rabe (rapini), cut into 3-inch pieces
  2 tablespoons chopped fresh parsley
  2 tablespoons capers, rinsed and drained
  4 lemon slices (optional)
     Parsley sprigs (optional)

1. Heat olive oil in a large nonstick skillet over medium-high heat.
2. Combine breadcrumbs and pepper in a shallow dish; dredge chicken in breadcrumb mixture. Add chicken to pan; cook 3 minutes on each side or until done. Remove from pan; keep warm.
3. Add wine, broth, juice, and butter to pan, scraping pan to loosen browned bits. Stir in broccoli rabe; cover and cook 3 minutes or until tender. Stir in chopped parsley and capers. Garnish with lemon slices and parsley sprigs, if desired. **YIELD:** 4 servings (serving size: 1 chicken cutlet and ½ cup broccoli rabe mixture).

CALORIES 318 (21% from fat); FAT 7.4g (sat 1.7g, mono 3.3g, poly 1g); PROTEIN 44.3g; CARB 14g; FIBER 3.9g; CHOL 101mg; IRON 2.9mg; SODIUM 577mg; CALC 102mg

Chicken Scaloppine with Broccoli Rabe

Black Pepper Citrus Chicken

Be sure to use fresh coarsely ground black pepper in this dish; finely ground pepper will overpower the chicken.

- 1 tablespoon canola oil, divided
- 1¼ teaspoons freshly ground black pepper, divided
- ¼ teaspoon salt
- 4 (6-ounce) skinless, boneless chicken breast halves
- 1 cup vertically sliced onion
- 2 teaspoons bottled minced garlic
- ¼ cup white wine
- 2 tablespoons fresh orange juice
- 1 tablespoon fresh lemon juice
- 2 tablespoons chopped fresh parsley

1. Heat 1 teaspoon oil in a large nonstick skillet over medium-high heat. Sprinkle ½ teaspoon pepper and salt over chicken. Add chicken to pan; cook 2 minutes on each side or until browned. Remove chicken from pan; keep warm. Add remaining 2 teaspoons oil to pan. Add onion and garlic to pan; sauté 2 minutes. Add wine; cook 1 minute. Return chicken to pan. Add remaining ¾ teaspoon pepper and juices. Cover, reduce heat, and simmer 4 minutes or until chicken is done. Sprinkle with parsley.
YIELD: 4 servings (serving size: 1 chicken breast half and 2 tablespoons onion mixture).

CALORIES 240 (22% from fat); FAT 5.9g (sat 0.8g, mono 2.6g, poly 1.5g); PROTEIN 39.6g; CARB 3.8g; FIBER 0.5g; CHOL 99mg; IRON 1.5mg; SODIUM 259mg; CALC 29mg

ORGANIC TIP
More involved organic consumers expand their organic purchases beyond produce, dairy, and meat in time, especially as they come to appreciate the environmental as well as health benefits of organic foods.

Easy Schnitzel

This is a simpler, lighter version of the German specialty Wiener schnitzel.

- 4 (6-ounce) skinless, boneless chicken breast halves
- ¼ teaspoon salt
- ¼ teaspoon freshly ground black pepper
- 2 tablespoons all-purpose flour
- 2 tablespoons Dijon mustard
- 1 large egg, lightly beaten
- ½ cup dry breadcrumbs
- 1½ tablespoons grated fresh Parmesan cheese
- 2 teaspoons finely chopped fresh parsley
- 2 teaspoons chopped fresh chives
- 1 garlic clove, minced
- 1 tablespoon olive oil
- 4 lemon wedges (optional)

1. Preheat oven to 350°.
2. Place each chicken breast half between 2 sheets of heavy-duty plastic wrap; pound to ½-inch thickness using a meat mallet or rolling pin. Sprinkle chicken with salt and pepper.
3. Place flour in a shallow bowl. Combine mustard and egg in a shallow dish. Combine breadcrumbs, cheese, parsley, chives, and garlic in a shallow dish. Dredge 1 chicken breast half in flour, turning to coat; shake off excess flour. Dip in egg mixture; dredge in breadcrumb mixture. Repeat procedure with remaining chicken, flour, egg mixture, and breadcrumb mixture.
4. Heat oil in a large ovenproof nonstick skillet over medium-high heat. Add chicken; sauté 2½ minutes or until browned. Remove from heat. Turn chicken over; place pan in oven. Bake at 350° for 10 minutes or until chicken is done. Serve with lemon wedges, if desired.
YIELD: 4 servings (serving size: 1 chicken breast half).

CALORIES 328 (22% from fat); FAT 8.1g (sat 1.9g, mono 3.8g, poly 1.3g); PROTEIN 45.3g; CARB 16.7g; FIBER 0.7g; CHOL 153mg; IRON 2.6mg; SODIUM 636mg; CALC 85mg

Greek Chicken with Capers, Raisins, and Feta

4   (6-ounce) skinless, boneless chicken breast halves
2   tablespoons all-purpose flour
1   teaspoon dried oregano
1   tablespoon olive oil
1   cup thinly sliced onion
1½ cups fat-free, less-sodium chicken broth
⅓   cup golden raisins
2   tablespoons lemon juice
2   tablespoons capers
¼   cup (1 ounce) crumbled feta cheese
4   thin lemon slices (optional)

1. Place each chicken breast half between 2 sheets of heavy-duty plastic wrap; flatten to ¼-inch thickness using a meat mallet or rolling pin. Combine flour and dried oregano in a shallow dish, and dredge chicken in flour mixture.

2. Heat oil in a large nonstick skillet over medium-high heat. Add chicken; cook 4 minutes on each side. Remove chicken from pan; keep warm. Add onion to pan; sauté 2 minutes. Stir in broth, raisins, and lemon juice; cook 3 minutes, scraping pan to loosen browned bits. Return chicken to pan. Cover, reduce heat, and simmer 8 minutes or until chicken is done.

3. Place a chicken breast on each of 4 serving plates. Add capers to sauce in pan. Spoon ⅓ cup sauce over each serving; top with 1 tablespoon cheese. Garnish with lemon slices, if desired. **YIELD:** 4 servings.

CALORIES 319 (22% from fat); FAT 7.7g (sat 2.5g, mono 3.4g, poly 1g); PROTEIN 43.1g; CARB 18.5g; FIBER 1.5g; CHOL 107mg; IRON 2.1mg; SODIUM 559mg; CALC 89mg

Herbed Chicken Breasts with Tomatillo Salsa and Queso Fresco

SALSA:

- 2 quarts water
- ½ pound tomatillos (about 10 small), husks and stems removed
- 1 garlic clove
- ½ to 1 serrano chile
- ½ cup chopped fresh cilantro
- ¼ cup coarsely chopped onion
- 1 teaspoon fresh lime juice
- ¼ teaspoon salt

CHICKEN:

- 3 (1-ounce) slices white bread
- 4 (6-ounce) skinless, boneless chicken breast halves
- ½ teaspoon salt
- ½ teaspoon ground cumin
- ¼ teaspoon ground red pepper
- 1 large egg, lightly beaten
- 1 tablespoon olive oil
- ½ cup (2 ounces) crumbled queso fresco cheese

Cilantro sprigs (optional)

Lime wedges (optional)

1. Preheat oven to 350°.

2. To prepare salsa, bring water to a boil. Add tomatillos, garlic, and chile; cook 7 minutes. Drain and rinse with cold water. Combine tomatillos, garlic, chile, chopped cilantro, onion, lime juice, and ¼ teaspoon salt in a food processor or blender; pulse 4 or 5 times or until ingredients are coarsely chopped. Set aside.

3. To prepare chicken, place bread in a food processor, and pulse 10 times or until coarse crumbs measure 1½ cups. Arrange crumbs on a baking sheet; bake at 350° for 3 minutes or until lightly browned. Cool completely.

4. Place each chicken breast half between 2 sheets of heavy-duty plastic wrap; pound to ½-inch thickness using a meat mallet or rolling pin. Combine ½ teaspoon salt, cumin, and red pepper; sprinkle evenly over chicken.

5. Place breadcrumbs in a shallow dish. Place egg in another shallow dish. Dip chicken in egg; dredge in breadcrumbs.

6. Heat oil in a large nonstick skillet over medium-high heat. Add chicken; cook 4 minutes on each side or until done. Top chicken with salsa; sprinkle with queso fresco cheese. Garnish with cilantro sprigs and lime wedges, if desired. **YIELD:** 4 servings (serving size: 1 chicken breast half, ¼ cup salsa, and 2 tablespoons cheese).

CALORIES 364 (26% from fat); FAT 10.7g (sat 3.2g, mono 4.5g, poly 1.6g); PROTEIN 47.1g; CARB 17.7g; FIBER 2g; CHOL 162mg; IRON 3mg; SODIUM 770mg; CALC 169mg

Mexican Chicken with Almond-Chile Cream

The almond nut meal, made in the blender, lends a creamy richness to the sauce, even with minimal added fat. Look for ground ancho chile pepper in the spice section. If you can't find it, substitute 1½ teaspoons regular chili powder and ½ teaspoon ground chipotle chile pepper. Crema Mexicana is similar to crème fraîche but has a thinner consistency and a sweeter flavor. Slice the chicken, and serve with flour tortillas and a tossed salad.

    3 tablespoons sliced almonds
    2 teaspoons ground ancho chile pepper
    4 (6-ounce) skinless, boneless chicken breast halves
    ¼ teaspoon salt, divided
    ¼ teaspoon freshly ground black pepper
    2 teaspoons butter
    1 teaspoon canola oil
    1 garlic clove, minced
    1 cup fat-free, less-sodium chicken broth
    2 tablespoons crema Mexicana
    Cilantro sprigs (optional)

1. Combine almonds and chile pepper in a blender or food processor, and process until mixture resembles coarse meal.
2. Place each chicken breast half between 2 sheets of heavy-duty plastic wrap, and pound to ½-inch thickness using a heavy skillet. Sprinkle with ⅛ teaspoon salt and black pepper.
3. Heat butter and oil in a large nonstick skillet over medium heat. Add chicken; cook 6 minutes on each side or until done. Remove chicken from pan, and keep warm.
4. Add minced garlic to pan; cook 1 minute, stirring constantly. Add almond mixture, remaining ⅛ teaspoon salt, and broth; bring to a boil, scraping pan to loosen browned bits. Cook until broth mixture is reduced to ½ cup (about 3 minutes). Remove from heat. Stir in crema Mexicana. Serve sauce over chicken. Garnish with cilantro sprigs, if desired. **YIELD:** 4 servings (serving size: 1 chicken breast half and 2 tablespoons sauce).

CALORIES 269 (30% from fat); FAT 8.9g (sat 2.8g, mono 3.1g, poly 1.4g); PROTEIN 41.3g; CARB 2.8g; FIBER 1.2g; CHOL 109mg; IRON 1.4mg; SODIUM 387mg; CALC 35mg

Chicken in Cherry-Marsala Sauce

If you can't find dried cherries, use dried cranberries. The microwave is ideal for heating small amounts of liquid to rehydrate dried fruit.

    ⅓ cup dried cherries
    ⅓ cup Marsala
    2 teaspoons olive oil
    4 (6-ounce) skinless, boneless chicken breast halves
    ½ teaspoon salt, divided
    ½ teaspoon black pepper, divided
    1 teaspoon butter
    ¼ cup finely chopped shallots
    1 tablespoon chopped fresh thyme
    ½ cup fat-free, less-sodium chicken broth

1. Combine dried cherries and Marsala in a small microwave-safe bowl. Microwave at HIGH 45 seconds; set aside.
2. Heat olive oil in a large nonstick skillet over medium-high heat. Add chicken; cook 4 minutes on each side or until done. Remove chicken from pan; sprinkle with ¼ teaspoon salt and ¼ teaspoon pepper. Cover and keep warm.
3. Add butter to pan; cook until butter melts. Add shallots and thyme; sauté 1 minute or until tender. Stir in broth, scraping pan to loosen browned bits. Add cherry mixture, remaining ¼ teaspoon salt, and remaining ¼ teaspoon pepper; bring to a boil. Reduce heat to medium; simmer 2 minutes or until sauce is slightly thick. Serve chicken with sauce. **YIELD:** 4 servings (serving size: 1 chicken breast half and about ¼ cup sauce).

CALORIES 297 (16% from fat); FAT 5.4g (sat 1.4g, mono 2.6g, poly 0.8g); PROTEIN 40.5g; CARB 13.7g; FIBER 1.1g; CHOL 101mg; IRON 2.1mg; SODIUM 464mg; CALC 33mg

ORGANIC FACT
Conventional agriculture's routine use of antibiotics and growth hormones in livestock handling has motivated many consumers to seek organically derived dairy and meat products.

Chicken with Summer Squash and Lemon-Chive Sauce

You can serve up a side of quinoa or egg noodles to complete the meal.

  2   teaspoons canola oil
  4   (6-ounce) skinless, boneless chicken breast halves
  ¼   teaspoon salt
  ¼   teaspoon black pepper
  2   cups (½-inch) cubed yellow squash
  1½ cups (½-inch) cubed zucchini
  1   cup fat-free, less-sodium chicken broth
  1   tablespoon chopped fresh chives
  ½   teaspoon grated lemon rind
  1   tablespoon fresh lemon juice
  2   teaspoons cornstarch
  2   teaspoons honey mustard

1. Heat oil in a large nonstick skillet over medium-high heat. Sprinkle chicken with salt and pepper; add chicken to pan. Cook 4 minutes on each side; remove from pan. Keep warm.
2. Reduce heat to medium. Add cubed squash and zucchini to pan, and cook 2 minutes, stirring frequently. Return chicken to pan.
3. Combine broth and next 5 ingredients in a small bowl, stirring with a whisk. Add broth mixture to pan. Cover, reduce heat to medium-low, and cook 3 minutes. **YIELD:** 4 servings (serving size: 1 chicken breast half and ½ cup squash mixture).

CALORIES 237 (17% from fat); FAT 4.6g (sat 0.8g, mono 1.9g, poly 1.3g); PROTEIN 41.3g; CARB 5.8g; FIBER 1.2g; CHOL 99mg; IRON 1.6mg; SODIUM 419mg; CALC 36mg

ECO FACT
Organic meats take a lot of time and a lot of energy to produce. When it comes to chickens, they are the most efficient animals when converting fossil energy to food energy.

Chicken with Duxelles

Duxelles is a thick mixture of finely chopped mushrooms, shallots, and seasonings cooked slowly to evaporate the liquid and intensify the mushroom flavor. Drizzling with half-and-half at the end pulls the flavors together. Using the microwave shortens the cooking time significantly. A food processor relieves you of tedious chopping.

  3   cups fresh parsley leaves (about 1 bunch)
  2   large shallots, peeled and quartered
  4   cups coarsely chopped mushrooms
        (about ¾ pound)
  1   tablespoon olive oil, divided
  ½   teaspoon salt, divided
  ¼   teaspoon black pepper, divided
  ⅛   teaspoon ground red pepper
  2   teaspoons bottled minced garlic
  4   (6-ounce) skinless, boneless chicken breast halves
  ¼   cup half-and-half

1. Place parsley leaves and shallots in a food processor; process until shallots are finely chopped. Add mushrooms, and process until finely chopped, scraping sides of bowl occasionally. Place mushroom mixture in a deep-dish 10-inch pie plate. Microwave at HIGH 12 minutes, stirring every 4 minutes. Stir in 1 teaspoon oil, ¼ teaspoon salt, ⅛ teaspoon black pepper, and red pepper.
2. Combine remaining 2 teaspoons oil, remaining ¼ teaspoon salt, remaining ⅛ teaspoon black pepper, minced garlic, and chicken in a bowl; toss well. Arrange chicken spokelike on top of mushroom mixture. Drizzle with half-and-half. Cover with plastic wrap; vent. Microwave at HIGH 7 minutes or until done. **YIELD:** 4 servings (serving size: 1 chicken breast half and about ½ cup duxelles).

CALORIES 284 (25% from fat); FAT 7.9g (sat 2.1g, mono 3.5g, poly 1g); PROTEIN 43.2g; CARB 8.8g; FIBER 1.4g; CHOL 104mg; IRON 4.6mg; SODIUM 430mg; CALC 101mg

Cuban-Style Chicken

The simple addition of a mojo marinade lends a Latin flair to this easy dish. Look for the marinade in the ethnic-foods aisle.

4 (6-ounce) skinless, boneless chicken breast halves
3 tablespoons commercial mojo marinade
½ cup finely chopped onion
¼ cup finely chopped fresh parsley
1 teaspoon canola oil
4 teaspoons fresh lime juice
Lime wedges (optional)

1. Combine chicken and mojo in a large zip-top plastic bag; seal and marinate in refrigerator 2 hours, turning bag occasionally.

2. While chicken marinates, combine onion and parsley; refrigerate.

3. Remove chicken from bag; pat chicken dry. Heat oil in a large nonstick skillet over medium-high heat. Add chicken; cook 4 minutes on each side or until done. Drizzle each breast with 1 teaspoon lime juice; top each serving with 2 tablespoons onion mixture. Serve with lime wedges, if desired. **YIELD:** 4 servings.

CALORIES 212 (14% from fat); FAT 3.3g (sat 0.7g, mono 1.2g, poly 0.8g); PROTEIN 39.6g; CARB 3.3g; FIBER 0.4g; CHOL 99mg; IRON 1.6mg; SODIUM 282mg; CALC 48mg

Spiced Chicken with Black-Eyed Peas and Rice

Spiced Chicken with Black-Eyed Peas and Rice

For juicier chicken, sear it on the stove top first, and then finish the cooking in the oven.

      1 tablespoon olive oil, divided
      1 teaspoon paprika
      1 teaspoon Old Bay seasoning
      ½ teaspoon sugar
      ½ teaspoon salt, divided
      4 (6-ounce) skinless, boneless chicken breast
         halves
      1 cup chopped onion
      1 garlic clove, minced
   1½ cups cooked long-grain rice
      1 teaspoon hot pepper sauce
      1 (15.8-ounce) can black-eyed peas, undrained
      ¼ cup sliced green onions

1. Preheat oven to 350°.
2. Heat 2 teaspoons olive oil in a large nonstick skillet over medium-high heat. Combine paprika, seasoning, sugar, and ¼ teaspoon salt; sprinkle over chicken. Add chicken to pan; cook 2 minutes on each side. Wrap handle of pan with foil. Place pan in oven. Bake at 350° for 6 minutes or until chicken is done. Cover and keep warm.
3. Heat 1 teaspoon olive oil in a large saucepan over medium-high heat. Add onion and garlic; sauté 3 minutes. Stir in rice, ¼ teaspoon salt, 1 teaspoon hot pepper sauce, and peas; cook 3 minutes or until thoroughly heated, stirring frequently. Spoon about ¾ cup rice mixture into each of 4 bowls; top each serving with 1 chicken breast half. Sprinkle each serving with 1 tablespoon green onions. **YIELD:** 4 servings.

CALORIES 405 (14% from fat); FAT 6.5g (sat 1.3g, mono 3.1g, poly 1.2g); PROTEIN 47g; CARB 37.5g; FIBER 5g; CHOL 99mg; IRON 3.4mg; SODIUM 868mg; CALC 64mg

Maple-Orange Chicken

      Cooking spray
      4 (6-ounce) skinless, boneless chicken breast
         halves
      3 tablespoons water
      3 tablespoons 100% pure maple syrup
      2 tablespoons low-sodium soy sauce
      2 tablespoons cider vinegar
   1½ teaspoons grated orange rind

1. Heat a large nonstick skillet over medium heat. Coat pan with cooking spray. Add chicken to pan; cook 6 minutes on each side or until done.
2. Combine water and remaining ingredients; add to pan. Cook 1 minute, turning chicken to coat. **YIELD:** 4 servings (serving size: 1 chicken breast half and about 1 tablespoon sauce).

CALORIES 233 (8% from fat); FAT 2.1g (sat 0.6g, mono 0.5g, poly 0.5g); PROTEIN 39.8g; CARB 11.3g; FIBER 0.1g; CHOL 99mg; IRON 1.5mg; SODIUM 415mg; CALC 31mg

ORGANIC FACT
Organic standards vary by country, thus constraining growth of the industry. Fortunately, Canada and the United States developed an equivalency agreement in June 2009 that enables each country to accept the organic certification of the other.

Source: Organic Trade Association

Sweet-and-Sour Chicken

      4 (6-ounce) skinless, boneless chicken breast halves
      2 cups teriyaki marinade, divided
      2 cups (1-inch) cubed fresh pineapple
   1½ cups yellow or orange bell pepper strips
   1½ cups red bell pepper strips
      2 cups vertically sliced Vidalia onion
      2 cups cherry tomatoes
      ¼ cup chopped fresh cilantro

1. Place chicken in a large zip-top plastic bag; add 1 cup marinade. Seal bag; toss gently to coat. Place pineapple, bell peppers, and onion in another large zip-top plastic bag; add 1 cup marinade. Seal; toss gently. Refrigerate 2 hours, turning bags occasionally.
2. Prepare grill.
3. Drain pineapple mixture, discarding marinade. Place pineapple mixture and tomatoes in a large foil cooking bag. Drain chicken, discarding marinade. Place chicken on top of pineapple mixture. Seal and cut 6 (½-inch) slits in top of cooking bag. Place bag on grill. Grill 25 minutes or until chicken is done. Cut bag open with a sharp knife or cooking shears. Carefully peel back foil. Sprinkle with cilantro. **YIELD:** 4 servings (serving size: 1 chicken breast half and 1 cup pineapple mixture).

CALORIES 336 (8% from fat); FAT 3.2g (sat 0.7g, mono 0.6g, poly 0.9g); PROTEIN 43g; CARB 35g; FIBER 7g; CHOL 99mg; IRON 3mg; SODIUM 279mg; CALC 72mg

Easy Puebla-Style Chicken Mole

Easy Puebla-Style Chicken Mole

This version of the Mexican classic comes together in minutes. To save time, use an immersion blender to puree the sauce while it's still in the pan. Serve with black beans and yellow rice, or as a filling for enchiladas. Garnish with sliced green onions, if you wish.

1 teaspoon olive oil
1 cup thinly sliced onion
1 teaspoon ground cumin
1 teaspoon ground coriander
½ teaspoon ground cinnamon
2 stemmed dried seeded ancho chiles, torn into 2-inch pieces (about ¼ cup)
2 garlic cloves, thinly sliced
3 cups fat-free, less-sodium chicken broth
1⅓ cups coarsely chopped tomato (about 1 medium)
¼ cup golden raisins
3 tablespoons sliced almonds, toasted
3 (½ x 2–inch) orange rind strips
¾ pound skinless, boneless chicken breast halves
¾ pound skinless, boneless chicken thighs
½ ounce unsweetened chocolate
¼ teaspoon salt
¼ teaspoon black pepper

1. Heat oil in a Dutch oven over medium-high heat. Add onion; cook 5 minutes or until almost tender. Combine cumin, coriander, and cinnamon in a small bowl; sprinkle over onion in pan. Cook 1 minute. Add chiles and garlic to pan; cook 2 minutes or until chiles soften. Add broth and next 4 ingredients to pan; bring to a boil. Add chicken to pan; cover, reduce heat, and simmer 10 minutes or until chicken is done. Remove chicken from pan; shred with 2 forks. Set aside.
2. Add chocolate to chile mixture; let stand until chocolate melts. Using an immersion blender in pan, puree chocolate mixture until smooth. Cook over medium heat 20 minutes or until reduced to 3½ cups, stirring occasionally. Add chicken to sauce; stir in salt and pepper. **YIELD:** 6 servings (serving size: about 1 cup chicken mixture).

CALORIES 211 (29% from fat); FAT 6.8g (sat 1.8g; mono 2.8g; poly 1.3g); PROTEIN 27.2g; CARB 10.5g; FIBER 2.5g; CHOL 80mg; IRON 2.1mg; SODIUM 380mg; CALC 50mg

Oven-Fried Chicken

(pictured on page 116)

Marinating in buttermilk results in tender, juicy chicken, and double breading gives a crisp crust even without the skin. For a smoky taste, use ground chipotle pepper in place of the ground red pepper.

¾ cup low-fat buttermilk
2 bone-in chicken breast halves (about 1 pound), skinned
2 chicken drumsticks (about ½ pound), skinned
2 chicken thighs (about ½ pound), skinned
½ cup all-purpose flour (about 2¼ ounces)
1 teaspoon salt
½ teaspoon ground red pepper
¼ teaspoon white pepper
¼ teaspoon ground cumin
Cooking spray

1. Combine first 4 ingredients in a large zip-top plastic bag; seal. Marinate in refrigerator 1 hour, turning occasionally.
2. Preheat oven to 450°.
3. Lightly spoon flour into a dry measuring cup; level with a knife. Combine flour, salt, peppers, and cumin in a second large zip-top plastic bag. Remove chicken from first bag, discarding marinade. Add chicken, one piece at a time, to flour mixture, shaking bag to coat chicken. Remove chicken from bag, shaking off excess flour; lightly coat each chicken piece with cooking spray. Return chicken, one piece at a time, to flour mixture, shaking bag to coat chicken. Remove chicken from bag, shaking off excess flour.
4. Place chicken on a baking sheet lined with parchment paper. Lightly coat chicken with cooking spray. Bake at 450° for 35 minutes or until done, turning after 20 minutes. **YIELD:** 4 servings (serving size: 1 breast half or 1 thigh and 1 drumstick).

CALORIES 263 (15% from fat); FAT 4.4g (sat 1.2g, mono 1.1g, poly 0.9g); PROTEIN 38.4g; CARB 14.9g; FIBER 0.8g; CHOL 110mg; IRON 2.2mg; SODIUM 754mg; CALC 73mg

Slow Cooker
Sweet-and-Sour Chicken

Pork tenderloin can be used in place of chicken thighs.

  1 cup chopped onion
  ⅓ cup sugar
  ⅓ cup ketchup
  ¼ cup orange juice
  3 tablespoons cornstarch
  3 tablespoons cider vinegar
  2 tablespoons low-sodium soy sauce
  1 tablespoon grated peeled fresh ginger
  1 pound skinless, boneless chicken thighs, cut into
      1-inch pieces
  2 (8-ounce) cans pineapple chunks in juice, drained
  1 large green bell pepper, cut into ¾-inch pieces
  1 large red bell pepper, cut into ¾-inch pieces
  3 cups hot cooked white rice

1. Combine first 12 ingredients in an electric slow
cooker. Cover and cook on LOW 6 hours or HIGH
4 hours. Serve over rice. **YIELD:** 6 servings (serving size:
⅔ cup chicken mixture and ½ cup rice).

CALORIES 381 (21% from fat); FAT 8.7g (sat 2.3g, mono 3.2g, poly 2g); PROTEIN 23.2g;
CARB 51.9g; FIBER 2.1g; CHOL 72mg; IRON 2.5mg; SODIUM 396mg; CALC 29mg

ORGANIC FACT
Organic food sales only represent about 3% of all
food sales in the United States today. So the potential for the market to grow and have an impact on
the environment is enormous.

Margarita-Braised
Chicken Thighs

Stir chopped cilantro and green onions into steamed rice for
an easy side.

  ½ cup flour (about 2¼ ounces)
  1 tablespoon paprika
  2 teaspoons garlic powder
  8 skinless, boneless chicken thighs (about 1½
      pounds)
  ½ teaspoon salt
  1 tablespoon olive oil
Cooking spray
  1 cup thinly sliced onion (about 1 medium)
  5 garlic cloves, minced
  ½ cup dried tropical fruit
  ½ cup orange juice
  ¼ cup tequila
  1 lime, thinly sliced

1. Preheat oven to 400°.
2. Combine first 3 ingredients in a small baking dish.
Sprinkle chicken with salt; dredge chicken in flour
mixture.
3. Heat oil in a large nonstick skillet over medium-high
heat. Add chicken to pan; cook 4 minutes on each side or
until lightly browned. Transfer chicken to an 11 x 7–inch
baking dish coated with cooking spray. Add onion to
pan; cook 3 minutes. Add garlic to pan; sauté 1 minute.
4. Combine fruit, juice, and tequila in a microwave-safe
dish; microwave at HIGH 2 minutes. Pour fruit mixture
into pan; bring to a boil, scraping pan to loosen browned
bits. Cook 1 minute. Pour onion mixture over chicken;
top with lime slices. Bake at 400° for 20 minutes or until
chicken is done. **YIELD:** 4 servings (serving size: 2 chicken
thighs and about ⅓ cup fruit mixture).

CALORIES 350 (25% from fat); FAT 9.9g (sat 2.2g, mono 4.3g, poly 2.1g); PROTEIN 25.1g;
CARB 37.9g; FIBER 2.7g; CHOL 94mg; IRON 2.7mg; SODIUM 416mg; CALC 55mg

Margarita-Braised
Chicken Thighs

Chicken Paprikash–Topped Potatoes

The traditional Hungarian dish of chicken and onion in a creamy paprika sauce makes a hearty topping for baked potatoes. Dark-meat chicken complements the bold flavors.

4 baking potatoes (about 1½ pounds)
4 skinless, boneless chicken thighs (about 12 ounces), cut into bite-sized pieces
2 tablespoons all-purpose flour
2 teaspoons paprika
¾ teaspoon salt
¼ teaspoon ground red pepper
1 tablespoon butter
½ cup coarsely chopped onion
1 (8-ounce) package presliced mushrooms
2 garlic cloves, minced
½ cup fat-free, less-sodium chicken broth
¼ cup reduced-fat sour cream
2 tablespoons chopped fresh parsley

1. Pierce potatoes with a fork, and arrange in a circle on paper towels in a microwave oven. Microwave at HIGH 16 minutes or until done, rearranging potatoes after 8 minutes. Wrap each potato in foil; let stand 5 minutes.
2. Combine chicken, flour, paprika, salt, and pepper in a large zip-top plastic bag; seal and shake to coat.
3. Melt butter in a large nonstick skillet over medium-high heat. Add chicken mixture, onion, mushrooms, and garlic; sauté 5 minutes. Add broth; bring to a boil. Cook 6 minutes or until chicken is done and sauce thickens, stirring frequently. Remove from heat; stir in sour cream.
4. Remove foil from potatoes, and split open with a fork. Fluff pulp. Divide chicken mixture evenly over potatoes; sprinkle with parsley. **YIELD:** 4 servings (serving size: 1 potato, ½ cup chicken mixture, and 1½ teaspoons parsley).

CALORIES 311 (25% from fat); FAT 8.6g (sat 3.9g, mono 1.9g, poly 1.2g); PROTEIN 22.9g; CARB 36.3g; FIBER 3.4g; CHOL 86mg; IRON 2.6g; SODIUM 619mg; CALC 56mg

Yakitori

The Japanese term "yakitori" refers to small pieces of marinated chicken that are skewered and grilled. We preferred dark-meat chicken with the soy-ginger mixture.

¼ cup sake (rice wine)
¼ cup low-sodium soy sauce
3 tablespoons sugar
2 tablespoons grated peeled fresh ginger
¼ teaspoon crushed red pepper
2 garlic cloves, minced
1 pound skinless, boneless chicken thighs, cut into 24 bite-sized pieces
5 green onions, each cut into 4 (2-inch) pieces
Cooking spray

1. Combine first 6 ingredients in a small saucepan. Bring to a boil; cook until reduced to ¼ cup (about 2½ minutes). Remove from heat; cool.
2. Combine soy sauce mixture and chicken in a zip-top plastic bag, and seal. Marinate in refrigerator 1 hour.
3. Heat a large grill pan over medium-high heat.
4. Thread 6 chicken pieces and 5 green onion pieces alternately onto each of 4 (10-inch) skewers. Brush kebabs with soy mixture. Coat pan with cooking spray. Place kebabs in pan; cook 4 minutes on each side or until browned and chicken is done. **YIELD:** 4 servings (serving size: 1 kebab).

CALORIES 172 (24% from fat); FAT 4.5g (sat 1.1g, mono 1.4g, poly 1.1g); PROTEIN 22.9g; CARB 6.7g; FIBER 0.3g; CHOL 94mg; IRON 1.5mg; SODIUM 366mg; CALC 19mg

Braised Chicken Thighs with Figs and Bay Leaves

Chicken thighs are more succulent than breasts, but you can use the latter if you prefer. Serve this entrée with couscous to capture the tangy sauce.

8 chicken thighs (about 2¼ pounds), skinned
½ teaspoon salt
¼ teaspoon black pepper
8 bay leaves
2 teaspoons olive oil
3 tablespoons water
½ cup sliced shallots
⅓ cup dry red wine
1 tablespoon red wine vinegar
1 teaspoon honey
16 fresh figs, halved

1. Sprinkle chicken with salt and black pepper. Place 1 bay leaf on each chicken thigh. Heat oil in a heavy 10-inch skillet over medium-high heat. Place chicken, bay leaf sides down, in pan. Cook 5 minutes or until browned. Turn chicken over; cook 3 minutes. Add 3 tablespoons water; cover, reduce heat, and simmer 5 minutes. Remove chicken from pan. Add shallots; cook 2 minutes. Add chicken, wine, vinegar, and honey to pan; bring to a boil. Cook for 1 minute. Cover, reduce heat, and simmer 5 minutes or until chicken is done. Add figs; cover and simmer 5 minutes or until figs are tender. **YIELD:** 4 servings (serving size: 2 chicken thighs, 8 fig halves, and ¼ cup sauce).

CALORIES 393 (26% from fat); FAT 11.4g (sat 2.6g, mono 4.5g, poly 2.5g); PROTEIN 42.4g; CARB 27.4g; FIBER 4.4g; CHOL 163mg; IRON 2.9mg; SODIUM 472mg; CALC 74mg

ORGANIC FACT
Honey bees play an important role in the ecosystem. Conventional beekeepers commonly exterminate bees at the end of a season, whereas organic bee-keepers typically keep the bees to help promote environmental sustainability.

Chicken Thighs with Roasted Apples

142

Chicken Thighs with Roasted Apples

The roasted apples create a flavorful chunky sauce for this rustic dish. Gala apples are a good substitute for Braeburn.

5 cups chopped Braeburn apple (about 1½ pounds)
1 teaspoon chopped fresh sage
¼ teaspoon ground cinnamon
⅛ teaspoon ground nutmeg
4 garlic cloves, chopped
½ teaspoon salt, divided
Cooking spray
8 chicken thighs (about 2½ pounds), skinned
¼ teaspoon black pepper
Chopped parsley (optional)

1. Preheat oven to 475°.
2. Combine first 5 ingredients in a large bowl. Sprinkle ¼ teaspoon salt over apple mixture; toss well to coat. Spread apple mixture on a jelly-roll pan coated with cooking spray.
3. Sprinkle chicken with ¼ teaspoon salt and pepper; arrange on top of apple mixture. Bake at 475° for 25 minutes or until chicken is done and apple is tender. Remove chicken from pan; set aside, and keep warm.
4. Partially mash apple mixture with a potato masher; serve with chicken. Sprinkle with parsley, if desired.

YIELD: 4 servings (serving size: 2 chicken thighs and about ⅔ cup roasted apples).

CALORIES 257 (20% from fat); FAT 5.7g (sat 1.4g, mono 1.6g, poly 1.4g); PROTEIN 25.9g; CARB 26.6g; FIBER 3.5g; CHOL 107mg; IRON 1.7mg; SODIUM 405mg; CALC 30mg

Jamaican-Spiced Jerk Chicken

Slow cooking chicken thighs in a classic Caribbean seasoning mixture yields tender morsels in a spicy jus. Serve over yellow rice.

1 Scotch bonnet chile
1 cup chopped green onions
2 tablespoons sugar
2 tablespoons cider vinegar
2 tablespoons low-sodium soy sauce
1 teaspoon ground allspice
¼ teaspoon ground cinnamon
¼ teaspoon dried thyme
½ teaspoon salt
2 garlic cloves, crushed
6 chicken thighs (about 2 pounds), skinned

1. Remove stem from chile; cut chile in half. Combine chile, chopped green onions, and next 8 ingredients in a food processor; process until smooth.
2. Place chicken in an electric slow cooker; top with onion mixture, stirring gently to coat. Cover and cook on LOW 6 hours. Remove chicken thighs from slow cooker with a slotted spoon. Remove meat from bones, and shred meat into bite-sized pieces using 2 forks.
3. Place a zip-top plastic bag inside a 2-cup glass measure. Pour liquid from slow cooker into bag; let stand 10 minutes (fat will rise to the top). Seal bag; carefully snip off 1 bottom corner of bag. Drain drippings into a bowl, stopping before fat layer reaches opening; discard fat. Serve chicken with jus. **YIELD:** 4 servings (serving size: 4 ounces chicken and ¼ cup jus).

CALORIES 317 (26% from fat); FAT 9g (sat 2.3g, mono 2.8g, poly 2.3g); PROTEIN 45.8g; CARB 10.9g; FIBER 1.3g; CHOL 188mg; IRON 3.2mg; SODIUM 763mg; CALC 53mg

ORGANIC RESOURCE
The Organic Trade Association (OTA) started in 1985 in order to promote and protect the growth of organic trade to benefit the environment, farmers, the public, and the economy in North America.

Source: Organic Trade Association

Chicken and Dumplings from Scratch

Creating a chicken and dumplings recipe that's creamy, rich, and thick is a challenge, especially thickening the base. Relying solely on cornstarch produced a gluey consistency and a thin flavor, and using all flour created pasty results. A little of each achieved the perfect thickness and texture. Toasting the flour, a process similar to making a dry roux, adds richness. Finish the dish with a splash of cream for flavor.

STEW:

1 (4-pound) whole chicken
3 quarts water
3 cups chopped onion
1 cup chopped celery
1 cup chopped carrot
1 teaspoon salt
¼ teaspoon freshly ground black pepper
10 garlic cloves, peeled
4 thyme sprigs
2 bay leaves
¼ cup all-purpose flour (about 1 ounce)
2 teaspoons cornstarch
3 tablespoons heavy cream

DUMPLINGS:

¾ cup 1% low-fat milk
1 large egg
1½ cups all-purpose flour (about 6¾ ounces)
1 tablespoon baking powder
1 tablespoon cornmeal
½ teaspoon salt

REMAINING INGREDIENTS:

1 tablespoon chopped parsley
Freshly ground black pepper

1. To prepare stew, remove and discard giblets and neck from chicken. Rinse chicken with cold water; place chicken in an 8-quart stockpot. Add 3 quarts water and next 8 ingredients; bring to a simmer. Reduce heat, and simmer 45 minutes; skim surface occasionally, discarding solids. Remove chicken from pot; cool. Strain stock through a sieve into a large bowl; discard solids. Remove chicken meat from bones; tear chicken meat into 2-inch pieces, and store in refrigerator. Let stock cool to room temperature.

2. Pour stock into 2 zip-top plastic bags. Let stand 15 minutes. Working with one bag at a time, snip off 1 bottom corner of bag; drain liquid into stockpot, stopping before fat layer reaches opening. Discard fat. Repeat procedure with remaining bag. Bring stock to a boil over medium-high heat; reduce heat, and simmer until reduced to 8 cups (about 15 minutes).

3. Heat a cast-iron skillet over medium-high heat 5 minutes. Lightly spoon ¼ cup flour into a dry measuring cup; level with a knife. Add flour to pan; cook 1 minute or until lightly browned, stirring constantly. Combine browned flour and cornstarch in a large bowl; add ⅔ cup stock to flour mixture, stirring with a whisk until smooth. Add flour mixture to remaining stock in pan; bring to a boil over medium-high heat. Cook 2 minutes or until slightly thick. Reduce heat; stir in cream. Add chicken; keep warm over low heat.

4. To prepare dumplings, combine milk and egg in a medium bowl. Lightly spoon 1½ cups flour into dry measuring cups; level with a knife. Combine flour, baking powder, cornmeal, and ½ teaspoon salt. Add flour mixture to milk mixture, stirring with a fork just until dry ingredients are moistened.

5. Drop one-third of dumpling batter by 8 heaping teaspoonfuls onto chicken mixture. Cover and cook 3 minutes or until dumplings are done (do not allow chicken mixture to boil). Remove dumplings with a slotted spoon; place in a large serving bowl or on a deep serving platter. Keep warm. Repeat procedure with remaining dumpling batter.

6. Remove pan from heat; slowly pour stew over dumplings. Sprinkle with parsley and freshly ground black pepper. Serve immediately. **YIELD:** 6 servings (serving size: 1⅓ cups stew and 4 dumplings).

CALORIES 334 (21% from fat); FAT 7.9g (sat 3.2g, mono 2.4g, poly 1.2g); PROTEIN 31.4g; CARB 32.2g; FIBER 1.2g; CHOL 130mg; IRON 3.3mg; SODIUM 755mg; CALC 211mg

ORGANIC QUOTE

"I advocate feeding kids organic foods whenever possible. Growing children are developing brain function and internal organs to last a lifetime, so their food should be the purest and most nutritious available."

—Dr. Alan Greene, pediatrician and board member of The Organics Center

Rosemary-Lemon Cornish Hens with Roasted Potatoes

You can easily vary this recipe by using thyme in place of rosemary or sprinkling ground red pepper and garlic powder over the potatoes.

    2 teaspoons crushed dried rosemary
    ½ teaspoon salt, divided
    ¼ teaspoon black pepper, divided
    2 (1¼-pound) Cornish hens
    ½ lemon, halved and divided
    Cooking spray
    2 cups cubed Yukon gold or red potato
    2 teaspoons olive oil

1. Preheat oven to 375°.

2. Combine rosemary, ¼ teaspoon salt, and ⅛ teaspoon pepper.

3. Remove and discard giblets from hens. Rinse hens with cold water; pat dry. Remove skin; trim excess fat. Working with 1 hen at a time, place 1 lemon piece in cavity of each hen; tie ends of legs together with twine. Lift wing tips up and over back; tuck under hen. Repeat procedure with remaining hen and lemon piece. Rub hens with rosemary mixture. Place hens, breast sides up, on a broiler pan coated with cooking spray.

4. Toss potato with oil; sprinkle with remaining ¼ teaspoon salt and ⅛ teaspoon pepper. Arrange potato around hens.

5. Insert a thermometer into meaty part of thigh, making sure not to touch bone. Remove twine. Bake at 375° for 1 hour or until thermometer registers 165°. **YIELD:** 2 servings (serving size: 1 hen and about ¾ cup potatoes).

CALORIES 372 (28% from fat); FAT 11.4g (sat 2.4g, mono 5.5g, poly 2.1g); PROTEIN 41.8g; CARB 24.1g; FIBER 2.7g; CHOL 180mg; IRON 3mg; SODIUM 702mg; CALC 47mg

Seared Duck Breast with Ginger-Rhubarb Sauce

The sweet, spicy heat from the ginger preserves is balanced by tart rhubarb and wine. Chicken breasts can be substituted for the duck, if desired.

    2 cups dry red wine
    1 cup finely chopped rhubarb
    2 tablespoons finely chopped shallots
    1 bay leaf
    1 star anise
    ½ cup ginger preserves
    ½ teaspoon kosher salt, divided
    2 (12-ounce) packages boneless whole duck breast, thawed, skinned, and cut in half
    ½ teaspoon freshly ground black pepper
    2 teaspoons olive oil

1. Combine first 5 ingredients in a large saucepan; bring to a boil. Cook until reduced to 1 cup (about 18 minutes). Stir in preserves and ¼ teaspoon salt; cook 1 minute. Strain wine mixture through a sieve over a bowl; discard solids.

2. Sprinkle duck with ¼ teaspoon salt and pepper. Heat oil in a large nonstick skillet over medium heat. Add duck; cook 5 minutes on each side or until desired degree of doneness. Cut duck diagonally across grain into thin slices; serve with sauce. **YIELD:** 4 servings (serving size: 1 duck breast half and about 2 tablespoons sauce).

CALORIES 380 (23% from fat); FAT 9.5g (sat 2.6g, mono 3.7g, poly 1.2g); PROTEIN 34.2g; CARB 23.1g; FIBER 0.6g; CHOL 131mg; IRON 8.3mg; SODIUM 347mg; CALC 29mg

ORGANIC HISTORY

"Sir Albert Howard is widely considered to be the father of organic farming. Despite his avoidance of the term 'organic' to describe these [organic farming] principles, Howard was among the first to suggest that plants grown in chemically fertilized soils were lacking in health and vigor."

Source: www.organicguide.com

Seared Duck Breast with Ginger-Rhubarb Sauce

Turkey–Jasmine Rice Meatballs with Baby Bok Choy

Use a box grater to shred the ginger after you've peeled away the brown outer layer. Jasmine rice has a pleasant aroma that underscores the other Asian ingredients, but any long-grain white rice will work to help keep the meatballs moist and add a bit of texture. Chopped bok choy can substitute for whole baby bok choy.

MEATBALLS:

  1 cup water
  ⅓ cup uncooked jasmine rice
  ¼ cup dry breadcrumbs
  ¼ cup chopped green onions
  ¾ teaspoon salt
  ¼ teaspoon freshly ground black pepper
1¼ pounds ground turkey
  2 large egg whites
  1 garlic clove, minced
     Cooking spray

BOK CHOY:

  6 baby bok choy (about 1⅓ pounds)
  2 teaspoons vegetable oil
  ¼ cup chopped green onions
  1 tablespoon shredded peeled fresh ginger
  1 garlic clove, minced
  1 cup water
  ¾ cup fat-free, less-sodium chicken broth
  3 tablespoons low-sodium soy sauce
1½ teaspoons sugar
  ½ teaspoon crushed red pepper
1½ tablespoons dry sherry
  2 teaspoons cornstarch

1. To prepare meatballs, bring 1 cup water to a boil in a small saucepan. Stir in jasmine rice; reduce heat, and simmer 15 minutes or until rice is almost tender. Drain; cool. Combine rice, breadcrumbs, and next 6 ingredients. Shape mixture into 18 meatballs.

2. Heat a large nonstick skillet over medium-high heat. Coat pan with cooking spray. Add meatballs; cook 5 minutes, browning on all sides. Cover, reduce heat to medium, and cook 10 minutes or until done, turning often. Remove pan from heat; keep warm.

3. While meatballs cook, prepare bok choy. Cut each bok choy in half lengthwise. Rinse under cold running water; drain well. Arrange bok choy in a steamer basket, overlapping pieces.

4. Heat oil in a Dutch oven over medium-high heat. Add ¼ cup onions, ginger, and 1 garlic clove; sauté 30 seconds. Place steamer basket in pan. Combine water and next 4 ingredients; pour over bok choy. Bring to a boil; cover, reduce heat, and steam over medium-low heat 20 minutes or until bok choy is tender, rearranging bok choy after 10 minutes. Remove bok choy and steamer basket from pan; cover and keep warm.

5. Combine 1½ tablespoons sherry and 2 teaspoons cornstarch; add to pan. Bring to a boil; cook 1 minute or until slightly thick. **YIELD:** 6 servings (serving size: 3 meatballs, 2 bok choy halves, and 3 tablespoons sauce).

CALORIES 251 (35% from fat); FAT 9.8g (sat 2.4g, mono 3.4g, poly 2.9g); PROTEIN 21.3g; CARB 18g; FIBER 1.9g; CHOL 75mg; IRON 2.6mg; SODIUM 832mg; CALC 135mg

Joe's Special

This San Francisco specialty turns straightforward scrambled eggs into a distinctive dinner. To stay true to the recipe's roots, serve with toasted sourdough bread.

½   teaspoon dried basil
¼   teaspoon salt
4   large egg whites
3   large eggs
4   ounces hot turkey Italian sausage
2   cups chopped onion
6   cups chopped Swiss chard
4   (1½-ounce) slices sourdough bread, toasted

1. Combine first 4 ingredients in a medium bowl, stirring with a whisk.

2. Remove casings from sausage. Cook sausage in a large nonstick skillet over medium-high heat until lightly browned; stir to crumble. Add onion; cook 3 minutes or until onion is tender. Stir in chard; cover and cook 3 minutes or until chard wilts, stirring occasionally. Uncover and cook 1 minute or until liquid evaporates. Stir in egg mixture; cook 3 minutes or until eggs are set, stirring frequently. Serve with toast. **YIELD:** 4 servings (serving size: 1 cup egg mixture and 1 slice toast).

CALORIES 335 (23% from fat); FAT 8.6g (sat 2.4g, mono 3.3g, poly 1.8g); PROTEIN 20.9g; CARB 43.2g; FIBER 4.3g; CHOL 183mg; IRON 3.7mg; SODIUM 931mg; CALC 116mg

Breakfast Sausage Casserole

This satisfying recipe is a good choice if you have weekend guests. Assemble and refrigerate the casserole the night before, and just pop it in the oven the next morning. Look for turkey sausage near other breakfast-style sausage in the frozen foods section of your supermarket.

Cooking spray
1 (16-ounce) package frozen turkey sausage, thawed (such as Louis Rich)
8 (1½-ounce) slices sourdough bread, cut into ½-inch cubes (about 8 cups)
⅔ cup (about 2½ ounces) shredded sharp Cheddar cheese
3 cups 1% low-fat milk, divided
1 cup egg substitute
1 tablespoon Dijon mustard
1 (10.75-ounce) can condensed 30% reduced-sodium, 98% fat-free cream of mushroom soup, undiluted

1. Heat a large nonstick skillet over medium-high heat. Coat pan with cooking spray. Add sausage to pan; cook 5 minutes or until browned, stirring well to crumble.
2. Arrange bread in a 13 x 9–inch baking dish coated with cooking spray. Top evenly with cooked turkey sausage and Cheddar cheese. Combine 2½ cups milk, egg substitute, and Dijon mustard, stirring with a whisk. Pour over bread mixture in dish. Cover and refrigerate 8 hours or overnight.
3. Preheat oven to 350°.
4. Uncover casserole. Combine remaining ½ cup milk and cream of mushroom soup, stirring with a whisk. Pour over bread mixture. Bake at 350° for 1 hour and 5 minutes or until set and lightly browned. Let stand 15 minutes before serving. **YIELD:** 8 servings.

CALORIES 321 (30% from fat); FAT 10.8g (sat 5.3g, mono 2.5g, poly 1.1g); PROTEIN 22g; CARB 32.2g; FIBER 1.6g; CHOL 58mg; IRON 2.8mg; SODIUM 968mg; CALC 238mg

Tamale Pie

Once a staple in Northern Italian kitchens, polenta is now a popular item on American tables. Precooked polenta comes ready-packed in 16-ounce tubes and eliminates the need for lengthy preparation. Use a fork or pastry blender to crumble the firm polenta.

1½ (16-ounce) tubes polenta, crumbled
Cooking spray
2 (15-ounce) cans low-fat turkey chili
1 cup (4 ounces) preshredded sharp Cheddar cheese
6 tablespoons salsa
6 tablespoons reduced-fat sour cream

1. Preheat oven to 475°.
2. Place polenta in an 11 x 7–inch baking dish coated with cooking spray. Top with chili and cheese. Bake at 475° for 13 minutes or until bubbly. Top each serving with 1 tablespoon salsa and 1 tablespoon sour cream.
YIELD: 6 servings.

CALORIES 324 (27% from fat); FAT 9.7g (sat 5.5g, mono 2.5g, poly 1g); PROTEIN 18.8g; CARB 40.6g; FIBER 6.6g; CHOL 46mg; IRON 2.8mg; SODIUM 881mg; CALC 223mg

ORGANIC FACT
The production of organic corn requires one-third less fossil-fuel energy than its conventional counterpart.

Source: CCOF

Grilled Vegetable Salad with
Creamy Blue Cheese Dressing, page 173

Cooking Light with **O** ORGANICS

SOUPS, SALADS & SANDWICHES

Chilled Vegetable Basil Soup
with Vegetable Confetti

154

Chilled Vegetable Basil Soup with Vegetable Confetti

To make a spicier version of this gazpacho-style soup, use a spicy or hot variety of tomato or vegetable juice. For the best texture and freshest flavor, chill the soup several hours ahead. Don't stir in the zucchini and remaining vegetables until you're ready to serve.

    2   teaspoons olive oil
    ½   teaspoon fennel seeds
    2   garlic cloves, minced
    1   (46-ounce) can no-salt-added tomato juice
    1   cup basil leaves
    1   teaspoon hot pepper sauce
    ¼   teaspoon salt
    ½   cup finely chopped zucchini
    ½   cup finely chopped cucumber
    ½   cup chopped yellow bell pepper
    1   cup halved cherry tomatoes
    ½   cup chopped green onions
    ¼   cup chopped fresh basil
    2   tablespoons reduced-fat sour cream
    Chopped green onions (optional)

1. Heat olive oil in a large saucepan over medium heat. Add fennel seeds and garlic; cook 1 minute, stirring frequently. Add juice, and bring to a boil. Reduce heat, and simmer 2 minutes. Remove from heat; stir in 1 cup basil, hot pepper sauce, and ¼ teaspoon salt. Place soup in a large bowl; cover and chill 6 hours or overnight.
2. Strain mixture through a sieve over a bowl; discard solids. Stir in zucchini and next 5 ingredients. Spoon 1 cup into each of 6 shallow bowls; top each serving with 1 teaspoon sour cream and green onions, if desired. Serve immediately. **YIELD:** 6 servings.

CALORIES 69 (25% from fat); FAT 1.9g (sat 0.3g, mono 1.2g, poly 0.3g); PROTEIN 2.7g; CARB 12.9g; FIBER 2.2g; CHOL 0mg; IRON 1.7mg; SODIUM 130mg; CALC 54mg

ORGANIC FACT

It is important to remember that choosing organic is not just of benefit to ourselves but to farm workers as well. The National Cancer Institute found that farmers exposed to herbicides had six times more risk of contracting cancer than non-farmers.

Source: CCOF

Radish Vichyssoise

After chilling overnight, this soup is refreshing on a warm day. Radishes add an earthy, turniplike flavor. Use white pepper to keep the soup creamy white. You can cut the recipe in half if you're not serving a crowd.

    1   tablespoon butter
    1½   cups thinly sliced onion
    20   radishes, halved (about 1 pound)
    1½   pounds baking potatoes, peeled and cut into
         1-inch pieces
    3   cups fat-free, less-sodium chicken broth
    2   cups 2% reduced-fat milk
    ¾   cup reduced-fat sour cream
    1   teaspoon salt
    ¼   teaspoon black pepper
    ⅛   teaspoon ground nutmeg
    ¼   cup chopped fresh chives

1. Melt 1 tablespoon butter in a large saucepan over medium heat. Add onion, and cook 5 minutes or until tender, stirring frequently. Add radishes and potatoes, tossing to coat with butter. Stir in broth and 2 cups milk; bring to a boil. Cover, reduce heat, and simmer 15 minutes or until potatoes are tender. Cool 10 minutes.
2. Place half of radish mixture in a blender. Remove center piece of blender lid (to allow steam to escape); secure blender lid on blender. Place a clean towel over opening in blender lid (to avoid splatters). Blend until smooth. Pour pureed soup into a large bowl. Repeat procedure with remaining radish mixture. Cover and chill at least 2 hours.
3. Add sour cream, salt, pepper, and nutmeg, stirring with a whisk. Cover and chill at least 4 hours or overnight. Sprinkle with chives. **YIELD:** 12 servings (serving size: ¾ cup).

CALORIES 119 (29% from fat); FAT 3.9g (sat 2.3g, mono 1.1g, poly 0.2g); PROTEIN 4.2g; CARB 17.2g; FIBER 1.9g; CHOL 13mg; IRON 0.4mg; SODIUM 359mg; CALC 91mg

Golden Potato-Leek Soup
with Cheddar Toasts

Golden Potato-Leek Soup with Cheddar Toasts

Yukon gold potatoes are key to the rich, buttery flavor.

SOUP:
- 1 tablespoon butter
- 3 cups thinly sliced leek (about 3 medium)
- 6 cups cubed peeled Yukon gold potato (about 2¼ pounds)
- 2 cups water
- ½ teaspoon salt
- 2 (14-ounce) cans organic vegetable broth
- 2 thyme sprigs

CHEDDAR TOASTS:
- 8 (¼-inch-thick) slices diagonally cut sourdough French bread baguette
- Cooking spray
- ½ cup (2 ounces) shredded sharp Cheddar cheese
- ⅛ teaspoon ground red pepper

REMAINING INGREDIENTS:
- ⅓ cup whipping cream
- ¼ teaspoon freshly ground black pepper
- Thyme sprigs (optional)

1. Preheat oven to 375°.

2. To prepare soup, melt butter in a Dutch oven over medium heat. Add leek; cook 10 minutes or until tender, stirring occasionally (do not brown).

3. Add potato, water, salt, broth, and 2 thyme sprigs. Bring to a boil; reduce heat, and simmer 20 minutes or until potatoes are very tender.

4. To prepare Cheddar toasts, place baguette slices in a single layer on a baking sheet. Bake at 375° for 7 minutes or until toasted. Turn slices over; coat with cooking spray, and sprinkle 1 tablespoon cheese over each slice. Bake 5 minutes or until cheese melts. Sprinkle evenly with red pepper.

5. Remove pan from heat; discard thyme sprigs. Partially mash potatoes with a potato masher; stir in cream. Sprinkle with black pepper. Serve with Cheddar toasts. Garnish with thyme sprigs, if desired. **YIELD:** 8 servings (serving size: about 1 cup soup and 1 toast).

CALORIES 299 (25% from fat); FAT 8.6g (sat 4.7g, mono 2.7g, poly 0.6g); PROTEIN 7.5g; CARB 48.4g; FIBER 3.9g; CHOL 25mg; IRON 2mg; SODIUM 660mg; CALC 113mg

Golden Corn Chowder with Roasted Chiles

With sweet corn, potatoes, and tomatoes at their garden best, corn chowder is certainly the soup for the season. Roast the peppers ahead to save time later.

- 6 jalapeño peppers
- 3 cups cubed peeled Yukon gold or red potato (about 1 pound)
- 2 tablespoons butter
- 1 cup chopped onion
- ⅔ cup diced orange or yellow bell pepper
- 3 tablespoons chopped celery
- 3 cups fresh corn kernels (about 6 ears)
- 3 cups 1% low-fat milk
- 2 cups chopped seeded yellow tomato (about 1 pound)
- ¾ teaspoon salt
- ¼ teaspoon white pepper
- 6 tablespoons (1½ ounces) reduced-fat shredded Monterey Jack cheese
- 2 tablespoons chopped fresh cilantro

1. Preheat broiler.

2. Place jalapeño peppers on a foil-lined baking sheet; broil 10 minutes or until blackened, turning occasionally. Place in a zip-top plastic bag; seal. Let stand 15 minutes. Peel peppers; cut in half lengthwise, discarding seeds and membranes. Finely chop jalapeño peppers; set aside.

3. Place potato in a medium saucepan, and cover with water; bring to a boil. Reduce heat, and simmer 15 minutes or until tender. Drain; partially mash potato with a potato masher.

4. Melt butter in a Dutch oven over medium heat. Add onion, bell pepper, and celery; cook 10 minutes, stirring frequently. Add jalapeño peppers, potato, corn, milk, tomato, salt, and white pepper; cook until thick (about 30 minutes), stirring occasionally. Ladle soup into each of 6 bowls, and sprinkle with cheese and cilantro. **YIELD:** 6 servings (serving size: 1⅓ cups soup, 1 tablespoon cheese, and 1 teaspoon cilantro).

CALORIES 265 (26% from fat); FAT 7.8g (sat 4.2g, mono 2.3g, poly 0.8g); PROTEIN 11.4g; CARB 41.5g; FIBER 5.4g; CHOL 20mg; IRON 1.8mg; SODIUM 466mg; CALC 230mg

French Onion Soup

French Onion Soup

Allowing the soup to simmer for a couple of hours tenderizes each piece of onion until it's perfectly infused with the broth.

- 2 teaspoons olive oil
- 4 cups thinly vertically sliced Walla Walla or other sweet onion
- 4 cups thinly vertically sliced red onion
- ½ teaspoon sugar
- ½ teaspoon freshly ground black pepper
- ¼ teaspoon salt
- ¼ cup dry white wine
- 8 cups less-sodium beef broth
- ¼ teaspoon chopped fresh thyme
- 8 (1-ounce) slices French bread, cut into 1-inch cubes
- 8 (1-ounce) slices reduced-fat, reduced-sodium Swiss cheese

1. Heat olive oil in a Dutch oven over medium-high heat. Add onions to pan; sauté 5 minutes or until tender. Stir in sugar, pepper, and ¼ teaspoon salt. Reduce heat to medium; cook 20 minutes, stirring frequently. Increase heat to medium-high, and sauté 5 minutes or until onion is golden brown. Stir in wine, and cook 1 minute. Add broth and thyme; bring to a boil. Cover, reduce heat, and simmer 2 hours.
2. Preheat broiler.
3. Place bread cubes in a single layer on a baking sheet; broil 2 minutes or until toasted, turning cubes after 1 minute.
4. Place 8 ovenproof soup bowls on a jelly-roll pan. Ladle 1 cup soup into each bowl. Divide bread evenly among bowls, and top each serving with 1 cheese slice. Broil 3 minutes or until cheese begins to brown. **YIELD:** 8 servings.

CALORIES 290 (30% from fat); FAT 9.6g (sat 4.8g, mono 1.9g, poly 0.7g); PROTEIN 16.8g; CARB 33.4g; FIBER 3.1g; CHOL 20mg; IRON 1.6mg; SODIUM 359mg; CALC 317mg

ORGANIC TIP

If you can't buy organic produce, try to stay away from those that are most likely to contain pesticides (see "The Dirty Dozen" on page 14). Also, be sure to wash any non-organic produce and peel if possible.

Quick Fall Minestrone

This easy soup brims with fresh vegetables; canned beans and orzo make it hearty and filling. Use a vegetable peeler to quickly remove the skin from the squash.

- 1 tablespoon vegetable oil
- 1 cup chopped onion
- 2 garlic cloves, minced
- 6 cups vegetable broth
- 2½ cups (¾-inch) cubed peeled butternut squash
- 2½ cups (¾-inch) cubed peeled baking potato
- 1 cup (1-inch) cut green beans (about ¼ pound)
- ½ cup diced carrot
- 1 teaspoon dried oregano
- ¼ teaspoon black pepper
- ¼ teaspoon salt
- 4 cups chopped kale
- ½ cup uncooked orzo (rice-shaped pasta)
- 1 (16-ounce) can cannellini beans or other white beans, rinsed and drained
- ½ cup (2 ounces) grated fresh Parmesan cheese

1. Heat oil in a large Dutch oven over medium-high heat. Add onion and garlic; sauté 2½ minutes. Add broth and next 7 ingredients; bring to a boil. Reduce heat; simmer 3 minutes. Add kale, orzo, and cannellini beans; cook 5 minutes or until vegetables are tender. Sprinkle with cheese. **YIELD:** 8 servings (serving size: 1½ cups soup and 1 tablespoon cheese).

CALORIES 212 (21% from fat); FAT 5g (sat 1.6g, mono 1g, poly 1.2g); PROTEIN 9.6g; CARB 36g; FIBER 3.9g; CHOL 5mg; IRON 1.9mg; SODIUM 961mg; CALC 164mg

White Chicken Chili

Cooking spray

2 pounds skinless, boneless chicken breast, cut into bite-sized pieces

2 cups finely chopped onion

2 garlic cloves, minced

2 teaspoons ground cumin

½ teaspoon dried oregano

1 teaspoon ground coriander

2 (4.5-ounce) cans chopped green chiles, undrained

1 cup water

2 (15.5-ounce) cans cannellini beans, rinsed and drained

1 (14-ounce) can fat-free, less-sodium chicken broth

½ teaspoon hot pepper sauce

1 cup (4 ounces) shredded Monterey Jack cheese

½ cup chopped fresh cilantro

½ cup chopped green onions

1. Heat a large nonstick skillet over medium-high heat. Coat pan with cooking spray. Add chicken to pan; cook 10 minutes or until browned on all sides.

2. Heat a large Dutch oven over medium-high heat. Coat pan with cooking spray. Add onion to pan; sauté 6 minutes or until tender, stirring frequently. Add garlic, and sauté 2 minutes, stirring frequently. Stir in cumin, dried oregano, and coriander; sauté 1 minute. Stir in chiles; reduce heat to low, and cook 10 minutes, partially covered. Add chicken, water, beans, and broth; bring to a simmer. Cover and simmer 10 minutes. Stir in hot sauce. Ladle 1 cup chili into each of 8 bowls; sprinkle each serving with 2 tablespoons cheese, 1 tablespoon cilantro, and 1 tablespoon green onions. **YIELD:** 8 servings.

CALORIES 233 (23% from fat); FAT 5.9g (sat 3.1g, mono 1.6g, poly 0.5g); PROTEIN 32.7g; CARB 11.7g; FIBER 3.4g; CHOL 78mg; IRON 3.2mg; SODIUM 694mg; CALC 180mg

Tuscan Chicken Soup

1 cup chopped onion
2 tablespoons tomato paste
¼ teaspoon salt
¼ teaspoon freshly ground black pepper
1 (15-ounce) can cannellini beans, rinsed and drained
1 (14-ounce) can fat-free, less-sodium chicken broth
1 (7-ounce) bottle roasted red bell peppers, rinsed and drained, and cut into ½-inch pieces
1 pound skinless, boneless chicken thighs, cut into 1-inch pieces
3 garlic cloves, minced
½ teaspoon chopped fresh rosemary
1 (6-ounce) package fresh baby spinach
8 teaspoons grated Parmesan cheese

1. Combine first 9 ingredients in an electric slow cooker. Cover and cook on HIGH 1 hour; reduce heat to low, and cook 3 hours. Stir in rosemary and spinach; cook on LOW 10 minutes. Ladle 1½ cups soup into each of 4 bowls; top each serving with 2 teaspoons cheese. **YIELD:** 4 servings.

CALORIES 239 (17% from fat); FAT 5.8g (sat 1.8g, mono 1.7g, poly 1.4g); PROTEIN 28.6g; CARB 16.3g; FIBER 4.6g; CHOL 97mg; IRON 3.9mg; SODIUM 768mg; CALC 126mg

Chicken-Vegetable Soup with Orzo

This homey soup shows just how quickly you can make chicken broth in the microwave. It also shows off the microwave's fabulous way with vegetables; they not only keep more color but they also retain more vitamins.

5 cups water
2 pounds chicken drumsticks, skinned
2 cups small broccoli florets
2 cups presliced mushrooms
1½ cups sliced carrot
1 cup chopped onion
¼ cup chopped fresh basil
¼ cup uncooked orzo (rice-shaped pasta)
1 teaspoon salt
⅛ teaspoon black pepper
6 tablespoons (1½ ounces) grated fresh Parmesan cheese

1. Combine 5 cups water and chicken in a 3-quart casserole. Cover with lid, and microwave at HIGH 30 minutes or until chicken is done, stirring after 15 minutes. Drain in a colander over a bowl, reserving cooking liquid. Cool chicken slightly. Remove chicken from bones; discard bones. Shred chicken with 2 forks to measure 2½ cups.
2. Combine broccoli and next 4 ingredients in casserole. Cover; microwave at HIGH 8 minutes or until tender, stirring after 4 minutes. Add reserved cooking liquid, chicken, pasta, salt, and pepper. Cover; microwave at HIGH 6 minutes or until pasta is tender. Ladle 1 cup soup into each of 6 bowls; sprinkle each serving with 1 tablespoon cheese. **YIELD:** 6 servings.

CALORIES 277 (24% from fat); FAT 7.5g (sat 2.6g, mono 2.2g, poly 1.5g); PROTEIN 36.9g; CARB 14.5g; FIBER 3g; CHOL 121mg; IRON 2.8mg; SODIUM 658mg; CALC 134mg

Italian Sausage Soup

This soup has that simmered-all-day flavor but takes just minutes to prepare. Serve it with hot crusty bread.

8 ounces hot or sweet turkey Italian sausage
2 cups fat-free, less-sodium chicken broth
1 (14.5-ounce) can diced tomatoes with basil, garlic, and oregano
½ cup uncooked small shell pasta
2 cups bagged baby spinach leaves
2 tablespoons grated fresh Parmesan or Romano cheese
2 tablespoons chopped fresh basil

1. Heat a large saucepan over medium heat. Remove casings from sausage. Add sausage to pan; cook about 5 minutes or until browned, stirring to crumble. Drain; return to pan.
2. Add broth, tomatoes, and pasta to pan; bring to a boil over high heat. Cover, reduce heat, and simmer 10 minutes or until pasta is done. Remove from heat; stir in spinach until wilted. Sprinkle each serving with cheese and basil. **YIELD:** 4 servings (serving size: 1⅓ cups soup, 1½ teaspoons cheese, and 1½ teaspoons basil).

CALORIES 216 (30% from fat); FAT 7.1g (sat 2.6g, mono 2.5g, poly 1.8g); PROTEIN 17.4g; CARB 20g; FIBER 1.6g; CHOL 52mg; IRON 3.2mg; SODIUM 1,020mg; CALC 153mg

Slow-Cooker Sausage-and-Vegetable Chili

With the help of ready-to-use convenience products and a little creativity, preparing a healthful meal just got easier.

CHILI:
1¼ cups bottled salsa
1 cup (1-inch) pieces red bell pepper
1 cup (1-inch) pieces yellow bell pepper
1 tablespoon chili powder
1 (15.5-ounce) can whole-kernel corn, drained
1 (12-ounce) package chicken sausages with
   habanero chiles and tequila, cut into ½-inch pieces
REMAINING INGREDIENTS:
2 cups hot cooked long-grain rice
¼ cup crushed baked tortilla chips
¼ cup chopped fresh cilantro
¼ cup chopped green onions
¼ cup fat-free sour cream

1. To prepare chili, combine salsa, peppers, chili powder, corn, and sausages in an electric slow cooker. Cover with lid; cook on LOW 8 hours.
2. Spoon ½ cup rice into each of 4 bowls; top each serving with about 1¼ cups chili, 1 tablespoon crushed tortilla chips, 1 tablespoon fresh cilantro, 1 tablespoon onions, and 1 tablespoon sour cream. **YIELD:** 4 servings.
NOTE: Smoked turkey sausage can be substituted for the chicken sausage.

CALORIES 412 (23% from fat); FAT 10.6g (sat 2.7g, mono 3.8g, poly 3.2g); PROTEIN 18.1g; CARB 63.1g; FIBER 9.6g; CHOL 66mg; IRON 4mg; SODIUM 1,111mg; CALC 85mg

All-American Beef Stew

2 tablespoons uncooked granulated tapioca
1 tablespoon sugar
1 tablespoon garlic powder
1 teaspoon salt
3 (5.5-ounce) cans tomato juice
4 cups chopped onion
3 cups chopped celery
2½ cups (¼-inch-thick) slices carrot
2 (8-ounce) packages presliced mushrooms
2 pounds beef stew meat

1. Place first 5 ingredients in a blender; process until smooth.
2. Combine onion, celery, carrot, mushrooms, and beef in an electric slow cooker; add juice mixture. Cover and cook on HIGH 5 hours or until beef is tender. **YIELD:** 6 servings (serving size: about 1¾ cups).

CALORIES 345 (29% from fat); FAT 11.1g (sat 4g, mono 4.7g, poly 0.7g); PROTEIN 34.1g; CARB 28.8g; FIBER 5.9g; CHOL 95mg; IRON 5.3mg; SODIUM 811mg; CALC 81mg

Udon-Beef Noodle Bowl

This entrée falls somewhere between a soup and a noodle dish. You can eat it with chopsticks, but be sure to have a spoon to catch the broth.

8 ounces uncooked udon noodles (thick, round
   fresh Japanese wheat noodles) or spaghetti
1½ teaspoons bottled minced garlic
½ teaspoon crushed red pepper
2 (14-ounce) cans less-sodium beef broth
3 tablespoons low-sodium soy sauce
3 tablespoons sake (rice wine) or dry sherry
1 tablespoon honey
Cooking spray
2 cups sliced shiitake mushroom caps
   (about 4 ounces)
½ cup thinly sliced carrot
8 ounces top round steak, thinly sliced
¾ cup diagonally cut green onions
1 (6-ounce) package fresh baby spinach

1. Cook noodles according to package directions; drain.
2. Place garlic, pepper, and broth in a large saucepan. Bring to a boil; reduce heat, and simmer 10 minutes.
3. Combine soy sauce, sake, and honey in a small bowl; stir with a whisk.
4. Heat a large nonstick skillet over medium-high heat. Coat pan with cooking spray. Add mushrooms and carrot, and sauté 2 minutes. Stir in soy sauce mixture; cook 2 minutes, stirring constantly. Add vegetable mixture to broth mixture. Stir in beef; cook 2 minutes or until beef loses its pink color. Stir in noodles, green onions, and spinach. Serve immediately. **YIELD:** 5 servings (serving size: about 1½ cups).

CALORIES 306 (16% from fat); FAT 5.6g (sat 1.8g, mono 2g, poly 0.4g); PROTEIN 22.4g; CARB 36.6g; FIBER 2.4g; CHOL 39mg; IRON 3.4mg; SODIUM 707mg; CALC 59mg

Chunky Minestrone with Beef

Stir in the cooked pasta at the end to help the shells keep their shape. A slow cooker makes this a versatile hands-off recipe.

1 pound beef stew meat, trimmed
1 cup chopped onion
½ cup chopped carrot
2 (14.5-ounce) cans no-salt-added diced tomatoes with roasted garlic, undrained
2 (14-ounce) cans fat-free, less-sodium chicken broth
1 teaspoon dried Italian seasoning
½ teaspoon salt
¼ teaspoon black pepper
2 cups chopped cabbage
1 cup thinly sliced yellow squash
1 (15.5-ounce) can chickpeas (garbanzo beans), rinsed and drained
2 cups cooked seashell pasta
6 tablespoons (1½ ounces) grated fresh Parmesan cheese

1. Combine first 8 ingredients in an electric slow cooker. Cover and cook on HIGH 1 hour. Reduce heat to LOW, and cook 5 hours or until meat is tender.

2. Stir in cabbage, squash, and chickpeas. Cook on HIGH 45 minutes or until vegetables are tender. Stir in cooked pasta. Top each serving with 1 tablespoon cheese. **YIELD:** 6 servings (serving size: 1½ cups soup and 1 tablespoon cheese).

CALORIES 253 (29% from fat); FAT 8.2g (sat 3.2g, mono 2.3g, poly 0.3g); PROTEIN 22.1g; CARB 21.8g; FIBER 3.7g; CHOL 53mg; IRON 3.1mg; SODIUM 590mg; CALC 136mg

Melon, Berry, and Pear Salad with
Cayenne-Lemon-Mint Syrup

Melon, Berry, and Pear Salad with Cayenne-Lemon-Mint Syrup

Simple and nutrient-packed, this fruit salad is a deliciously healthful way to satisfy a sweet tooth. The ground red pepper provides an unexpected heat that balances the sweetness of the fruit. This recipe makes 15 cups and is a perfect make-ahead dish for summer picnics or other social gatherings. If you don't need that much, you can easily cut the salad ingredients in half. But go ahead and make the whole recipe for the syrup, and just store it in an airtight container in the refrigerator for later use.

SYRUP:
- ⅓ cup sugar
- ⅓ cup water
- ¼ cup fresh lemon juice
- 3 tablespoons honey
- ½ teaspoon ground red pepper
- ¼ cup chopped fresh mint
- 1 tablespoon grated lemon rind

SALAD:
- 6 cups cubed cantaloupe
- 6 cups cubed honeydew melon
- 2 cups fresh blueberries
- 2 cups quartered fresh strawberries
- 1½ cups cubed ripe pear (about 2 medium)
- 1 cup fresh blackberries
- 1 tablespoon chopped fresh mint
- ⅛ teaspoon freshly ground black pepper

1. To prepare syrup, combine first 5 ingredients in a small saucepan. Bring to a boil; cook 3 minutes or until mixture is slightly syrupy. Remove from heat; stir in ¼ cup mint and rind. Let stand 30 minutes. Strain syrup through a sieve over a small bowl; discard solids.

2. To prepare salad, combine cantaloupe and next 7 ingredients in a large bowl. Add syrup; toss gently to coat. Cover and refrigerate 2 hours, stirring occasionally.

YIELD: 10 servings (serving size: about 1½ cups).

CALORIES 168 (4% from fat); FAT 0.7g (sat 0.1g, mono 0.1g, poly 0.3g); PROTEIN 2.3g; CARB 42.6g; FIBER 3.1g; CHOL 0mg; IRON 0.8mg; SODIUM 37mg; CALC 33mg

Salad of Papaya, Mango, and Grapefruit

If pressed for time, use bottled grapefruit sections from the produce department. Combine the ingredients a few hours ahead, but stir in the mint just before serving.

- 2 cups grapefruit sections (about 2 large grapefruit)
- 2 peeled ripe mangoes, each cut into 12 wedges
- 1 peeled ripe papaya, cut into thin slices
- 2 to 3 tablespoons fresh lime juice
- 2 tablespoons extravirgin olive oil
- ¼ teaspoon salt
- ⅛ teaspoon black pepper
- 3 tablespoons chopped fresh mint

1. Combine first 3 ingredients in a large bowl. Combine juice, oil, salt, and pepper, stirring with a whisk. Drizzle dressing over fruit; sprinkle with mint. Toss gently to combine. **YIELD:** 12 servings (serving size: about ¾ cup).

CALORIES 77 (28% from fat); FAT 2.4g (sat 0.3g, mono 1.7g, poly 0.2g); PROTEIN 0.7g; CARB 15.2g; FIBER 3.5g; CHOL 0mg; IRON 0.1mg; SODIUM 50mg; CALC 18mg

Green Salad with Apples and Maple-Walnut Dressing

This salad contains sweet, spicy, nutty, and salty notes. Walnut oil adds depth; you can substitute extravirgin olive oil—albeit with milder results.

- 6 cups gourmet salad greens
- 1 cup (2-inch) julienne-cut Braeburn apple
- 2 tablespoons cider vinegar
- 2 tablespoons maple syrup
- 2 teaspoons whole-grain Dijon mustard
- 1½ teaspoons walnut oil
- ⅛ teaspoon salt
- ⅛ teaspoon ground red pepper

1. Combine salad greens and apple in a large bowl.

2. Combine vinegar and next 5 ingredients, stirring with a whisk. Drizzle over salad; toss gently to coat.

YIELD: 4 servings (serving size: about 1¼ cups).

CALORIES 73 (27% from fat); FAT 2.2g (sat 0.2g, mono 0.5g, poly 1.3g); PROTEIN 1.6g; CARB 13.7g; FIBER 2.5g; CHOL 0mg; IRON 1.4mg; SODIUM 159mg; CALC 58mg

Fig-and-Arugula Salad with Parmesan

The combination of flavors in this recipe—sweet figs, sharp cheese, and peppery arugula—couldn't be better; it received the highest rating in our Test Kitchens.

  2 tablespoons minced shallots
1½ tablespoons balsamic vinegar
  1 tablespoon extravirgin olive oil
  ¼ teaspoon salt
16 fresh figs, each cut in half lengthwise
  6 cups trimmed arugula (about 6 ounces)
  ¼ teaspoon freshly ground black pepper
  ¼ cup (1 ounce) shaved fresh Parmesan cheese

1. Combine first 4 ingredients in a large bowl, and stir well with a whisk. Add figs; cover and let stand 20 minutes. Add arugula and pepper, and toss well. Top with cheese. Serve immediately. **YIELD:** 4 servings (serving size: 1½ cups).

CALORIES 156 (33% from fat); FAT 5.8g (sat 1.7g, mono 3.1g, poly 0.5g); PROTEIN 4.6g; CARB 25.1g; FIBER 4.9g; CHOL 5mg; IRON 1.1mg; SODIUM 273mg; CALC 194mg

ORGANIC FACT

Organic agriculture minimizes children's exposure to toxic and persistent pesticides in the air they breathe, the water they drink, the foods they eat, and the soil on which they play.

Source: Organic Trade Association

Arugula Salad with Port-Cooked Pears and Roquefort Cheese

Sweet wine infuses pears with flavor that marries well with the pungent cheese. Serve with pork tenderloin.

  2 peeled Bartlett pears, cored and quartered
Cooking spray
  ½ cup port or other sweet red wine
  1 teaspoon sugar
  1 tablespoon white wine vinegar
  1 teaspoon walnut oil
  ¼ teaspoon salt
  ¼ teaspoon freshly ground black pepper
  8 cups trimmed arugula (about 8 ounces)
  2 cups (½-inch) slices Belgian endive (about ½ pound)
  ¼ cup (1 ounce) crumbled Roquefort or other blue cheese
  2 tablespoons chopped walnuts, toasted

1. Preheat oven to 400°.
2. Arrange pears in a 13 x 9–inch baking dish coated with cooking spray, and drizzle with port. Sprinkle evenly with sugar. Cover and bake at 400° for 10 minutes. Uncover and bake an additional 15 minutes or until pears are almost tender. Cool completely, and reserve 1 tablespoon liquid from pan. Thinly slice pears; set aside. Combine reserved 1 tablespoon liquid, vinegar, oil, salt, and pepper, stirring with a whisk.
3. Combine sliced pears, arugula, and endive in a large bowl. Drizzle vinegar mixture over arugula mixture; toss gently to coat. Arrange about 1⅓ cups salad on each of 8 plates. Sprinkle each serving with 1½ teaspoons cheese and ¾ teaspoon nuts. **YIELD:** 8 servings.

CALORIES 88 (31% from fat); FAT 3g (sat 0.9g, mono 0.6g, poly 1.4g); PROTEIN 2g; CARB 11g; FIBER 2.5g; CHOL 3mg; IRON 0.6mg; SODIUM 131mg; CALC 62mg

Autumn Apple, Pear, and Cheddar Salad with Pecans

Serve this classic flavor combination with roast chicken or a pork roast. Double the dressing to have extra on hand.

1 cup apple juice
2 tablespoons cider vinegar
1 teaspoon extravirgin olive oil
½ teaspoon salt
¼ teaspoon freshly ground black pepper
10 cups gourmet salad greens (about 10 ounces)
1 cup seedless red grapes, halved
1 medium McIntosh apple, cored and cut into 18 wedges
1 medium Bartlett pear, cored and cut into 18 wedges
¼ cup (1 ounce) finely shredded sharp Cheddar cheese
3 tablespoons chopped pecans, toasted

1. Place apple juice in a small saucepan; bring to a boil over medium-high heat. Cook until reduced to about 3 tablespoons (about 10 minutes). Combine reduced apple juice, cider vinegar, olive oil, salt, and black pepper, stirring with a whisk until well blended. Set aside.

2. Combine greens, grapes, apple, and pear in a large bowl. Drizzle with apple juice mixture; toss gently to coat. Arrange salad on individual plates; sprinkle each serving with cheese and nuts. **YIELD:** 6 servings (serving size: about 1⅔ cups salad, 2 teaspoons cheese, and 1½ teaspoons nuts).

CALORIES 134 (36% from fat); FAT 5.4g (sat 1.2g, mono 2.6g, poly 1.1g); PROTEIN 3.4g; CARB 21.1g; FIBER 4.1g; CHOL 5mg; IRON 1.5mg; SODIUM 255mg; CALC 93mg

Pike Place Market Salad

168

Pike Place Market Salad

This flavorful salad calls for an herb salad mix, which can be found prebagged in the produce section of the supermarket. Or you can use any combination of lettuces and herbs. Cherries or any fresh berry will also do nicely. The dressing and caramelized walnuts can be made a day ahead (store the nuts in an airtight container and the dressing in the refrigerator). The salad gets its name from Seattle's Pike Place Market—an icon of fresh, seasonal bounty.

WALNUTS:
1 tablespoon sugar
3 tablespoons coarsely chopped walnuts
Cooking spray

DRESSING:
½ cup apple cider
3 tablespoons water
¼ teaspoon cornstarch
1 tablespoon finely chopped shallots
1 tablespoon champagne vinegar
⅛ teaspoon salt
⅛ teaspoon freshly ground black pepper

REMAINING INGREDIENTS:
8 cups herb salad mix
2 cups fresh blackberries
¼ cup (1 ounce) crumbled blue cheese

1. To prepare nuts, place sugar in a small skillet over medium heat; cook 90 seconds or until sugar dissolves, stirring as needed so sugar dissolves evenly and doesn't burn. Reduce heat; stir in walnuts. Cook over low heat 30 seconds or until golden. Spread mixture onto foil coated with cooking spray. Cool completely; break into small pieces.

2. To prepare dressing, place cider in a small saucepan over medium-high heat; bring to a boil. Cook until reduced to 2 tablespoons (about 5 minutes). Combine 3 tablespoons water and cornstarch; add to pan. Bring cider mixture to a boil, stirring constantly; cook 30 seconds. Remove from heat. Stir in shallots, vinegar, salt, and pepper; cool.

3. To prepare salad, place salad mix in a large bowl. Drizzle with dressing; toss gently to coat. Divide evenly among 4 plates; top with berries, cheese, and walnuts. Serve immediately. **YIELD:** 4 servings (serving size: 2 cups salad, ½ cup berries, 1 tablespoon cheese, and 2¼ teaspoons walnuts).

CALORIES 165 (37% from fat); FAT 6.7g (sat 1.8g, mono 0.7g, poly 3g); PROTEIN 5.2g; CARB 24.6g; FIBER 4.5g; CHOL 6mg; IRON 1.9mg; SODIUM 199mg; CALC 116mg

Mixed Greens Salad with Honey-Orange Dressing

The sweetness in the citrus-based dressing balances the bitterness of the radicchio. This easy, all-purpose salad goes with almost any dinner.

3 tablespoons fresh orange juice
1 tablespoon honey
2 teaspoons minced shallots
2 teaspoons white wine vinegar
½ teaspoon Dijon mustard
¼ teaspoon salt
¼ teaspoon freshly ground black pepper
4 cups chopped romaine lettuce
4 cups torn radicchio
3 cups bagged baby spinach leaves

1. Combine first 7 ingredients in a large bowl, stirring with a whisk. Add romaine lettuce, radicchio, and spinach; toss gently to coat. **YIELD:** 8 servings (serving size: about 1 cup).

CALORIES 24 (8% from fat); FAT 0.2g (sat 0g, mono 0g, poly 0.1g); PROTEIN 1.1g; CARB 5.3g; FIBER 1.1g; CHOL 0mg; IRON 0.8mg; SODIUM 97mg; CALC 26mg

ORGANIC FACT
Compared to conventional, organic orange juice contains up to 30% more vitamin C. Besides having higher amounts of nutrients and antioxidants, organic oranges can intensify flavor in a dish and make it simply taste better.

Source: American Chemical Society

Escarole Salad with Melons and Crispy Prosciutto

The Italian combination of melon and prosciutto pairs nicely in this first-course salad. Serve alongside pork tenderloin, green beans, and corn custards.

  4   thin slices prosciutto (about 1½ ounces), coarsely chopped
  3   tablespoons minced shallots
  2   tablespoons balsamic vinegar
  1   tablespoon red wine vinegar
1½   teaspoons extravirgin olive oil
  ¼   teaspoon salt
  ¼   teaspoon freshly ground black pepper
 12   cups torn escarole (about 1¼ pounds)
  2   cups torn radicchio (about 4 ounces)
  2   cups cubed honeydew melon
  2   cups cubed cantaloupe
  2   tablespoons sliced almonds, toasted

1. Preheat oven to 400°.

2. Arrange prosciutto in a single layer on a baking sheet. Bake at 400° for 6 minutes or until crisp.

3. Combine shallots and next 5 ingredients in a large bowl, stirring with a whisk. Add escarole and radicchio; toss to coat. Add honeydew and cantaloupe; toss well.

4. Place 2 cups escarole mixture on each of 6 plates; top each serving with about 2 teaspoons prosciutto. Sprinkle each serving with 1 teaspoon almonds. **YIELD:** 6 servings.

CALORIES 105 (32% from fat); FAT 3.7g (sat 0.7g, mono 2.1g, poly 0.6g); PROTEIN 3.6g; CARB 16.4g; FIBER 4g; CHOL 4mg; IRON 1.1mg; SODIUM 228mg; CALC 68mg

Field Greens with Mississippi Caviar

Nutritious, inexpensive black-eyed peas have been a southern kitchen staple for three centuries. This salad's bright seasonings make it a good side for grilled meat or chicken.

¾ cup water
1 garlic clove, minced
Dash of black pepper
4 cups fresh or frozen black-eyed peas
1 cup (1-inch) julienne-cut yellow bell pepper
1 cup chopped tomato
½ cup bottled reduced-calorie Italian dressing
⅓ cup chopped fresh parsley
¼ cup chopped red onion
¼ teaspoon salt
6 cups mixed salad greens

1. Combine water, garlic, and black pepper in a large saucepan; bring to a boil. Add peas; cover and cook over medium-low heat 30 minutes or until tender. Drain.

2. Combine peas, bell pepper, and next 5 ingredients in a large bowl; toss gently to combine. Cover and chill 3 hours or overnight. Serve over salad greens.

YIELD: 6 servings (serving size: 1 cup pea mixture and 1 cup greens).

CALORIES 197 (14% from fat); FAT 3g (sat 0.5g, mono 0.5g, poly 1.7g); PROTEIN 11.2g; CARB 33.5g; FIBER 9.3g; CHOL 1mg; IRON 3.7mg; SODIUM 281mg; CALC 68mg

Creole Tomato Salad

Creole Tomato Salad

SALAD:

3 ripe tomatoes, cut into ¼-inch-thick slices (about 2 pounds)
1 Vidalia or other sweet onion, thinly sliced and separated into rings
¼ teaspoon salt
1 tablespoon thinly sliced fresh mint
2 teaspoons chopped fresh chives

VINAIGRETTE:

4 teaspoons olive oil
4 teaspoons red wine vinegar
1 teaspoon Dijon mustard
½ teaspoon minced fresh garlic

1. To prepare salad, alternate tomato and onion slices on a platter. Sprinkle with salt. Top with mint and chives.
2. To prepare vinaigrette, combine olive oil, vinegar, mustard, and garlic in a jar. Cover tightly; shake vigorously. Drizzle vinaigrette over salad. Serve at room temperature. **YIELD:** 4 servings.

CALORIES 73 (55% from fat); FAT 4.8g (sat 0.7g, mono 3.4g, poly 0.6g); PROTEIN 1.4g; CARB 7.5g; FIBER 1.5g; CHOL 0mg; IRON 0.6mg; SODIUM 185mg; CALC 13mg

Grilled Vegetable Salad with Creamy Blue Cheese Dressing

(pictured on page 152)

DRESSING:

⅓ cup low-fat mayonnaise
⅓ cup plain low-fat yogurt
¼ cup (1 ounce) crumbled blue cheese
¼ cup 1% low-fat milk
¼ teaspoon freshly ground black pepper
⅛ teaspoon salt

SALAD:

¼ pound green beans, trimmed
¼ pound sugar snap peas, trimmed
¼ pound carrots, peeled and cut diagonally into ½-inch-thick pieces
1 cup (½-inch-thick) slices red onion
Cooking spray
½ teaspoon freshly ground black pepper
¼ teaspoon garlic salt
6 cups torn romaine lettuce
½ cup thinly sliced radishes

1. To prepare dressing, combine first 6 ingredients, stirring with a whisk until blended. Cover and chill.
2. Prepare grill.
3. To prepare salad, cook beans, peas, and carrots in boiling water 3 minutes or until crisp-tender. Drain and plunge into ice water; drain. Place mixture in a large bowl; add onion slices. Lightly coat vegetable mixture with cooking spray. Sprinkle with ½ teaspoon black pepper and garlic salt; toss gently to coat.
4. Place vegetable mixture in a wire grilling basket coated with cooking spray. Place grilling basket on grill rack; grill 7 minutes on each side or until lightly browned. Arrange 1½ cups lettuce on each of 4 salad plates. Divide grilled vegetables and radishes evenly among servings. Serve ¼ cup dressing with each salad.
YIELD: 4 servings.

CALORIES 144 (29% from fat); FAT 4.7g (sat 2g, mono 0.8g, poly 0.3g); PROTEIN 6.8g; CARB 20.4g; FIBER 5.2g; CHOL 8mg; IRON 2.4mg; SODIUM 497mg; CALC 187mg

Marinated-Vegetable Salad

3 cups diagonally sliced carrot (about 1 pound)
2 cups (2-inch) julienne-cut zucchini
1 cup vertically sliced red onion
½ cup (2-inch) julienne-cut red bell pepper
¼ cup red wine vinegar
2 tablespoons finely grated fresh Parmesan cheese
1 tablespoon chopped fresh parsley
1 tablespoon water
1 tablespoon olive oil
¼ teaspoon dried basil
¼ teaspoon dried oregano
¼ teaspoon salt
⅛ teaspoon black pepper

1. Place carrot in a microwave-safe dish; cover with plastic wrap. Microwave at HIGH 4 minutes or until crisp-tender; cool.
2. Place zucchini in a microwave-safe dish; cover with plastic wrap. Microwave at HIGH 1½ minutes or until crisp-tender; cool.
3. Combine carrot, zucchini, onion, and bell pepper in a large bowl. Combine vinegar and next 8 ingredients in a small bowl, stirring with a whisk. Pour vinegar mixture over vegetables, tossing to coat. Cover and marinate in refrigerator 2 hours. **YIELD:** 7 servings (serving size: 1 cup).

CALORIES 59 (40% from fat); FAT 2.6g (sat 0.6g, mono 1.6g, poly 0.3g); PROTEIN 1.8g; CARB 8.1g; FIBER 2.2g; CHOL 1mg; IRON 0.6mg; SODIUM 129mg; CALC 44mg

Southwestern Falafel with Avocado Spread

Inspired by the traditional Middle Eastern sandwich of chickpea patties in pita bread, this southwestern version features cumin-flavored pinto bean patties and a spread that is much like guacamole. Serve with tomato soup.

PATTIES:
- 1 (15-ounce) can pinto beans, rinsed and drained
- ½ cup (2 ounces) shredded Monterey Jack cheese
- ¼ cup finely crushed baked tortilla chips (about ¾ ounce)
- 2 tablespoons finely chopped green onions
- 1 tablespoon finely chopped cilantro
- ⅛ teaspoon ground cumin
- 1 large egg white
- 1½ teaspoons canola oil

AVOCADO SPREAD:
- ¼ cup mashed peeled avocado
- 2 tablespoons finely chopped plum tomato
- 1 tablespoon finely chopped red onion
- 2 tablespoons fat-free sour cream
- 1 teaspoon fresh lime juice
- ⅛ teaspoon salt
- 2 (6-inch) pitas, each cut in half crosswise

1. To prepare patties, place pinto beans in a medium bowl; partially mash with a fork. Add Monterey Jack cheese and next 5 ingredients; stir until well combined. Form into 4 (½-inch-thick) oval patties.

2. Heat oil in a large nonstick skillet over medium-high heat. Add patties; cook 3 minutes on each side or until patties are browned and thoroughly heated.

3. To prepare avocado spread, while patties cook, combine avocado, tomato, red onion, sour cream, juice, and salt. Place 1 patty in each pita half. Spread about 2 tablespoons avocado spread over patty in each pita half.

YIELD: 4 servings (serving size: 1 stuffed pita half).

CALORIES 281 (30% from fat); FAT 9.5g (sat 3.4g, mono 3.9g, poly 1.5g); PROTEIN 12.2g; CARB 37.4g; FIBER 5.9g; CHOL 13mg; IRON 2.4mg; SODIUM 625mg; CALC 188mg

Grilled Vegetable and Mozzarella Sandwich

You can use a grilling basket to make it easier to handle the vegetables as they cook. If you can't find a loaf of ciabatta, use focaccia.

  3 cups (⅛-inch-thick) diagonally cut zucchini
     (about 1 pound)
  3 (⅛-inch-thick) slices red onion
  1 red bell pepper, seeded and cut into 4 pieces
  2 tablespoons balsamic vinegar
  1 teaspoon extravirgin olive oil
  ½ teaspoon salt
  ¼ teaspoon freshly ground black pepper
Cooking spray
  1 (1-pound) loaf ciabatta, cut in half horizontally
  1 cup gourmet salad greens
  5 ounces fresh mozzarella cheese, sliced
  8 fresh basil leaves

1. Prepare grill.
2. Combine first 7 ingredients in a large bowl, tossing to coat. Remove vegetables from bowl, reserving vinegar mixture. Place onion and bell pepper on grill rack coated with cooking spray; grill 7 minutes on each side or until tender. Grill zucchini 3 minutes on each side or until tender.
3. Hollow out bottom half of bread, leaving a ½-inch-thick shell; reserve torn bread for another use. Layer vegetables, greens, cheese, and basil in loaf; drizzle reserved vinegar mixture on top. Cover with top of bread; press lightly.
4. Place filled loaf on grill rack; grill 4 minutes on each side or until cheese melts. Cut into quarters. **YIELD:** 4 servings (serving size: 1 sandwich quarter).

CALORIES 338 (30% from fat); FAT 11.1g (sat 5.7g, mono 3.5g, poly 1g); PROTEIN 14.3g; CARB 44.8g; FIBER 4.4g; CHOL 28mg; IRON 2.9mg; SODIUM 785mg; CALC 287mg

Eggplant-and-Portobello Mushroom Melts

  4 portobello mushrooms (about 10 ounces)
  4 (½-inch-thick) slices peeled eggplant
     (about 8 ounces)
  ¼ cup balsamic vinaigrette, divided
  ¼ cup chopped bottled roasted red bell peppers
  2 tablespoons chopped fresh basil
  4 (½-ounce) slices provolone cheese
  4 (2-ounce) onion rolls, halved
  ½ cup spinach leaves

1. Preheat broiler.
2. Remove stems from mushrooms; discard stems. Remove brown gills from undersides of mushrooms using a sharp knife, and discard gills. Place mushrooms and eggplant on a broiler pan; brush vegetables with 1 tablespoon vinaigrette. Broil 6 minutes. Turn vegetables over, and brush with 1 tablespoon vinaigrette. Broil an additional 5 minutes or until tender.
3. Combine bell peppers and basil. Spoon 1 tablespoon pepper mixture over each eggplant slice. Top each mushroom with 1 cheese slice. Broil 1 minute or until cheese melts. Brush 2 tablespoons vinaigrette evenly over cut sides of onion rolls. Arrange spinach evenly on bottom halves of rolls. Top each roll half with 1 mushroom and 1 eggplant slice; cover with roll tops. **YIELD:** 4 servings.

CALORIES 276 (30% from fat); FAT 9.3g (sat 3.5g, mono 2.5g, poly 2.5g); PROTEIN 12g; CARB 39.6g; FIBER 3.9g; CHOL 15mg; IRON 2.9mg; SODIUM 564mg; CALC 205mg

ORGANIC FACT
California Certified Organic Farmers (CCOF) is one of several certifiers that ensures the USDA National Organic Program standards are met before a grower or producer can obtain USDA organic certification.

Source: USDA National Organic Program

Spicy Pork and Sauerkraut Sandwiches

Packaged coleslaw mix creates easy, speedy "sauerkraut" that's more colorful and less salty than the traditional recipe.

½ teaspoon salt, divided
½ teaspoon dried oregano
½ teaspoon dried thyme
½ teaspoon black pepper
1 pound pork tenderloin, trimmed and cut crosswise into ¼-inch-thick slices
1 tablespoon canola oil, divided
Cooking spray
4 cups packaged cabbage-and-carrot coleslaw (about 8 ounces)
1 tablespoon prepared horseradish
1 tablespoon red wine vinegar
½ teaspoon crushed red pepper
1½ teaspoons Worcestershire sauce
⅓ cup fat-free mayonnaise
1 tablespoon Dijon mustard
4 (2-ounce) Kaiser rolls or hamburger buns
16 (⅛-inch-thick) slices cucumber

1. Combine ¼ teaspoon salt, oregano, thyme, and black pepper; sprinkle pork with spice mixture. Heat 1½ teaspoons oil in a large nonstick skillet coated with cooking spray over medium-high heat. Add pork; cook 2 minutes on each side or until done. Remove pork from pan; keep warm.
2. Heat 1½ teaspoons oil in pan over medium-high heat. Add ¼ teaspoon salt, coleslaw, and next 4 ingredients; cook 2 minutes, stirring frequently. Remove from heat.
3. Combine mayonnaise and mustard; spread mixture evenly over cut sides of rolls. Divide coleslaw mixture, pork, and cucumber slices evenly among bottom halves of rolls. Cover with top halves of rolls. **YIELD:** 4 servings.

CALORIES 366 (27% from fat); FAT 10.8g (sat 2.6g, mono 3.2g, poly 3.8g); PROTEIN 29.9g; CARB 37.5g; FIBER 4.1g; CHOL 76mg; IRON 3.7mg; SODIUM 989mg; CALC 108mg

Chipotle Pulled-Pork Barbecue Sandwiches

Sweet-and-sour pickles are a tasty balance to the smoky barbecue sauce in this updated southern-style sandwich. Serve with coleslaw.

1 (7-ounce) can chipotle chiles in adobo sauce
¼ cup barbecue sauce
1 teaspoon garlic powder
1½ teaspoons ground cumin
1 (1-pound) pork tenderloin, trimmed and cut into ½-inch cubes
1 (14.5-ounce) can diced tomatoes, undrained
1 tablespoon olive oil
3 cups thinly sliced onion
2 teaspoons chopped fresh thyme
1 teaspoon sugar
6 (½-ounce) slices provolone cheese
12 sandwich-cut bread-and-butter pickles
6 (2½-ounce) Kaiser rolls

1. Remove 1 chile from can; reserve remaining chiles and sauce for another use. Finely chop chile.
2. Place chopped chile, barbecue sauce, and next 4 ingredients in a medium saucepan; bring to a boil over medium-high heat. Cover, reduce heat, and simmer 45 minutes, stirring occasionally. Uncover and cook 10 minutes or until sauce thickens and pork is very tender; remove from heat. Remove pork from sauce; shred pork. Return pork to sauce.
3. Heat oil in a large nonstick skillet over medium-high heat. Add onion, thyme, and sugar; cook 10 minutes or until golden, stirring occasionally.
4. Heat a large nonstick skillet over medium heat. Place 1 cheese slice, ½ cup pork mixture, about 2 tablespoons onions, and 2 pickle slices on bottom half of each roll. Cover with top halves of rolls. Add 3 sandwiches to pan. Place a cast-iron or heavy skillet on top of sandwiches; press gently to flatten. Cook 2 minutes on each side or until cheese melts and bread is toasted (leave cast-iron skillet on sandwiches while they cook). Repeat procedure with remaining sandwiches. **YIELD:** 6 servings (serving size: 1 sandwich).

CALORIES 431 (26% from fat); FAT 12.4g (sat 3.9g, mono 3.7g, poly 1.8g); PROTEIN 28.3g; CARB 51.4g; FIBER 4.7g; CHOL 59mg; IRON 4.1mg; SODIUM 910mg; CALC 207mg

Chipotle Pulled-Pork
Barbecue Sandwiches

Cashew Chicken
Salad Sandwiches

Cashew Chicken Salad Sandwiches

These chicken sandwiches come together quickly. Add lettuce and tomato, if you'd like.

  ¼ cup fat-free sour cream
  1 tablespoon light mayonnaise
  ¼ teaspoon curry powder
  2 cups chopped roasted skinless, boneless chicken breast (about 2 breasts)
  ⅓ cup chopped celery
  2 tablespoons chopped dry-roasted cashews
  1 tablespoon finely chopped green onions
  2 (2-ounce) whole wheat hamburger buns

1. Combine first 3 ingredients in a large bowl, stirring until well blended. Add chicken, celery, cashews, and green onions; stir well. Serve on buns. **YIELD:** 2 servings (serving size: ⅔ cup chicken salad and 1 bun).

CALORIES 353 (26% from fat); FAT 10.3g (sat 2.6g, mono 1.5g, poly 1.8g); PROTEIN 31.6g; CARB 35.8g; FIBER 4.8g; CHOL 69mg; IRON 1.8mg; SODIUM 925mg; CALC 115mg

Smoky Bacon and Blue Cheese Chicken Salad Pitas

You can make the chicken salad ahead; place it in pita halves just before serving.

  ¾ cup plain fat-free yogurt
  ¼ cup (1 ounce) crumbled blue cheese
  2 tablespoons light mayonnaise
  ½ teaspoon freshly ground black pepper
  3 cups shredded romaine lettuce
  1½ cups shredded cooked chicken (about 6 ounces)
  4 bacon slices, cooked and crumbled
  2 medium tomatoes, seeded and chopped
  4 (6-inch) whole wheat pitas, cut in half

1. Combine first 4 ingredients, stirring well. Combine lettuce, chicken, bacon, and tomatoes in a medium bowl, stirring well. Drizzle yogurt mixture over chicken mixture; toss gently to coat. Spoon ½ cup salad into each pita half. Serve immediately. **YIELD:** 4 servings (serving size: 2 stuffed pita halves).

CALORIES 375 (29% from fat); FAT 12.1g (sat 3.7g, mono 3.6g, poly 3.1g); PROTEIN 26.1g; CARB 43.8g; FIBER 6.3g; CHOL 55mg; IRON 3.5mg; SODIUM 696mg; CALC 130mg

Balsamic-Glazed Chicken Sandwiches with Red Onions and Goat Cheese

You'll need less than half an hour to prepare these tangy chicken sandwiches.

¾ cup balsamic vinegar
½ cup dry red wine
2 teaspoons brown sugar
1 teaspoon low-sodium soy sauce
2 (6-ounce) skinless, boneless chicken breast halves
½ teaspoon salt
¼ teaspoon freshly ground black pepper
Cooking spray
1 tablespoon olive oil
1½ cups thinly vertically sliced red onion
1 (3-ounce) package goat cheese
4 (2-ounce) hoagie or Kaiser rolls
1 cup trimmed arugula

1. Combine first 4 ingredients in a small saucepan over medium heat. Bring mixture to a boil, stirring until sugar dissolves. Cook until reduced to ⅓ cup (about 12 minutes). Remove from heat; cool slightly.
2. Heat a large nonstick skillet over medium-high heat. Sprinkle chicken with salt and pepper. Coat pan with cooking spray. Add chicken to pan; cook 4 minutes on each side or until done. Remove chicken from pan; thinly slice. Cover and keep warm.
3. Add oil to pan; reduce temperature to medium-low. Add onion; cook 5 minutes or until onion is soft and beginning to brown, stirring frequently. Remove from heat.
4. Spread about 1½ tablespoons goat cheese evenly over bottom half of each roll; divide sliced chicken and onion evenly over rolls. Drizzle each serving with about 1 tablespoon balsamic mixture; top with ¼ cup trimmed arugula and top halves of rolls. Serve immediately.
YIELD: 4 servings (serving size: 1 sandwich).

CALORIES 424 (25% from fat); FAT 11.0g (sat 4.2g, mono 4.4g, poly 1.7g); PROTEIN 30.1g; CARB 43.9g; FIBER 2.2g; CHOL 59mg; IRON 3.7mg; SODIUM 796mg; CALC 129mg

Chicken and Bacon Roll-Ups

Made hearty with shredded chicken, these easy sandwiches can be endlessly adapted to suit any taste. Substitute chopped fresh basil or chives for the tarragon, use flavored wraps, or try applewood-smoked bacon for a smoky punch.

½ cup reduced-fat mayonnaise
1 teaspoon minced fresh tarragon
2 teaspoons fresh lemon juice
4 (2.8-ounce) whole wheat flatbreads
2 cups shredded romaine lettuce
2 cups chopped tomato (about 2 medium)
4 center-cut bacon slices, cooked and drained
2 cups shredded skinless, boneless rotisserie chicken breast

1. Combine reduced-fat mayonnaise, minced tarragon, and fresh lemon juice in a small bowl. Spread 2 tablespoons mayonnaise mixture over each flatbread. Top each with ½ cup shredded romaine lettuce, ½ cup chopped tomato, 1 bacon slice, crumbled, and ½ cup chicken. Roll up. **YIELD:** 4 servings (serving size: 1 wrap).

CALORIES 433 (27% from fat); FAT 13g (sat 2.6g, mono 2g, poly 0.9g); PROTEIN 34.8g; CARB 44.2g; FIBER 5.5g; CHOL 66mg; IRON 3.1mg; SODIUM 925mg; CALC 49mg

ORGANIC FACT
Organic food does not have to break your budget. Prioritize grocery items that are most important to you and think about which ones might have the most pesticides. Consider referring to "The Dirty Dozen" on page 14 to find more information on produce items that contain the most pesticides.

Source: Environmental Working Group

Turkey Philly Sandwiches

You can also add sliced mushrooms to the pan with the onion and bell pepper. Serve with dill pickles and chips.

> 2 teaspoons butter
> 1 cup thinly sliced onion
> 1 cup thinly sliced green bell pepper
> ¼ teaspoon black pepper
> ¾ pound thinly sliced deli turkey breast
> 4 (2-ounce) sandwich rolls
> 4 (1-ounce) slices low-sodium mozzarella or
>   provolone cheese

1. Preheat oven to 375°.
2. Melt butter in a large nonstick skillet over medium-high heat. Add onion and bell pepper; sauté 5 minutes or until tender. Stir in black pepper.
3. Divide onion mixture and turkey evenly among bottom halves of rolls; top each serving with 1 cheese slice. Cover with top halves of rolls.
4. Place sandwiches on a baking sheet. Bake at 375° for 5 minutes or until cheese melts. **YIELD:** 4 servings (serving size: 1 sandwich).

CALORIES 380 (30% from fat); FAT 12.9g (sat 6.9g, mono 2.7g, poly 1.4g); PROTEIN 28.5g; CARB 40.6g; FIBER 2.6g; CHOL 52mg; IRON 2.2mg; SODIUM 1,042mg; CALC 277mg

Turkey-Vegetable Wraps

> 2 cups coarsely chopped smoked turkey breast
>   (about 8 ounces)
> 2 cups gourmet salad greens
> ½ cup fresh corn kernels (about 1 ear)
> ½ cup chopped red bell pepper
> ¼ cup thinly sliced green onions
> 3 tablespoons light ranch dressing
> 4 (8-inch) flour tortillas

1. Combine first 6 ingredients in a large bowl, tossing well to coat. Warm tortillas according to package directions. Top each tortilla with 1 cup turkey mixture; roll up. Cut each wrap in half diagonally. **YIELD:** 4 servings (serving size: 1 wrap).

CALORIES 252 (26% from fat); FAT 7.2g (sat 1.2g, mono 2.3g, poly 3.3g); PROTEIN 18.2g; CARB 29.8g; FIBER 3g; CHOL 32mg; IRON 2.4mg; SODIUM 741mg; CALC 76mg

Barbecue Turkey Burgers

As long as you have the grill pan out, add Spicy Grilled Sweet Potatoes (recipe on page 207) for an easy side.

> ¼ cup chopped onion
> ¼ cup barbecue sauce, divided
> 2 tablespoons dry breadcrumbs
> 2 teaspoons prepared mustard
> ¾ teaspoon chili powder
> ½ teaspoon garlic powder
> ¼ teaspoon salt
> 1 pound ground turkey
> Cooking spray
> 4 large leaf lettuce leaves
> 4 (¼-inch-thick) slices tomato
> 4 (1½-ounce) hamburger buns

1. Combine onion, 2 tablespoons barbecue sauce, breadcrumbs, and next 5 ingredients in a medium bowl. Divide turkey mixture into 4 equal portions, shaping each portion into a 1½-inch-thick patty.
2. Heat a grill pan over medium-high heat. Coat pan with cooking spray. Place patties in pan; cook 7 minutes on each side or until done.
3. Place 1 lettuce leaf, 1 tomato slice, and 1 patty on bottom half of each bun. Spread each patty with 1½ teaspoons barbecue sauce. Cover with top halves of buns. **YIELD:** 4 servings (serving size: 1 burger).

CALORIES 310 (22% from fat); FAT 7.6g (sat 2.1g, mono 1.7g, poly 2.8g); PROTEIN 29.9g; CARB 28.5g; FIBER 2.1g; CHOL 65mg; IRON 3.5mg; SODIUM 642mg; CALC 102mg

Barbecue
Turkey Burgers

Jamaican Jerk Turkey Burgers with Papaya-Mango Salsa

Fruity salsa is a good match for these spicy burgers. Be sure to coat the burgers and the grill rack with cooking spray to prevent sticking. Prepare the salsa up to a day in advance; refrigerate in a covered container.

SALSA:
- ⅔ cup diced peeled mango
- ⅔ cup diced peeled papaya
- ¼ cup finely chopped red bell pepper
- ¼ cup finely chopped red onion
- 2 tablespoons chopped fresh cilantro
- ½ teaspoon grated lime rind
- 2 tablespoons fresh lime juice

BURGERS:
- 1 cup finely chopped red onion
- ½ cup dry breadcrumbs
- ⅓ cup bottled sweet-and-sour sauce
- ¼ cup finely chopped red bell pepper
- 1 tablespoon Jamaican jerk seasoning
- 1 large egg white
- 1 pound ground turkey
- Cooking spray
- 4 (2-ounce) Kaiser rolls or hamburger buns, split

1. To prepare salsa, combine first 7 ingredients. Let stand at room temperature at least 30 minutes.

2. Prepare grill.

3. To prepare burgers, combine 1 cup onion and next 5 ingredients, stirring well. Add turkey, and mix well to combine. Divide turkey mixture into 4 equal portions, shaping each into a 1-inch-thick patty. Cover and refrigerate patties 20 minutes.

4. Lightly coat both sides of patties with cooking spray, and place patties on a grill rack coated with cooking spray. Grill 7 minutes on each side or until done.

5. Place Kaiser rolls, cut sides down, on grill rack; grill 1 minute or until lightly toasted. Place 1 patty on bottom half of each roll; top with ½ cup salsa and top half of roll.

YIELD: 4 servings (serving size: 1 burger).

CALORIES 424 (22% from fat); FAT 10.4g (sat 2.5g, mono 3.7g, poly 2.9g); PROTEIN 24.1g; CARB 58g; FIBER 3.9g; CHOL 67mg; IRON 4mg; SODIUM 818mg; CALC 121mg

California Burgers

Alfalfa sprouts and avocados crown these juicy burgers. A combination of regular ground turkey and ground turkey breast offers superior texture. If you don't need this many burgers, wrap individual patties in plastic wrap and again in foil; freeze. Thaw as many as you need in the refrigerator; cook as directed. The sauce can also be made ahead; cover and chill.

SAUCE:
- ½ cup ketchup
- 1 tablespoon Dijon mustard
- 1 tablespoon fat-free mayonnaise

PATTIES:
- ½ cup finely chopped shallots
- ¼ cup dry breadcrumbs
- 1 teaspoon salt
- 1 teaspoon Worcestershire sauce
- ¼ teaspoon freshly ground black pepper
- 3 garlic cloves, minced
- 1¼ pounds ground turkey breast
- 1¼ pounds ground turkey
- Cooking spray

REMAINING INGREDIENTS:
- 10 (2-ounce) hamburger buns
- 10 red leaf lettuce leaves
- 20 bread-and-butter pickles
- 10 (¼-inch-thick) slices red onion, separated into rings
- 2 peeled avocados, each cut into 10 slices
- 3 cups alfalfa sprouts

1. Prepare grill or broiler.

2. To prepare sauce, combine first 3 ingredients; set aside.

3. To prepare patties, combine shallots and next 7 ingredients, mixing well. Divide mixture into 10 equal portions, shaping each into a ½-inch-thick patty. Place patties on grill rack or broiler pan coated with cooking spray; grill 4 minutes on each side or until done.

4. Spread 1 tablespoon sauce on top half of each hamburger bun. Layer bottom half of each bun with 1 lettuce leaf, 1 patty, 2 pickles, 1 onion slice, 2 avocado slices, and about ⅓ cup of sprouts. Cover with top halves of buns. **YIELD:** 10 servings (serving size: 1 burger).

CALORIES 384 (29% from fat); FAT 12.4g (sat 2.6g, mono 5.1g, poly 2.8g); PROTEIN 31.4g; CARB 37.5g; FIBER 3.9g; CHOL 68mg; IRON 4mg; SODIUM 828mg; CALC 94mg

Sausage and Egg Burrito

Use two beaten large eggs in place of the egg substitute, if desired. Keep in mind however, that this will increase the total fat to 14.6 grams per serving.

- Cooking spray
- ½ cup chopped red bell pepper
- ¼ cup chopped onion
- 3 ounces turkey breakfast sausage
- ½ cup egg substitute
- ¼ cup (1 ounce) reduced-fat shredded Cheddar cheese
- 6 tablespoons bottled salsa, divided
- 2 (8-inch) fat-free flour tortillas
- ¼ cup reduced-fat sour cream

1. Heat a medium skillet over medium-high heat. Coat pan with cooking spray. Add bell pepper, onion, and sausage; cook 4 minutes or until browned, stirring to crumble sausage. Add egg substitute; cook 2 minutes, stirring frequently. Remove from heat; stir in cheese and 2 tablespoons salsa. Remove from heat. Cover and let stand 2 minutes.

2. Heat tortillas according to package directions. Spoon half of egg mixture down center of each tortilla; roll up. Serve with remaining salsa and sour cream. **YIELD:** 2 servings (serving size: 1 burrito, 2 tablespoons salsa, and 2 tablespoons sour cream).

CALORIES 314 (28% from fat); FAT 9.6g (sat 4.4g, mono 3.1g, poly 1.8g); PROTEIN 20.7g; CARB 26.9g; FIBER 3.9g; CHOL 50mg; IRON 2.6mg; SODIUM 915mg; CALC 148mg

ORGANIC FACT

One of the more intriguing facts about organic agriculture is that its increased antioxidant content is a result of its having to fight off pests. That's one more reason why the use of toxic synthetic pesticides to kill off pests is undesirable. They prevent this antioxidant-developing process from taking place.

Source: Organic Consumers Association

SIDE DISHES

Boston Baked Beans, page 190

185

Baked Apples

Serve these juicy baked apples as a topping for oatmeal or pancakes, or as a side with pork. Any sweet-tart apple, such as Ida Red and McIntosh, will also work well in place of Galas.

  2 cups dried cranberries
1¼ cups coarsely chopped walnuts
  1 cup packed brown sugar
  1 cup water
  2 teaspoons ground cinnamon
  6 Gala apples, cored and chopped (about 3 pounds)

1. Combine all ingredients in a large microwave-safe dish. Microwave at HIGH 20 minutes or until apples are soft, stirring occasionally. **YIELD:** 6 cups (serving size: ¼ cup).

CALORIES 126 (29% from fat); FAT 4.1g (sat 0.4g, mono 0.6g, poly 3g); PROTEIN 1g; CARB 23.7g; FIBER 2.3g; CHOL 0mg; IRON 0.5mg; SODIUM 4mg; CALC 16mg

Baked Apples

Rum-Spiked Grilled Pineapple

Grilling caramelizes the natural sugars in the fresh pineapple. Serve this as a side dish with barbecued chicken or pork for summer cookouts.

  1 pineapple, peeled, cored, halved lengthwise, and sliced lengthwise into 12 wedges (about 1½ pounds)
  2 tablespoons butter, melted
  ¼ cup packed light brown sugar
  ¼ cup dark rum
  ¼ teaspoon ground cinnamon
Cooking spray
Lime wedges

1. Prepare grill.
2. Brush pineapple with 2 tablespoons butter. Combine brown sugar, rum, and ¼ teaspoon cinnamon in a microwave-safe bowl. Microwave at HIGH 1½ minutes or until sugar dissolves. Brush rum mixture evenly over pineapple wedges. Place pineapple on grill rack coated with cooking spray. Grill 3 minutes on each side or until grill marks form and pineapple is thoroughly heated. Serve with lime wedges. **YIELD:** 6 servings (serving size: 2 pineapple wedges).

CALORIES 146 (25% from fat); FAT 4g (sat 2.4g, mono 1g, poly 0.2g); PROTEIN 0.7g; CARB 23.4g; FIBER 1.6g; CHOL 10mg; IRON 0.5mg; SODIUM 32g; CALC 25mg

Raspberry-Asparagus Medley

  1 tablespoon white wine vinegar
  2 tablespoons raspberry preserves
1½ teaspoons Dijon mustard
  ⅛ teaspoon salt
  ½ teaspoon grated lemon rind
2½ cups (1-inch) slices asparagus (about 1 pound)
1½ cups fresh raspberries
  2 tablespoons finely chopped pecans, toasted

1. Combine first 4 ingredients in a small saucepan; bring to a boil. Remove from heat; stir in rind.
2. Cook asparagus in boiling water 2 minutes or until crisp-tender. Drain and plunge into ice water, and drain. Combine preserves mixture, asparagus, and raspberries in a bowl; toss gently to coat. Sprinkle with pecans. **YIELD:** 6 servings (serving size: about ½ cup).

CALORIES 65 (30% from fat); FAT 2.2g (sat 0.2g, mono 1.1g, poly 0.7g); PROTEIN 2.3g; CARB 10.8g; FIBER 3.9g; CHOL 0mg; IRON 1mg; SODIUM 82mg; CALC 27mg

Rum-Spiked Grilled Pineapple

Haricots Verts and Grape Tomato Salad with Crème Fraîche Dressing

Haricots verts (ah-ree-koh VEHR) are tender, young French green beans. If not labeled as such in your market, look for slim, petite green beans. Crème fraîche adds a nutty flavor and rich texture to the dressing; look for it near the gourmet cheeses in your supermarket. Whole sour cream is an acceptable substitute.

1 pound haricots verts, trimmed
¼ cup finely chopped fresh basil
2 tablespoons minced shallots
2 tablespoons fresh lemon juice
2 tablespoons crème fraîche or whole sour cream
1 tablespoon honey
½ teaspoon salt
1 pint grape or cherry tomatoes, halved
1 tablespoon pine nuts, toasted

1. Cook haricots verts in boiling water 2 minutes or until crisp-tender. Drain. Rinse with cold water; drain.
2. Combine basil and next 5 ingredients in a large bowl, stirring with a whisk. Add haricots verts and grape tomatoes; toss gently to coat. Divide salad mixture evenly among 6 plates, and sprinkle with nuts. **YIELD:** 6 servings (serving size: about ¾ cup salad and ½ teaspoon nuts).

CALORIES 74 (34% from fat); FAT 2.8g (sat 1.1g, mono 0.8g, poly 0.6g); PROTEIN 1.7g; CARB 11.4g; FIBER 3.5g; CHOL 7mg; IRON 0.7mg; SODIUM 203mg; CALC 47mg

ORGANIC TIP
Composting is a common technique used in organic farming. Put food, table scraps, and dried leaves into a composting bin. Turn it every few days and regulate the temperature. Within three to six months, the matter will decompose into soil, which can be reused for gardening.

Green Beans with Roasted Onion Vinaigrette

Serve these as a side with a rotisserie chicken for a simple summer meal. To simplify things, you can make and refrigerate the vinaigrette and steam and chill the green beans a day ahead.

2 pounds green beans, trimmed
2 red onions, peeled (about 1 pound)
4 teaspoons olive oil, divided
¼ teaspoon salt
¼ teaspoon black pepper
2 sprigs fresh thyme
1 tablespoon chopped fresh dill
3 tablespoons Champagne vinegar or white wine vinegar
1 tablespoon stone-ground mustard

1. Preheat oven to 400°.
2. Cook green beans in boiling water 5 minutes. Drain and plunge beans into ice water; drain. Place beans in a large bowl.
3. Cut onions in half vertically. Drizzle cut side of each onion half with ¼ teaspoon oil. Sprinkle halves evenly with salt and pepper. Place 1 thyme sprig on 1 onion half; top with other half. Wrap in foil. Repeat procedure with remaining thyme and onion halves. Bake wrapped onions at 400° for 1 hour or until tender. Cool to room temperature. Discard thyme; chop onions.
4. Combine remaining 1 tablespoon olive oil, onions, dill, vinegar, and mustard in a small bowl. Toss beans with onion mixture. **YIELD:** 8 servings (serving size: about 4 ounces green beans and ¼ cup onion vinaigrette).

CALORIES 83 (29% from fat); FAT 2.7g (sat 0.4g, mono 1.7g, poly 0.4g); PROTEIN 2.9g; CARB 14g; FIBER 4.8g; CHOL 0mg; IRON 1.6mg; SODIUM 109mg; CALC 65mg

Green Beans with
Roasted Onion Vinaigrette

189

Boston Baked Beans

(pictured on page 184)

Molasses was first shipped to Boston from the West Indies in the late 1600s and soon became a signature flavor in this New England recipe.

   1   cup chopped onion
   ½   cup ketchup
   ½   cup maple syrup
   2   tablespoons light brown sugar
   2   tablespoons molasses
   1   teaspoon dry mustard
   ½   teaspoon salt
   ¼   teaspoon ground allspice
   ⅛   teaspoon ground ginger
   3   (15-ounce) cans small white beans, rinsed and drained
   4   bacon slices, uncooked and chopped

1. Combine all ingredients in an electric slow cooker. Cover and cook on LOW 5 hours. **YIELD:** 10 servings (serving size: ½ cup).

CALORIES 141 (7% from fat); FAT 1.1g (sat 0.2g, mono 0.2g, poly 0.2g); PROTEIN 5.8g; CARB 32.4g; FIBER 4g; CHOL 2mg; IRON 1.5mg; SODIUM 531mg; CALC 64mg

Country Lima Beans

Humble ingredients create a flavorful, satisfying dish. Oven cooking works well and makes preparation a snap. Serve as a side with roast beef, pork, or chicken; or you can even enjoy this as a main dish with a simple green salad.

   2   cups dried lima beans (about 1 pound)
   1   teaspoon salt
   ½   teaspoon freshly ground black pepper
   3   bacon slices, chopped
   1   cup chopped onion
   1   cup finely chopped carrot
   2   cups water
   2   tablespoons butter, softened

1. Sort and wash beans; place in a large Dutch oven. Cover with water to 2 inches above beans; cover and let stand 8 hours or overnight. Drain beans. Return beans to pan; stir in salt and black pepper.
2. Preheat oven to 300°.

3. Cook bacon slices in a large nonstick skillet over medium heat until crisp. Remove bacon from pan with a slotted spoon; set bacon aside. Add onion and carrot to drippings in pan; sauté 5 minutes or until golden. Add onion mixture, bacon, 2 cups water, and butter to bean mixture in Dutch oven; stir well. Cover and bake at 300° for 2½ hours or until beans are tender, stirring every hour. **YIELD:** 8 cups (serving size: 1 cup).

CALORIES 248 (26% from fat); FAT 7.2g (sat 2.8g, mono 2.9g, poly 0.8g); PROTEIN 11.8g; CARB 35.4g; FIBER 11.2g; CHOL 13mg; IRON 3.3mg; SODIUM 404mg; CALC 53mg

Broccoli with Pan-Roasted Peppers

This colorful side dish is a fine way to perk up a weeknight rotisserie chicken dinner.

   4   cups broccoli florets (about 1½ pounds)
   1   tablespoon olive oil
   1¾ cups (1-inch) red bell pepper strips (2 medium)
   1¾ cups (1-inch) yellow bell pepper strips (2 medium)
   ¼   cup red wine vinegar
   1   teaspoon sugar
   ¾   teaspoon salt
   ¼   teaspoon freshly ground black pepper

1. Cook broccoli in boiling water 4 minutes or until crisp-tender, and drain. Rinse with cold water; drain.
2. Heat oil in a large nonstick skillet over medium-high heat. Add bell peppers and red wine vinegar. Cover, reduce heat to medium, and cook 15 minutes or until peppers are tender, stirring frequently. Uncover; sprinkle with sugar. Increase heat to medium-high; cook 2 minutes or until liquid evaporates and bell peppers begin to brown, stirring constantly. Add broccoli; cook 2 minutes or until thoroughly heated, tossing to combine. Remove from heat, and stir in salt and black pepper. **YIELD:** 6 servings (serving size: 1 cup).

CALORIES 65 (39% from fat); FAT 2.8g (sat 0.4g, mono 1.7g, poly 0.5g); PROTEIN 2.5g; CARB 9.9g; FIBER 1.4g; CHOL 0mg; IRON 1mg; SODIUM 311mg, CALC 31mg

Broccoli with Cheddar Sauce

This classic side dish is quick and easy. Steaming for the appropriate time ensures the broccoli is properly crisp-tender.

1   tablespoon all-purpose flour
1   cup fat-free milk
½   cup (2 ounces) shredded reduced-fat extrasharp
    Cheddar cheese
3   tablespoons grated fresh Parmesan cheese
½   teaspoon Dijon mustard
¼   teaspoon salt
¼   teaspoon freshly ground black pepper
¼   teaspoon chopped fresh thyme
1½ pounds broccoli florets (about 9 cups)

1. Place flour in a medium saucepan. Gradually add milk, stirring constantly with a whisk until smooth. Cook over medium-high heat 2 minutes or until mixture is bubbly and thickened, stirring constantly. Cook 1 additional minute, stirring constantly. Remove from heat. Add cheeses, mustard, salt, pepper, and thyme, stirring with a whisk until smooth. Keep warm.

2. Add water to a large saucepan to a depth of 1 inch; set a large vegetable steamer in pan. Bring water to a boil over medium-high heat. Add broccoli to steamer. Steam broccoli, covered, 4 minutes or until crisp-tender. Serve broccoli immediately with sauce. **YIELD:** 8 servings (serving size: about 1 cup broccoli and 2 tablespoons sauce).

CALORIES 69 (30% from fat); FAT 2.3g (sat 1.4g, mono 0.6g, poly 0.2g); PROTEIN 6.2g; CARB 7.1g; FIBER 2.5g; CHOL 7mg; IRON 0.8mg; SODIUM 204mg; CALC 143mg

Corn Fritter Casserole

Corn Fritter Casserole

This moist, sweet-savory side dish is a cross between corn bread and corn pudding.

    3 tablespoons butter, softened
    3 large egg whites
    1 (8-ounce) block fat-free cream cheese, softened
    ½ cup finely chopped onion
    ½ cup finely chopped red bell pepper
    1 (15¼-ounce) can whole-kernel corn, drained
    1 (14¾-ounce) can cream-style corn
    1 (8½-ounce) package corn muffin mix
    ¼ teaspoon black pepper
    Cooking spray

1. Preheat oven to 375°.
2. Combine first 3 ingredients in a large bowl, stirring with a whisk until smooth. Stir in onion, bell pepper, whole-kernel corn, and cream-style corn; mix well. Add muffin mix and black pepper, stirring until well combined. Pour into an 11 x 7–inch baking dish coated with cooking spray. Bake at 375° for 50 minutes or until a wooden pick inserted in center comes out clean. **YIELD:** 9 servings (serving size: about ⅔ cup).

CALORIES 247 (31% from fat); FAT 8.4g (sat 3.7g, mono 2.7g, poly 0.7g); PROTEIN 8.6g; CARB 36.7g; FIBER 1.9g; CHOL 31mg; IRON 1.3mg; SODIUM 629mg; CALC 72mg

Roasted Cauliflower with Fresh Herbs and Parmesan

Use any fresh herbs you have on hand for this recipe. While parsley, tarragon, and thyme make a nice combination, you can also try sage, chives, and rosemary. The recipe can easily be halved.

    12 cups cauliflower florets (about 2 heads)
    1½ tablespoons olive oil
    1 tablespoon chopped fresh parsley
    2 teaspoons chopped fresh thyme
    2 teaspoons chopped fresh tarragon
    3 garlic cloves, minced
    ¼ cup (1 ounce) grated fresh Parmesan cheese
    2 tablespoons fresh lemon juice
    ½ teaspoon salt
    ¼ teaspoon pepper

1. Preheat oven to 450°.

2. Place cauliflower in a large roasting pan or jelly-roll pan. Drizzle with oil; toss well to coat. Bake at 450° for 20 minutes or until tender and browned, stirring every 5 minutes. Sprinkle with parsley, thyme, tarragon, and garlic. Bake an additional 5 minutes. Combine cauliflower mixture, Parmesan cheese, and remaining ingredients in a large bowl; toss well to combine. **YIELD:** 8 servings (serving size: about 1 cup).

CALORIES 89 (35% from fat); FAT 3.5g (sat 0.8g, mono 2.1g, poly 0.4g); PROTEIN 5.2g; CARB 12.1g; FIBER 5.4g; CHOL 2mg; IRON 1.1mg; SODIUM 251mg; CALC 83mg

Fresh Corn Bread Pudding

Simple ingredients render this side dish versatile enough to serve for breakfast with country ham or as part of an elegant dinner with filet mignon and asparagus.

    1 (¾-pound) loaf country-style bread
    2 teaspoons butter
    3 cups fresh corn kernels (about 6 ears)
    3 garlic cloves, minced
    3 cups fat-free milk
    2 large eggs
    4 large egg whites
    1 teaspoon salt
    ¼ teaspoon freshly ground black pepper
    1¼ cups (5 ounces) shredded sharp Cheddar cheese
    Cooking spray

1. Preheat oven to 300°.
2. Trim crust from bread; discard crust. Cut bread into 2-inch cubes. Place bread cubes on a baking sheet. Bake at 300° for 30 minutes or until bread is toasted, turning occasionally.
3. Increase oven temperature to 425°.
4. Heat butter in a large nonstick skillet over medium-high heat. Add corn and garlic to pan; cook 4 minutes or until lightly browned, stirring occasionally. Combine milk, eggs, 1 teaspoon salt, and ¼ teaspoon black pepper in a large bowl, stirring with a whisk.
5. Add corn mixture and cheese to milk mixture; stir to combine. Fold in bread cubes.
6. Pour corn mixture into a 2-quart baking dish coated with cooking spray; let stand 10 minutes. Bake at 425° for 40 minutes or until puffed and set. **YIELD:** 8 servings (serving size: 1 cup).

CALORIES 314 (26% from fat); FAT 9.1g (sat 3.6g, mono 1.7g, poly 2.6g); PROTEIN 18.7g; CARB 42.3g; FIBER 3.8g; CHOL 62mg; IRON 2.2mg; SODIUM 609 mg; CALC 285 mg

Grilled Corn with
Creamy Chipotle Sauce

Grilled Corn with Creamy Chipotle Sauce

Instead of butter, try this smoky, spicy sauce—it's a savory complement to the sweet corn. To remove the silks from an ear of corn, rub with a damp paper towel or a damp, soft-bristled toothbrush. Though the corn needs to be grilled at the last minute, the sauce can be prepared a day ahead.

    ¼ teaspoon salt
    1 chipotle chile, canned in adobo sauce
    1 garlic clove
    ½ cup 2% reduced-fat cottage cheese
    2 tablespoons light mayonnaise
    2 tablespoons plain fat-free yogurt
    6 ears shucked corn
    Cooking spray

1. Prepare grill.
2. Place first 3 ingredients in a food processor; process until minced. Add cottage cheese; process until smooth, scraping sides of bowl occasionally. Add mayonnaise and yogurt; process until blended. Spoon sauce into a bowl; cover and chill.
3. Place corn on grill rack coated with cooking spray. Grill 10 minutes, turning frequently. Serve corn with sauce. **YIELD:** 6 servings (serving size: 1 ear of corn and 2 tablespoons sauce).

CALORIES 116 (25% from fat); FAT 3.2g (sat 0.7g, mono 0.7g, poly 1.5g); PROTEIN 5.7g; CARB 19g; FIBER 2.5g; CHOL 3.3mg; IRON 0.5mg; SODIUM 245mg; CALC 23mg

Basic Lentils

Try this simple yet versatile dish with chicken, fish, or as part of a vegetable plate. You can substitute low-sodium vegetable broth for a vegetarian version.

    2   cups dried lentils
    1½ cups chopped onion
    1½ cups water
    1   cup chopped celery
    1   cup chopped carrot
    1   tablespoon extravirgin olive oil
    1   teaspoon salt
    ½   teaspoon freshly ground black pepper
    2   (14-ounce) cans fat-free, less-sodium chicken broth
    2   bay leaves

1. Combine all ingredients in an electric slow cooker. Cover and cook on LOW 5 hours or until tender. Discard bay leaves. **YIELD:** 12 servings (serving size: ½ cup).

CALORIES 143 (10% from fat); FAT 1.6g (sat 0.2g, mono 1g, poly 0.3g); PROTEIN 9.3g; CARB 22.9g; FIBER 10.8g; CHOL 0mg; IRON 2.7mg; SODIUM 319mg; CALC 34mg

New Orleans Okra

Onion, celery, and green bell pepper are used so often in Louisiana that locals call them "the trinity." Here they're combined with another local staple: okra.

    1   tablespoon olive oil
    2   cups chopped onion
    ½   cup minced celery
    ½   cup minced green bell pepper
    1   tablespoon tomato paste
    2   (14.5-ounce) cans diced tomatoes, undrained
    ½   teaspoon ground red pepper
    1½   pounds small okra pods, trimmed and cut into
         ½-inch slices
    ¼   teaspoon salt

1. Heat oil in a Dutch oven over medium-high heat. Add onion; sauté 5 minutes. Add celery, bell pepper, and tomato paste; cook 2 minutes. Stir in diced tomatoes and red pepper; cook 10 minutes or until sauce thickens. Add okra pods. Cover, reduce heat, and simmer 20 minutes or until okra pods are tender. Stir in salt. **YIELD:** 8 servings (serving size: ¾ cup).

CALORIES 101 (16% from fat); FAT 1.9g (sat 0.3g, mono 1.3g, poly 0.2g); PROTEIN 4g; CARB 20.3g; FIBER 5.2g; CHOL 0mg; IRON 1.2mg; SODIUM 499mg; CALC 149mg

ORGANIC TIP

A fun way to get local, seasonal organic produce at a reasonable price is to join a CSA (Community Sponsored Agriculture) group. Fresh organic produce can be delivered to your door on a regular basis, often with recipes to encourage you to try unfamiliar produce and new dishes.

Fresh Peas with Pancetta

Fresh Peas with Pancetta

Avoid the temptation to substitute regular bacon for the pancetta because bacon's smoky quality will overwhelm the delicate flavor of the peas. The season for fresh baby peas is short; if you miss it, frozen will work in this dish.

 3 slices pancetta, chopped (about 1 ounce)
 ¾ cup finely chopped white onion
 1 garlic clove, minced
 3 cups shelled green peas or frozen petite green peas
 1 cup fat-free, less-sodium chicken broth
 2 teaspoons sugar
 ¼ teaspoon salt
 ¼ cup chopped fresh flat-leaf parsley

1. Heat a large nonstick skillet over medium-high heat. Add pancetta; sauté 5 minutes or until crispy. Remove pancetta from pan, reserving drippings in pan. Add onion and garlic to pan; sauté 2 minutes or until tender. Add peas, broth, sugar, and salt to pan. Simmer 5 minutes or until peas are tender, stirring occasionally. Stir in pancetta and chopped parsley. **YIELD:** 6 servings (serving size: ½ cup).

CALORIES 153 (23% from fat); FAT 3.9g (sat 1.6g, mono 0.1g, poly 0.2g); PROTEIN 8.4g; CARB 21.6g; FIBER 6.4g; CHOL 8mg; IRON 2mg; SODIUM 425mg; CALC 44mg

Okra-Pepper Sauté

 2 teaspoons butter
 1 cup yellow bell pepper strips
 1 cup red bell pepper strips
 3 cups okra pods, cut in half diagonally
   (about ½ pound)
 2 tablespoons chopped fresh cilantro
 ¼ teaspoon salt
 ¼ teaspoon black pepper

1. Heat butter in a large nonstick skillet over medium heat. Add bell peppers, and sauté 4 minutes. Add okra; cover, reduce heat, and cook 15 minutes or until okra is tender. Stir in cilantro, ¼ teaspoon salt, and black pepper. **YIELD:** 4 servings (serving size: ¾ cup).

CALORIES 52 (38% from fat); FAT 2.2g (sat 1.3g, mono 0.6g, poly 0.2g); PROTEIN 1.6g; CARB 7.2g; FIBER 1.4g; CHOL 5mg; IRON 1.2mg; SODIUM 173mg; CALC 53mg

Sherry-Braised Roasted Peppers

Serve this versatile side dish with flank steak or chicken, or toss it with pasta. Keep leftovers in the refrigerator for a few days. Reheat in the microwave, or serve at room temperature.

 2 large green bell peppers (about 1 pound)
 2 large red bell peppers (about 1 pound)
 2 large yellow bell peppers (about 1 pound)
 1 tablespoon olive oil
 2 tablespoons capers
 1 teaspoon minced fresh rosemary
 1 teaspoon minced fresh thyme
 2 large garlic cloves, minced
 2 tablespoons medium dry sherry
 ¼ teaspoon salt

1. Preheat broiler.
2. Cut peppers in half lengthwise; discard seeds and membranes. Place pepper halves, skin sides up, on a foil-lined baking sheet; flatten with hand. Broil 15 minutes or until blackened. Place in a zip-top plastic bag; seal. Let stand 15 minutes. Peel and cut pepper halves into ½-inch-wide strips.
3. Heat oil in a large nonstick skillet over medium-high heat. Add capers, rosemary, thyme, and garlic; sauté 1 minute. Reduce heat to medium. Add sherry; cook 1 minute. Add pepper strips and salt; cook 2 minutes or until thoroughly heated. Serve warm or at room temperature. **YIELD:** 6 servings (serving size: ½ cup).

CALORIES 70 (33% from fat); FAT 2.6g (sat 0.4g, mono 1.7g, poly 0.4g); PROTEIN 1.6g; CARB 11.1g; FIBER 2.3g; CHOL 0mg; IRON 0.9mg; SODIUM 186mg; CALC 19mg

ORGANIC TIP

"Something curious has happened to a lot of our fresh produce, which is that it has [fewer] nutrients in it than it did in 1950 and 1960, and nobody knows why." More nutrient-rich organic produce can help make up the difference.

Source: Michael Pollan

Camembert
Mashed Potatoes

Camembert Mashed Potatoes

The buttery taste and creamy texture of Camembert cheese glorifies these potatoes. The rind is easiest to remove if the cheese is well chilled.

1½ (8-ounce) rounds Camembert cheese
11 cups cubed peeled Yukon gold potato (about 4½ pounds)
½ cup 1% low-fat milk
¾ teaspoon salt
¾ teaspoon freshly ground black pepper
Chopped fresh chives (optional)
Freshly ground black pepper (optional)

1. Cut cheese into 6 wedges. Carefully remove rind from cheese; discard rind. Chop cheese; let stand at room temperature while potato cooks.
2. Place potato in a large Dutch oven; cover with water. Bring to a boil. Reduce heat; simmer 12 minutes or until tender. Drain in a colander; return potato to pan. Add cheese, milk, salt, and ¾ teaspoon pepper; mash with a potato masher to desired consistency. Garnish with chives and additional pepper, if desired. **YIELD:** 12 servings (serving size: about ⅔ cup).

CALORIES 198 (20% from fat); FAT 4.4g (sat 2.8g, mono 1.3g, poly 0.1g); PROTEIN 7.9g; CARB 30.7g; FIBER 2g; CHOL 13mg; IRON 1.5mg; SODIUM 310mg; CALC 82mg

Mashed Potatoes with Green Onions

Using a slow cooker to prepare the potatoes reduces the chance of them boiling over on the stove top. It also decreases the chance of them overcooking.

¾ cup water
3 tablespoons butter, divided
2 pounds baking potatoes, peeled and cut into ½-inch cubes (about 4½ cups)
¾ cup fat-free milk
½ cup chopped green onions
1 teaspoon salt
⅛ teaspoon freshly ground black pepper

1. Combine ¾ cup water, 2 tablespoons butter, and potato in an electric slow cooker. Cover and cook on HIGH 3 hours or until tender.
2. Stir in remaining 1 tablespoon butter and remaining ingredients; mash with a potato masher to desired consistency. **YIELD:** 10 servings (serving size: ½ cup).

CALORIES 123 (26% from fat); FAT 3.5g (sat 2.2g, mono 0.9g, poly 0.2g); PROTEIN 2.4g; CARB 20.9g; FIBER 1.6g; CHOL 9mg; IRON 0.3mg; SODIUM 274mg; CALC 33mg

ORGANIC RESOURCE

The Organic Farming Research Foundation (OFRF) was established to foster the improvement and widespread adoption of organic farming systems. It provides grant money to research better organic farming techniques.

Source: Organic Farming Research Foundation

Spicy Roasted Potatoes and Asparagus

We've simplified cooking for two by combining menu items in one dish. Move the potatoes to one side of the dish before you add the asparagus so the spears can cook in a single, even layer. Watch the spears closely, especially if they're thin.

  2 teaspoons olive oil, divided
  ¼ teaspoon sea salt, divided
  ¼ teaspoon chopped fresh or ⅛ teaspoon dried thyme
  ⅛ teaspoon freshly ground black pepper
  ⅛ teaspoon crushed red pepper
  6 small red potatoes (about ¾ pound), quartered
Cooking spray
  2 tablespoons grated fresh Parmesan cheese
  1 teaspoon minced garlic, divided
  ½ pound asparagus spears

1. Preheat oven to 450°.
2. Combine 1 teaspoon oil, ⅛ teaspoon salt, thyme, peppers, and potato in an 11 x 7–inch baking dish coated with cooking spray. Bake at 450° for 20 minutes, stirring occasionally. Stir in cheese and ½ teaspoon garlic.
3. Snap off tough ends of asparagus. Combine remaining 1 teaspoon oil, ⅛ teaspoon salt, ½ teaspoon garlic, and asparagus. Add asparagus mixture to dish. Bake 10 minutes or until asparagus is crisp-tender. **YIELD:** 2 servings.

CALORIES 223 (27% from fat); FAT 6.8g (sat 1.9g, mono 3.9g, poly 0.6g); PROTEIN 9.1g; CARB 34.2g; FIBER 4.6g; CHOL 5mg; IRON 3.6mg; SODIUM 419mg; CALC 136mg

ORGANIC FACT
Instead of spraying pesticides on fruits and vegetables, some organic farmers use ladybugs to eat aphids, scales, and mealybugs. One adult ladybug can eat as many as 50,000 aphids.

Walnut-Crusted Potato and Blue Cheese Cakes

To avoid dirtying another dish, mash the potatoes in the same pot you use to cook them. The cakes can be shaped a few hours ahead, covered, and chilled until you're ready to eat. After chilling, cook them in the pan for an extra minute to make sure the insides of the cakes are thoroughly heated.

  2 pounds small red potatoes, halved
  1 garlic clove, peeled
  ⅓ cup (about 1½ ounces) crumbled blue cheese
  ¼ cup 1% low-fat milk
  1 tablespoon chopped fresh parsley
  ¾ teaspoon salt
  ¼ teaspoon freshly ground black pepper
  3 tablespoons chopped walnuts
  2 (1½-ounce) slices sourdough bread
  1 tablespoon olive oil, divided

1. Place potato halves and garlic in a large saucepan; cover with water. Bring to a boil; reduce heat, and simmer 20 minutes or until tender. Drain. Return potato halves and garlic to pan. Add blue cheese and next 4 ingredients; mash with a potato masher until desired consistency. Cool slightly. Shape potato mixture into 12 (½-inch-thick) cakes; set aside.
2. Place walnuts and bread in a food processor; pulse 10 times or until coarse crumbs form. Place in a shallow bowl or pie plate. Dredge cakes in breadcrumb mixture.
3. Heat 1½ teaspoons oil in a large nonstick skillet over medium heat. Add 6 cakes, and cook 2 minutes on each side or until browned. Remove cakes from pan; cover and keep warm. Repeat procedure with remaining 1½ teaspoons oil and 6 cakes. **YIELD:** 6 servings (serving size: 2 potato cakes).

CALORIES 219 (30% from fat); FAT 7.4g (sat 2g, mono 2.6g, poly 2.2g); PROTEIN 6.7g; CARB 32.5g; FIBER 3.3g; CHOL 6mg; IRON 1.9mg; SODIUM 489mg; CALC 84mg

Potato-Peanut Cakes

Fresh corn teams with buttery Yukon gold potatoes and chopped peanuts in these patties. Preheat the griddle before coating with cooking spray so the patties will brown nicely. Serve with a grilled steak and coleslaw.

¾ pound Yukon gold potatoes
1 bacon slice
1 cup fresh corn kernels (about 2 ears)
¼ cup finely chopped onion
¼ cup finely chopped red bell pepper
1 teaspoon chopped fresh thyme
¼ cup sliced green onions
¼ cup chopped peanuts
½ teaspoon salt
1 large egg, lightly beaten
Cooking spray
Chopped fresh thyme (optional)

1. Place potatoes in a saucepan; cover with water. Bring to a boil; reduce heat, and simmer 15 minutes or until tender. Drain and cool. Shred potatoes into a large bowl.
2. Cook bacon in a large nonstick skillet over medium heat until crisp. Remove bacon from pan; crumble. Add corn, onion, bell pepper, and 1 teaspoon thyme to drippings in pan; cook 4 minutes or until onion is tender.
3. Combine potato, bacon, corn mixture, green onions, peanuts, salt, and egg; stir with a fork until well blended.
4. Heat a nonstick griddle or skillet over medium-high heat. Coat griddle with cooking spray. Spoon about ⅓ cup potato mixture onto hot griddle; flatten slightly with a spatula. Cook 5 minutes on each side or until golden brown. Garnish with thyme, if desired. **YIELD:** 8 servings (serving size: 1 cake).

CALORIES 110 (40% from fat); FAT 4.9g (sat 1.1g, mono 2.2g, poly 1.2g); PROTEIN 3.9g; CARB 14g; FIBER 1.9g; CHOL 28mg; IRON 1mg; SODIUM 183mg; CALC 16mg

Two-Potato Latkes

Two-Potato Latkes

You can use a food processor's shredding blade for fast preparation. Serve the latkes with applesauce and sour cream. Even though these are traditionally served during Hanukkah, you'll want to enjoy them year-round.

    2 tablespoons olive oil
    ¼ cup grated fresh onion
    1 pound shredded peeled baking potato
    ½ pound shredded peeled sweet potato
    ½ cup all-purpose flour (about 2¼ ounces)
    ⅓ cup finely chopped green onions
    ½ teaspoon salt
    ¼ teaspoon freshly ground black pepper
    1 garlic clove, minced
    1 large egg, lightly beaten
 Cooking spray
 Green onion strips (optional)

1. Preheat oven to 425°.
2. Drizzle a jelly-roll pan evenly with olive oil, tilting pan to coat.
3. Combine grated onion and potato in a sieve; squeeze out excess moisture. Lightly spoon flour into a dry measuring cup; level with a knife. Combine potato mixture, flour, and next 5 ingredients in a large bowl. Divide mixture into 8 equal portions, squeezing out excess liquid. Shape each portion into a ¼-inch-thick patty; place on prepared pan. Lightly coat tops of patties with cooking spray. Bake at 425° for 12 minutes. Carefully turn patties over; cook 30 minutes or until lightly browned, turning every 10 minutes. Garnish with green onion strips, if desired. **YIELD:** 4 servings (serving size: 2 latkes).

CALORIES 256 (29% from fat); FAT 8.3g (sat 1.4g, mono 5.5g, poly 1g); PROTEIN 5.7g; CARB 40g; FIBER 4g; CHOL 53mg; IRON 1.7mg; SODIUM 337mg; CALC 38mg

ORGANIC FACT
Potatoes are one of the top 12 produce items that contain traces of pesticides, so be sure to incorporate organic potatoes when preparing a meal. See "The Dirty Dozen" on page 14.

Source: Environmental Working Group

Winter Greens and Potato Casserole

Earthy kale, mustard greens, and potatoes make this hearty dish a comfort on a cold winter night. Provolone cheese is not typically used in an Appalachian dish, but we enjoyed its pronounced flavor. Use any kind of cheese you like.

    8 cups water
   12 cups chopped kale, stems removed (about ½ pound)
   12 cups chopped mustard greens, stems removed (about ½ pound)
    6 cups (⅛-inch-thick) slices red potatoes (about 2 pounds), divided
 Cooking spray
    2 cups vertically sliced onion, divided
    ¾ teaspoon salt, divided
    1 cup (4 ounces) shredded sharp provolone cheese, divided
    ½ cup canned vegetable broth

1. Preheat oven to 350°.
2. Bring water to a boil in a Dutch oven. Add kale and mustard greens, and cook 5 minutes or until tender, stirring occasionally. Drain; set aside.
3. Arrange 2 cups potato slices in a single layer in a 13 x 9-inch baking dish coated with cooking spray; top with 1 cup onion. Sprinkle with ¼ teaspoon salt; top with half of kale mixture. Sprinkle kale mixture with ½ cup cheese. Repeat layers once, ending with the kale mixture. Top kale mixture with remaining 2 cups potatoes, and sprinkle with remaining ½ cup cheese. Pour broth evenly over potato mixture, and sprinkle with remaining ¼ teaspoon salt. Cover with foil. Bake at 350° for 45 minutes. Uncover and bake 30 minutes or until lightly browned and potatoes are tender. **YIELD:** 8 servings.

CALORIES 170 (27% from fat); FAT 5.1g (sat 2.6g, mono 1.5g, poly 0.4g); PROTEIN 7.9g; CARB 25.2g; FIBER 4g; CHOL 14mg; IRON 1.9mg; SODIUM 472mg; CALC 191mg

Mashed Sweet Potatoes with Pecan Butter

This side dish tastes like the traditional streusel-topped sweet potato casserole but is much simpler to prepare with the help of the microwave. It can easily be multiplied to serve more.

  2 medium sweet potatoes (about 1 pound)
  3 tablespoons 1% low-fat milk
  2 tablespoons brown sugar, divided
 ⅛ teaspoon salt
  1 tablespoon butter, softened
  1 tablespoon chopped pecans, toasted
 ⅛ teaspoon ground cinnamon

1. Pierce potatoes with a fork; arrange on paper towels in microwave oven. Microwave potatoes at HIGH 10 minutes, rearranging potatoes after 5 minutes. Wrap potatoes in a towel; let stand 5 minutes. Scoop out pulp; discard skins. Combine pulp, milk, 1 tablespoon brown sugar, and salt in a medium bowl; mash.
2. Combine remaining 1 tablespoon brown sugar, butter, pecans, and cinnamon in a small bowl. Top each serving with pecan mixture. **YIELD:** 2 servings (serving size: ¾ cup potatoes and 1 tablespoon pecan mixture).

CALORIES 299 (27% from fat); FAT 9g (sat 4.1g, mono 3.3g, poly 1.1g); PROTEIN 3.9g; CARB 52g; FIBER 5.4g; CHOL 16mg; IRON 1.4mg; SODIUM 237mg; CALC 78mg

ORGANIC FACT
Organic farmers are allowed to use pesticides (but not toxic synthetic pesticides) if other means of pest control fail. Plant-derived botanicals have the advantage of breaking down quickly by oxygen and sunlight.

Source: The Organic Center

Asiago, Potato, and Bacon Gratin

Remember this secret when cooking potatoes: Instead of salting the water they boil in, sprinkle the potatoes with salt after draining for the most pronounced flavor.

 1½ pounds peeled Yukon gold potatoes, cut into ¼-inch-thick slices
  1 teaspoon salt, divided
Cooking spray
  2 tablespoons minced shallots
 ¼ cup all-purpose flour (about 1 ounce)
  2 cups 1% low-fat milk, divided
 ¾ cup (3 ounces) grated Asiago cheese
 ¼ cup chopped fresh chives
 ¼ teaspoon freshly ground black pepper
  4 bacon slices, cooked and crumbled
 ¼ cup (1 ounce) grated fresh Parmesan cheese

1. Preheat oven to 350°.
2. Place potato in a large saucepan; cover with water. Bring to a boil. Reduce heat, and simmer 5 minutes or until almost tender. Drain. Sprinkle potatoes evenly with ¼ teaspoon salt; set aside, and keep warm.
3. Heat a medium saucepan over medium heat. Coat pan with cooking spray. Add shallots; cook 2 minutes or until tender, stirring frequently. Lightly spoon flour into a dry measuring cup; level with a knife. Sprinkle flour over shallots. Gradually add ½ cup milk, stirring with a whisk until well blended. Gradually add remaining 1½ cups milk, stirring with a whisk. Cook over medium heat 9 minutes or until thick, stirring frequently. Remove from heat; stir in ¾ teaspoon salt, Asiago, chives, pepper, and bacon.
4. Arrange half of potato slices in an 8-inch square baking dish coated with cooking spray. Pour half of cheese sauce over potato slices. Top with remaining potato slices and cheese sauce; sprinkle with Parmesan cheese. Bake at 350° for 35 minutes or until cheese is bubbly and lightly browned. **YIELD:** 6 servings.

CALORIES 250 (30% from fat); FAT 8.2g (sat 4.6g, mono 2.7g, poly 0.5g); PROTEIN 12.3g; CARB 31.9g; FIBER 2.3g; CHOL 23mg; IRON 0.9mg; SODIUM 618mg; CALC 306mg

Wild Mushroom–and–Sweet Potato Gratin

Chanterelle mushrooms and fontina cheese contribute a delicate, nutty flavor that contrasts nicely with the sweet potatoes in this dish. Serve with roasted pork loin or ham.

2   teaspoons olive oil
4   cups (¼-inch-thick) slices cremini mushrooms (about 8 ounces)
3½ cups (¼-inch-thick) slices chanterelle mushrooms (about 8 ounces)
⅓   cup finely chopped shallots
½   teaspoon kosher salt, divided
½   teaspoon black pepper, divided
1½ tablespoons finely chopped fresh parsley, divided
1½ tablespoons chopped fresh chives, divided
4   cups peeled sweet potatoes, cut into ¼-inch-thick slices (about 1½ pounds)
Cooking spray
1   cup (4 ounces) shredded fontina cheese
½   cup fat-free, less-sodium chicken broth

1. Preheat oven to 425°.

2. Heat oil in a large skillet over medium-high heat. Add mushrooms, shallots, ¼ teaspoon salt, and ¼ teaspoon pepper; sauté 5 minutes or until moisture evaporates, stirring frequently. Remove from heat; stir in 1 tablespoon parsley and 1 tablespoon chives.

3. Arrange half of potato slices in a single layer in an 11 x 7–inch baking dish coated with cooking spray; sprinkle with ⅛ teaspoon salt and ⅛ teaspoon pepper. Spoon half of mushroom mixture over potato slices; sprinkle with half of cheese. Repeat layers, ending with cheese; add broth to dish. Cover and bake at 425° for 30 minutes. Uncover and bake an additional 20 minutes or until potato is tender. Sprinkle with remaining parsley and chives. **YIELD:** 8 servings.

CALORIES 193 (28% from fat); FAT 6.1g (sat 3g, mono 2.3g, poly 0.6g); PROTEIN 8g; CARB 26.8g; FIBER 4.7g; CHOL 17mg; IRON 1.6mg; SODIUM 282mg; CALC 110mg

Spicy Grilled Sweet Potatoes

Fast, easy, and economical, this recipe is nice as an "out of the ordinary" side dish. It has good zesty flavor.

 ¾ teaspoon ground cumin
 ½ teaspoon garlic powder
 ¼ teaspoon salt
 ⅛ teaspoon ground red pepper
 1 tablespoon olive oil
 1 pound peeled sweet potatoes, cut into ¼-inch-thick slices
 Cooking spray
 2 tablespoons chopped fresh cilantro

1. Combine first 4 ingredients in a small bowl.
2. Combine olive oil and sliced sweet potatoes in a medium bowl; toss to coat. Heat a large grill pan over medium heat. Coat pan with cooking spray. Add potato; cook 10 minutes, turning occasionally. Place potato in a bowl; sprinkle with cumin mixture and cilantro, tossing gently to coat. **YIELD:** 4 servings (serving size: ½ cup).

CALORIES 157 (25% from fat); FAT 4.3g (sat 0.6g, mono 2.7g, poly 0.7g); PROTEIN 2g; CARB 28.1g; FIBER 3.5g; CHOL 0mg; IRON 1.1mg; SODIUM 163mg; CALC 31mg

Sweet Potatoes in Picante Sauce

This Latin American dish is often made using a tropical sweet potato known as a boniato.

 1 tablespoon olive oil
 ½ cup minced celery
 ½ teaspoon crushed fennel seeds
 2 garlic cloves, minced
 ¾ cup finely chopped onion
 1 teaspoon salt
 ½ teaspoon ground turmeric
 ¼ teaspoon paprika
 1 dried red chile, crumbled (about ¼ ounce)
 6 cups (1½-inch) cubed peeled sweet potatoes (about 2 pounds)
 ½ cup water
 1 tablespoon chopped fresh cilantro

1. Heat oil in a Dutch oven over medium heat. Add celery, fennel, and garlic; cook 1 minute, stirring constantly. Add chopped onion and next 4 ingredients; cook 10 minutes, stirring frequently. Add potato and water; bring to a boil. Cover, reduce heat, and simmer 35 minutes or until potato is tender. Sprinkle with cilantro. **YIELD:** 10 servings (serving size: 1 cup).

CALORIES 105 (15% from fat); FAT 1.7g (sat 0.3g, mono 1g, poly 0.3g); PROTEIN 1.7g; CARB 21.5g; FIBER 3g; CHOL 0mg; IRON 0.7mg; SODIUM 252mg; CALC 26mg

Sweet Potato Hash

To save time, precook the sweet potatoes in the microwave, and then add them to the skillet for last-minute browning with the sausage and onions.

 1½ pounds sweet potatoes, peeled and diced
 ⅓ cup water
 1½ teaspoons olive oil
 2 (1-ounce) links turkey breakfast sausage
 1¼ cups chopped onion
 ¾ teaspoon salt, divided
 1½ tablespoons maple syrup
 1 tablespoon water
 ¼ teaspoon black pepper
 ⅛ teaspoon ground nutmeg

1. Place sweet potato and ⅓ cup water in a large microwave-safe bowl. Cover with plastic wrap; microwave at HIGH 10 minutes or until tender. Carefully uncover; drain and keep warm.
2. Heat oil in a large nonstick skillet over medium-high heat. Remove casings from sausage. Add onion to pan; sauté 6 minutes or until tender. Add sausage and ¼ teaspoon salt; cook 4 minutes or until sausage is done, stirring to crumble. Stir in sweet potato, ½ teaspoon salt, and remaining ingredients. Cook until liquid is absorbed and sweet potato begins to brown (about 5 minutes). **YIELD:** 4 servings (serving size: about 1 cup).

CALORIES 200 (16% from fat); FAT 3.6g (sat 0.8g, mono 1.8g, poly 0.7g); PROTEIN 5.2g; CARB 37.8g; FIBER 4.5g; CHOL 11mg; IRON 1.2mg; SODIUM 571mg; CALC 43mg

Honey-Roasted Root Vegetables

Honey amplifies the natural sweetness of the oven-caramelized vegetables.

 2 cups coarsely chopped peeled sweet potato
 (about 1 large)
1½ cups coarsely chopped peeled turnip (about
 2 medium)
1½ cups coarsely chopped parsnip (about 2 medium)
1½ cups coarsely chopped carrot (about 2 medium)
 ¼ cup honey
 2 tablespoons olive oil
 ½ teaspoon salt
 3 shallots, halved
Cooking spray

1. Preheat oven to 450°.
2. Combine first 8 ingredients in a large bowl; toss to coat. Place vegetable mixture in a jelly-roll pan coated with cooking spray. Bake at 450° for 35 minutes or until vegetables are tender and begin to brown, stirring every 15 minutes. **YIELD:** 8 servings (serving size: ½ cup).

CALORIES 118 (27% from fat); FAT 3.5g (sat 0.5g, mono 2.5g, poly 0.4g); PROTEIN 1.3g; CARB 21.7g; FIBER 2.3g; CHOL 0mg; IRON 0.5mg; SODIUM 171mg; CALC 33mg

Spinach and Parmesan Fallen Soufflé

Cooking spray
2 tablespoons dry breadcrumbs
2 garlic cloves, minced
1 (10-ounce) package fresh spinach
1 cup 1% low-fat milk
1 tablespoon cornstarch
⅓ cup (about 1½ ounces) grated fresh Parmigiano-Reggiano cheese
¼ teaspoon salt
⅛ teaspoon freshly ground black pepper
⅛ teaspoon grated whole nutmeg
3 large egg whites
1 large egg

1. Preheat oven to 375°.
2. Lightly coat an 11 x 7–inch baking dish with cooking spray; dust with breadcrumbs. Set aside.
3. Heat a large nonstick skillet over medium heat. Coat pan with cooking spray. Add garlic; cook 20 seconds, stirring constantly. Add spinach; cook 3 minutes or until spinach wilts, stirring occasionally. Remove from heat; cool slightly. Place spinach mixture on several layers of heavy-duty paper towels; squeeze until barely moist. Place spinach mixture, milk, and cornstarch in a blender; process until smooth. Add cheese, salt, pepper, and nutmeg; pulse until well blended. Pour into a large bowl.
4. Place egg whites and egg in a large bowl; beat with a mixer at high speed 5 minutes or until tripled in volume. Gently fold one-fourth of mixture into spinach mixture; gently fold in remaining egg mixture (mixture will seem slightly thin). Spoon into baking dish; smooth top with a spatula. Bake at 375° for 35 minutes or until set in center. Cool 5 minutes on a wire rack before serving. **YIELD:** 6 servings.

CALORIES 92 (34% from fat); FAT 3.5g (sat 1.8g, mono 1g, poly 0.3g); PROTEIN 8.5g; CARB 7.3g; FIBER 1.2g; CHOL 42mg; IRON 1.7mg; SODIUM 326mg; CALC 193mg

Yellow Squash Gratin

Cooking spray
2 cups chopped onion
3 garlic cloves, minced
3 pounds yellow squash, halved lengthwise and cut into ¼-inch-thick slices (about 12 cups)
½ cup chopped fresh flat-leaf parsley
1½ teaspoons salt
1 teaspoon chopped fresh thyme
½ teaspoon freshly ground black pepper
3 cups cooked long-grain rice
¾ cup (3 ounces) grated Gruyère or Swiss cheese
3 large eggs, lightly beaten
1 (1-ounce) slice white bread
¼ cup (1 ounce) grated fresh Parmesan cheese
1 tablespoon butter, melted

1. Preheat oven to 375°.
2. Heat a Dutch oven over medium-high heat. Coat pan with cooking spray. Add onion; sauté 5 minutes or until tender. Add garlic; sauté 30 seconds. Add yellow squash; sauté 7 minutes or just until tender. Remove from heat; stir in parsley, salt, thyme, and pepper. Add cooked rice, Gruyère, and eggs to squash mixture, stirring until well combined. Spoon squash mixture into a 13 x 9–inch baking dish coated with cooking spray.
3. Place bread in a food processor; pulse 10 times or until fine crumbs measure ½ cup. Combine breadcrumbs, Parmesan, and butter, tossing to combine. Sprinkle breadcrumb mixture over squash mixture. Bake at 375° for 30 minutes or until topping is lightly browned and filling is set. Let stand 5 minutes before serving. **YIELD:** 8 servings.

CALORIES 247 (29% from fat); FAT 8g (sat 4.1g, mono 2.5g, poly 0.6g); PROTEIN 11.2g; CARB 32.4g; FIBER 4.9g; CHOL 98mg; IRON 2.4mg; SODIUM 599mg; CALC 220mg

Double-Squash Basmati Gratin

Basmati rice and feta cheese distinguish this updated squash-rice casserole from its classic counterpart.

  4 cups zucchini, halved lengthwise and thinly sliced (about 1¼ pounds)
  4 cups yellow squash, halved lengthwise and thinly sliced (about 1¼ pounds)
  2 cups thinly sliced leek (about 2 large)
  ¼ cup fat-free, less-sodium chicken broth
  1 teaspoon salt, divided
  1 teaspoon freshly ground black pepper, divided
  3 garlic cloves, minced
  1 cup fat-free sour cream
  ⅔ cup 1% low-fat milk
  2 large egg whites
  3 cups cooked basmati rice
  1 cup (4 ounces) crumbed feta cheese
  ½ cup (2 ounces) grated fresh Parmesan cheese
  ¼ cup chopped fresh parsley
  2 teaspoons chopped fresh oregano
Cooking spray
25 onion or garlic melba snack crackers
  2 tablespoons butter, melted

1. Preheat oven to 375°.
2. Combine zucchini, squash, leek, broth, ½ teaspoon salt, ½ teaspoon pepper, and garlic in a Dutch oven. Cover and cook over medium-high heat 20 minutes or until squash is very tender, stirring occasionally. Uncover and remove from heat; cool slightly.
3. Combine remaining ½ teaspoon salt, remaining ½ teaspoon pepper, sour cream, milk, and egg whites in a large bowl, stirring with a whisk. Add squash mixture, basmati rice, cheeses, parsley, and oregano; stir well to combine. Pour mixture into a 13 x 9–inch baking dish coated with cooking spray.
4. Place crackers in a food processor; process until coarsely ground. Drizzle with butter; pulse 3 times or until moist. Sprinkle crumb mixture evenly over rice mixture. Bake at 375° for 25 minutes or until bubbly around edges. Let stand 10 minutes. **YIELD:** 9 servings (serving size: about 1 cup).

CALORIES 251 (29% from fat); FAT 8.1g (sat 4.7g, mono 2.3g, poly 0.5g); PROTEIN 11g; CARB 34.1g; FIBER 2.4g; CHOL 25mg; IRON 2.1mg; SODIUM 656mg; CALC 246mg

Swiss Chard with Pine Nuts and Raisins

  1¼ pounds Swiss chard, trimmed
   2 tablespoons fresh lemon juice
  1½ teaspoons extravirgin olive oil
   ½ teaspoon salt
   ⅛ teaspoon freshly ground black pepper
   ½ cup golden raisins
   2 tablespoons pine nuts

1. Slice Swiss chard leaves crosswise into thin strips; place in a large bowl. Combine lemon juice, olive oil, salt, and pepper, stirring with a whisk. Drizzle juice mixture over chard; toss to coat. Add raisins and pine nuts; toss to combine. Let stand 15 minutes before serving.
YIELD: 4 servings (serving size: 1 cup).

CALORIES 111 (29% from fat); FAT 3.6g (sat 0.5g, mono 1.9g, poly 0.9g); PROTEIN 3.5g; CARB 19.8g; FIBER 2.7g; CHOL 0mg; IRON 2.7mg; SODIUM 391mg; CALC 69mg

Roasted Tomatoes with Shallots and Herbs

  4 medium tomatoes, cut in half horizontally (about 2 pounds)
  ½ teaspoon salt, divided
Cooking spray
  ¼ cup minced shallots
  1 tablespoon chopped fresh flat-leaf parsley
  1 teaspoon chopped fresh or ¼ teaspoon dried oregano
  1 teaspoon chopped fresh or ¼ teaspoon dried thyme
  ½ teaspoon chopped fresh or ⅛ teaspoon dried rosemary
  ¼ teaspoon freshly ground black pepper
  2 teaspoons olive oil

1. Preheat oven to 350°.
2. Core and seed tomato halves. Sprinkle cut sides of tomato halves with ¼ teaspoon salt. Place tomato halves, cut sides down, on paper towels. Let stand 20 minutes.
3. Place tomato halves, cut sides up, in a 13 x 9–inch baking dish coated with cooking spray. Sprinkle with remaining salt, shallots, and next 5 ingredients. Drizzle with oil. Bake at 350° for 1 hour and 15 minutes. **YIELD:** 8 servings (serving size: 1 tomato half).

CALORIES 38 (36% from fat); FAT 1.5g (sat 0.2g, mono 0.9g, poly 0.3g); PROTEIN 1.1g; CARB 6.2g; FIBER 1.3g; CHOL 0mg; IRON 0.6mg; SODIUM 121mg; CALC 10mg

Roasted Tomatoes with
Shallots and Herbs

Creamy Parmesan Orzo

    1   tablespoon butter
    1   cup orzo
 1¼   cups fat-free, less-sodium chicken broth
 1¼   cups water
  ¼   cup (1 ounce) grated fresh Parmesan cheese
    2   tablespoons chopped fresh basil
  ¼   teaspoon salt
  ¼   teaspoon freshly ground black pepper
    4   teaspoons pine nuts, toasted

1. Heat butter in a medium saucepan over medium heat. Add orzo, and cook 3 minutes, stirring constantly. Stir in broth and water; bring to a boil. Reduce heat, and simmer until liquid is absorbed and orzo is done (about 15 minutes). Remove from heat; stir in cheese, basil, salt, and pepper. Sprinkle with pine nuts. Serve immediately. **YIELD:** 4 servings (serving size: ½ cup).

CALORIES 236 (24% from fat); FAT 6.4g (sat 3.2g, mono 1.8g, poly 0.8g); PROTEIN 9.9g; CARB 34.8g; FIBER 1.7g; CHOL 12mg; IRON 1.8mg; SODIUM 412mg; CALC 82mg

Basmati Rice with Basil and Mint

This foolproof cooking method also works with long-grain white rice and jasmine rice.

    1   cup uncooked basmati rice
    2   teaspoons canola oil
    2   teaspoons minced peeled fresh ginger
    2   garlic cloves, minced
 2¼   cups fat-free, less-sodium chicken broth
    1   tablespoon chopped fresh basil
    2   teaspoons chopped fresh mint
  ¼   teaspoon freshly ground black pepper

1. Preheat oven to 350°.
2. Place rice in a fine-mesh strainer. Rinse with cold water; drain.
3. Heat oil in a large saucepan over medium-high heat. Add ginger and garlic; cook 30 seconds, stirring constantly. Stir in rice; cook 1 minute, stirring constantly. Add broth and remaining ingredients, stirring to combine; bring to a boil. Cover; wrap handle of pan with foil. Bake at 350° for 25 minutes, stirring once. Remove rice from oven; fluff rice with a fork. **YIELD:** 4 servings (serving size: about ¾ cup).

CALORIES 215 (10% from fat); FAT 2.3g (sat 0.3g, mono 0.5g, poly 1.3g); PROTEIN 4.5g; CARB 46.7g; FIBER 1.5g; CHOL 0mg; IRON 1.5mg; SODIUM 254mg; CALC 5mg

Pistachio Rice

    2   cups water
    1   cup basmati rice
  ¾   teaspoon salt, divided
    2   tablespoons dried currants or golden raisins
 1½   tablespoons chopped pistachios
    1   tablespoon chopped fresh flat-leaf parsley
    2   tablespoons pistachio oil
  ¼   teaspoon freshly ground black pepper
Fresh flat-leaf parsley sprigs (optional)

1. Bring water to a boil in a medium saucepan; add rice and ¼ teaspoon salt. Cover, reduce heat, and simmer 18 minutes or until liquid is absorbed and rice is done. Remove from heat; fluff with a fork. Add ½ teaspoon salt, currants, and next 4 ingredients. Cover and let stand 5 minutes. Garnish with parsley sprigs, if desired. **YIELD:** 6 servings (serving size: about ½ cup).

CALORIES 186 (29% from fat); FAT 5.9g (sat 0.8g, mono 3.8g, poly 1.3g); PROTEIN 2.4g; CARB 33.1g; FIBER 1.3g; CHOL 0mg; IRON 1.2mg; SODIUM 294mg; CALC 8mg

Rice Pilaf with Shallots and Parmesan

We used basmati rice, but any long-grain rice works well in this recipe.

    2   teaspoons butter
    2   tablespoons minced shallots
    1   garlic clove, minced
  ½   cup uncooked basmati rice
    1   cup fat-free, less-sodium chicken broth
  ¼   cup dry white wine
    2   tablespoons grated fresh Parmesan cheese
    2   tablespoons minced fresh parsley
  ⅛   teaspoon freshly ground black pepper
Dash of sea salt

1. Melt butter in a small saucepan over medium-high heat. Add shallots and garlic; sauté 1 minute. Stir in rice; sauté 1 minute. Stir in broth and wine; bring to a boil. Cover, reduce heat, and simmer 15 minutes.
2. Remove from heat; stir in cheese, parsley, pepper, and salt. **YIELD:** 2 servings (serving size: about ¾ cup).

CALORIES 266 (21% from fat); FAT 6.3g (sat 3.8g, mono 1.8g, poly 0.4g); PROTEIN 8.4g; CARB 43.9g; FIBER 0.6g; CHOL 15mg; IRON 0.8mg; SODIUM 455mg; CALC 100mg

Pistachio Rice

Sausage and Mushroom Stuffing

This herbed bread stuffing is a welcome addition to a roast chicken dinner.

  5 cups (1-inch) cubed white bread (about 7 [1-ounce] slices)
  5 cups (1-inch) cubed whole wheat bread (about 7 [1-ounce] slices)
  1 pound turkey Italian sausage
Cooking spray
  1 teaspoon canola oil
  3 cups finely chopped onion
1½ cups finely chopped celery
  1 (8-ounce) package presliced mushrooms
  1 teaspoon dried thyme
  1 teaspoon dried rubbed sage
  1 teaspoon dried rosemary
½ teaspoon dried marjoram
½ teaspoon black pepper
⅓ cup chopped fresh parsley
1½ cups fat-free, less-sodium chicken broth

1. Preheat oven to 250°.
2. Place bread in a single layer on 2 baking sheets. Bake at 250° for 1 hour or until dry.
3. Remove casings from sausage. Cook sausage in a large nonstick skillet coated with cooking spray over medium heat until browned, stirring to crumble. Place sausage in a large bowl.
4. Heat canola oil in pan over medium heat. Add onion, celery, and mushrooms; cover and cook 10 minutes or until vegetables are tender, stirring occasionally. Remove from heat; stir in thyme and next 4 ingredients. Add onion mixture, bread, and parsley to sausage; toss gently to combine. Add broth; stir until moist.
5. Increase oven temperature to 350°.
6. Spoon bread mixture into a 13 x 9–inch baking dish coated with cooking spray. Cover and bake at 350° for 15 minutes. Uncover and bake an additional 20 minutes or until top is crusty. **YIELD:** 12 servings (serving size: about ¾ cup).

CALORIES 187 (28% from fat); FAT 5.9g (sat 1.6g, mono 2g, poly 1.5g); PROTEIN 12.4g; CARB 21.6g; FIBER 2.9g; CHOL 38mg; IRON 2.5mg; SODIUM 460mg; CALC 52mg

Sourdough Stuffing with Pears and Sausage

Sourdough bread gives the stuffing a tangier flavor than French or Italian bread, but you can use the latter in a pinch.

  8 cups (½-inch) cubed sourdough bread (about 12 ounces)
  1 pound turkey Italian sausage
Cooking spray
  5 cups chopped onion (about 2 pounds)
  2 cups chopped celery
  1 cup chopped carrot
  1 (8-ounce) package presliced mushrooms
  2 cups (½-inch) cubed peeled Bartlett pear (about 2 medium)
1½ tablespoons chopped fresh basil
  2 teaspoons chopped fresh tarragon
  1 teaspoon salt
1½ cups fat-free, less-sodium chicken broth
½ teaspoon freshly ground black pepper

1. Preheat oven to 425°.
2. Arrange bread in a single layer on a baking sheet. Bake at 425° for 9 minutes or until golden. Place in a large bowl.
3. Remove casings from sausage. Heat a large nonstick skillet over medium-high heat. Coat pan with cooking spray. Add sausage; cook 8 minutes or until browned, stirring to crumble. Add sausage to bread cubes, tossing to combine. Set aside.
4. Return pan to medium-high heat. Add onion, celery, and carrot; sauté 10 minutes or until onion begins to brown. Stir in mushrooms; cook 4 minutes. Stir in pear, basil, tarragon, and salt; cook 4 minutes or until pear begins to soften, stirring occasionally. Add pear mixture to bread mixture, tossing gently to combine. Stir in broth and pepper.
5. Place bread mixture in a 13 x 9–inch baking dish coated with cooking spray; cover with foil. Bake at 425° for 20 minutes. Uncover; bake an additional 15 minutes or until top is crisp. **YIELD:** 12 servings (serving size: about ¾ cup).

CALORIES 199 (24% from fat); FAT 5.2g (sat 1.6g, mono 1.5g, poly 1g); PROTEIN 10.7g; CARB 28.6g; FIBER 3.4g; CHOL 23mg; IRON 1.8mg; SODIUM 684mg; CALC 54mg

Sourdough Stuffing
with Pears and Sausage

Lemon-Blueberry Bundt Cake,
page 219

Cooking Light with O ORGANICS
DESSERTS

Espresso-Walnut Cake

Espresso-Walnut Cake

Cooking spray
  2 teaspoons all-purpose flour
  ¼ cup packed brown sugar
  3 tablespoons finely chopped walnuts
  1 teaspoon ground cinnamon
  1 tablespoon instant espresso or 2 tablespoons instant coffee granules, divided
  5 tablespoons butter
  1 cup granulated sugar
  2 large eggs
  ⅔ cup plain fat-free yogurt
  2 teaspoons vanilla extract
  ½ teaspoon baking soda
  ¼ teaspoon salt
  1⅓ cups all-purpose flour

1. Preheat oven to 350°.
2. Coat an 8-inch square baking pan with cooking spray, and dust with 2 teaspoons flour. Combine brown sugar, walnuts, cinnamon, and 1 teaspoon espresso granules in a small bowl.
3. Place the butter in a large microwave-safe bowl. Cover and microwave at HIGH for 1 minute or until butter melts. Add granulated sugar, stirring with a whisk. Add eggs; stir well. Stir in yogurt, vanilla, baking soda, and salt. Lightly spoon 1⅓ cups flour into dry measuring cups; level with a knife. Add flour and 2 teaspoons espresso granules, stirring just until blended (do not overstir).
4. Spread half of the batter into the prepared pan, and sprinkle with half of the brown sugar mixture. Carefully spread remaining batter over brown sugar mixture, and sprinkle with remaining brown sugar mixture.
5. Bake at 350° for 25 minutes or until a wooden pick inserted in center comes out clean. Cool for 10 minutes in pan on a wire rack. Cut into squares. **YIELD:** 9 servings (serving size: 1 cake square).

CALORIES 284 (30% from fat); FAT 9.4g (sat 4.5g, mono 2.6g, poly 1.7g); PROTEIN 5g; CARB 45.4g; FIBER 0.8g; CHOL 65mg; IRON 1.4mg; SODIUM 231mg; CALC 58mg

Lemon-Blueberry Bundt Cake
(pictured on page 216)

CAKE:
Cooking spray
  2 tablespoons granulated sugar
  3 cups all-purpose flour (about 13½ ounces)
  1½ teaspoons baking powder
  ½ teaspoon baking soda
  ¼ teaspoon salt
  1¾ cups granulated sugar
  ¼ cup butter, softened
  1 tablespoon grated lemon rind
  4 large eggs
  ½ teaspoon vanilla extract
  1 (16-ounce) carton reduced-fat sour cream
  2 cups fresh blueberries
GLAZE:
  1 cup powdered sugar
  2 tablespoons fresh lemon juice

1. Preheat oven to 350°.
2. To prepare cake, coat a 12-cup Bundt pan with cooking spray; dust with 2 tablespoons sugar. Lightly spoon flour into dry measuring cups; level with a knife. Combine flour, baking powder, baking soda, and salt, stirring with a whisk.
3. Place 1¾ cups granulated sugar, butter, and rind in a large bowl; beat with a mixer at medium speed until well blended. Add eggs, 1 at a time, beating well after each addition. Beat in vanilla and sour cream. Add flour mixture; beat at medium speed just until combined. Gently fold in blueberries. Spoon batter into prepared pan. Bake at 350° for 1 hour or until a wooden pick inserted in center comes out clean. Cool in pan 15 minutes on a wire rack; remove from pan. Cool completely on wire rack.
4. To prepare glaze, combine powdered sugar and juice, stirring well with a whisk. Drizzle over cake. **YIELD:** 16 servings (serving size: 1 slice).

CALORIES 299 (23% from fat); FAT 7.8g (sat 4g, mono 2.7g, poly 0.5g); PROTEIN 5g; CARB 53.2g; FIBER 1.1g; CHOL 71mg; IRON 1.5mg; SODIUM 172mg; CALC 68mg

ORGANIC FACT

"Organic grapes are shown to have an average of 30% more resveratrol, a phytochemical shown to prevent aging and help preserve sensitivity to insulin, a key step in preventing diabetes."

Source: The Organic Center

Warm Chocolate Soufflé Cakes with Raspberry Sauce

SAUCE:
⅔ cup granulated sugar
¼ cup fresh orange juice
1 (12-ounce) package frozen unsweetened raspberries, thawed

CAKES:
Cooking spray
2 tablespoons granulated sugar
¾ cup fat-free milk
¼ cup half-and-half
2 ounces unsweetened chocolate, chopped
¼ cup unsweetened cocoa
1 teaspoon vanilla extract
1¼ cups granulated sugar, divided
¼ cup butter, softened
3 large egg yolks
¼ cup all-purpose flour (about 1 ounce)
¼ teaspoon cream of tartar
5 large egg whites
1 tablespoon powdered sugar
Raspberries and mint sprigs (optional)

1. To prepare sauce, combine first 3 ingredients in a food processor; process until smooth. Strain through a sieve into a bowl; discard solids. Cover and chill.
2. To prepare cakes, coat 12 (6-ounce) ramekins with cooking spray; sprinkle evenly with 2 tablespoons granulated sugar. Set aside.
3. Combine milk and half-and-half in a small saucepan. Bring to a simmer over medium-high heat (do not boil). Remove from heat; add chocolate, stirring until chocolate melts. Add cocoa and vanilla; stir with a whisk. Pour into a bowl; cool completely.
4. Preheat oven to 325°.
5. Place 1 cup granulated sugar and butter in a medium bowl; beat with a mixer at high speed until light and fluffy. Beat in egg yolks. Add cooled chocolate mixture, and beat until blended. Lightly spoon flour into a dry measuring cup; level with a knife. Stir into chocolate mixture.
6. Place cream of tartar and egg whites in a large bowl; beat with a mixer at high speed until soft peaks form. Gradually add remaining ¼ cup granulated sugar, 1 tablespoon at a time, beating until stiff peaks form. Gently stir one-fourth egg white mixture into chocolate mixture; gently fold in remaining egg white mixture. Spoon into prepared ramekins.

7. Place ramekins in 2 (13 x 9–inch) baking pans; add hot water to pans to a depth of 1 inch. Bake at 325° for 35 minutes or until puffy and set. Loosen cakes from sides of ramekins using a narrow metal spatula. Invert onto 12 plates. Sprinkle evenly with powdered sugar; serve with sauce. Garnish with raspberries and mint, if desired. **YIELD:** 12 servings (serving size: 1 cake and 2 tablespoons sauce).

CALORIES 273 (27% from fat); FAT 8.1g (sat 4.3g, mono 2.3g, poly 0.4g); PROTEIN 4.5g; CARB 48.1g; FIBER 2.5g; CHOL 64mg; IRON 1.2mg; SODIUM 63mg; CALC 54mg

Frosted Pumpkin Cake

CAKE:
Cooking spray
1 tablespoon all-purpose flour
¾ cup egg substitute
⅓ cup granulated sugar
⅓ cup applesauce
1 (15-ounce) can pumpkin
2 teaspoons pumpkin-pie spice
1 (18.25-ounce) package yellow cake mix

FROSTING:
⅔ cup (6 ounces) tub-style light cream cheese
1¼ teaspoons vanilla extract
3½ cups powdered sugar

1. Preheat oven to 350°.
2. Coat a 13 x 9–inch baking pan with cooking spray; dust with flour.
3. To prepare cake, place egg substitute, granulated sugar, applesauce, and pumpkin in a large bowl; beat with a mixer at high speed 1 minute. Add pumpkin-pie spice and cake mix, beating at high speed 2 minutes. Pour batter into prepared pan. Bake at 350° for 35 minutes or until a wooden pick inserted in center comes out clean. Cool cake completely on a wire rack.
4. To prepare frosting, place cream cheese and vanilla in a large bowl; beat with a mixer at medium speed until smooth. Gradually add powdered sugar, beating just until blended (do not overbeat). Spread frosting evenly over top of cake. Cover and store cake in refrigerator.
YIELD: 24 servings (serving size: 1 piece).

CALORIES 202 (16% from fat); FAT 3.7g (sat 1.2g, mono 1.1g, poly 1g); PROTEIN 2.6g; CARB 40g; FIBER 1g; CHOL 4mg; IRON 1mg; SODIUM 236mg; CALC 47mg

Sour Cream Pound Cake with Rum Glaze

CAKE:

Cooking spray
- 3 tablespoons dry breadcrumbs
- 3 cups cake flour (about 12 ounces)
- 1 teaspoon baking powder
- ¼ teaspoon baking soda
- ¼ teaspoon salt
- ¾ cup butter, softened
- 2 cups granulated sugar
- 3 large eggs
- ¼ cup fat-free milk
- 1 tablespoon dark rum
- 2 teaspoons vanilla extract
- 1 cup fat-free sour cream

GLAZE:
- ⅓ cup packed brown sugar
- 2 tablespoons dark rum
- 2 tablespoons water
- 1½ tablespoons butter

1. Preheat oven to 350°.

2. To prepare cake, coat a 10-inch tube pan with cooking spray; dust with breadcrumbs. Set aside.

3. Lightly spoon flour into dry measuring cups, and level with a knife. Combine flour, baking powder, baking soda, and salt, stirring well with a whisk. Place butter and granulated sugar in a large bowl, and beat with a mixer at medium speed until light and fluffy. Add eggs, 1 at a time, beating well after each addition. Add milk, 1 tablespoon rum, and vanilla, and beat until combined. Beating at low speed, add flour mixture and sour cream alternately to sugar mixture, beginning and ending with flour mixture, and beat just until combined.

4. Spoon batter into prepared pan. Bake at 350° for 1 hour or until a wooden pick inserted in center comes out clean. Cool in pan 10 minutes. Loosen cake from sides of pan using a narrow metal spatula. Place a plate upside down on top of cake; invert onto plate. Invert cake again. Pierce cake liberally with a wooden pick.

5. While cake bakes, prepare glaze. Combine brown sugar, 2 tablespoons rum, and water in a small saucepan; bring to a boil, stirring until sugar dissolves. Add 1½ tablespoons butter, stirring until butter melts. Drizzle half of warm glaze evenly over warm cake; allow mixture to absorb into cake. Drizzle remaining glaze over cake. Cool cake completely. Store loosely covered.

YIELD: 16 servings (serving size: 1 slice).

CALORIES 325 (30% from fat); FAT 11g (sat 6.3g, mono 3.2g, poly 0.5g); PROTEIN 3.6g; CARB 52.8g; FIBER 0.6g; CHOL 68mg; IRON 1.5mg; SODIUM 232mg; CALC 58mg

Vanilla Cheesecake with Cherry Topping

We use the entire vanilla bean, so none of it is wasted. The seeds flavor the cheesecake, and the bean halves flavor the topping. Both the cheesecake and the topping can be made up to three days ahead and stored separately in the refrigerator. Or make the cheesecake up to two months ahead and freeze. Before freezing, chill the cooled cheesecake in the pan for two hours; then wrap the pan in heavy-duty plastic wrap. Thaw the cheesecake in the refrigerator.

CRUST:
- ¾ cup graham cracker crumbs
- ¼ cup sugar
- 2 tablespoons butter, melted
- 2 teaspoons water
- Cooking spray

FILLING:
- 3 (8-ounce) blocks fat-free cream cheese, softened
- 2 (8-ounce) blocks ⅓-less-fat cream cheese, softened
- 1 cup sugar
- 3 tablespoons all-purpose flour
- ¼ teaspoon salt
- 1 (8-ounce) carton fat-free sour cream
- 4 large eggs
- 2 teaspoons vanilla extract
- 1 vanilla bean, split lengthwise

TOPPING:
- ⅔ cup tawny port or other sweet red wine
- ½ cup sugar
- 2 (10-ounce) bags frozen pitted dark sweet cherries
- 2 tablespoons fresh lemon juice
- 4 teaspoons cornstarch
- 4 teaspoons water

1. Preheat oven to 400°.

2. To prepare crust, combine first 3 ingredients, tossing with a fork. Add 2 teaspoons water; toss with a fork until moist and crumbly. Gently press mixture into bottom and 1½ inches up sides of a 9-inch springform pan coated with cooking spray. Bake at 400° for 5 minutes; cool on a wire rack.

3. Reduce oven temperature to 325°.

4. To prepare filling, beat cheeses with a mixer at high speed until smooth. Combine 1 cup sugar, flour, and salt, stirring with a whisk. Add to cheese mixture; beat well. Add sour cream; beat well. Add eggs, 1 at a time, beating well after each addition. Stir in vanilla extract. Scrape seeds from vanilla bean; stir seeds into cheese mixture, reserving bean halves.

5. Pour cheese mixture into prepared pan; bake at 325° for 1 hour and 15 minutes or until cheesecake center barely moves when pan is touched. Remove cheesecake from oven; run a knife around outside edge. Cool to room temperature. Cover and chill at least 8 hours.

6. To prepare topping, combine port, ½ cup sugar, cherries, and reserved vanilla bean halves in a large saucepan; bring to a boil. Cook 5 minutes or until cherries are thawed and mixture is syrupy. Remove vanilla bean halves; discard.

7. Combine juice, cornstarch, and 4 teaspoons water, stirring with a whisk until well blended. Stir cornstarch mixture into cherry mixture; bring to a boil. Reduce heat; simmer 3 minutes or until mixture is slightly thickened and shiny. Remove from heat; cool to room temperature. Cover and chill. Serve over cheesecake.

YIELD: 16 servings (serving size: 1 slice cheesecake and about 2 tablespoons topping).

CALORIES 324 (30% from fat); FAT 10.7g (sat 6.1g, mono 3.2g, poly 0.7g); PROTEIN 12.2g; CARB 42.8g; FIBER 1g; CHOL 83mg; IRON 0.8mg; SODIUM 458mg; CALC 134mg

ORGANIC FACT

Organic farmers use creative ways to protect against pests. They can plant trap crops to attract pests to the "bait" instead of the crop they want to harvest. An example is using alfalfa to "trap" the western tarnished plant bug, which damages strawberries.

Source: Organic Farming Research Foundation

Vanilla Cheesecake with
Cherry Topping

223

Sweet Potato Pie

Making this fall favorite is reason enough to invite over a friend or two. You can bake it up to two days ahead; cool it completely, cover with plastic wrap, and chill. Before serving, reheat it for about 15 minutes at 325° to bring back its silky texture.

PASTRY:
1¼ cups all-purpose flour (about 5½ ounces)
2 tablespoons granulated sugar
½ teaspoon salt
5 tablespoons chilled butter, cut into small pieces
4 to 5 tablespoons ice water
Cooking spray

FILLING:
1 cup mashed cooked sweet potatoes
1 cup evaporated fat-free milk
¾ cup packed light brown sugar
2 tablespoons all-purpose flour
1 large egg white
½ cup 1% low-fat milk
1 tablespoon butter, melted
1 teaspoon vanilla extract
½ teaspoon ground cinnamon
¼ teaspoon ground nutmeg
Dash of salt

1. To prepare pastry, lightly spoon 1¼ cups flour into dry measuring cups; level with a knife. Place 1¼ cups flour, granulated sugar, and ½ teaspoon salt in a food processor. Process 10 seconds. Add butter; pulse 4 times or until mixture resembles coarse meal. Place flour mixture in a bowl. Sprinkle surface with ice water, 1 tablespoon at a time; toss with a fork until moist. Place pastry on a lightly floured surface; knead lightly 3 or 4 times. Gently press mixture into a 4-inch circle on plastic wrap; cover. Chill 30 minutes.
2. Slightly overlap 2 sheets of plastic wrap on a slightly damp surface. Unwrap and place chilled dough on plastic wrap. Cover with 2 additional sheets of overlapping plastic wrap. Roll dough, still covered, into an 11-inch circle. Place dough in freezer 5 minutes or until plastic wrap can be easily removed.
3. Preheat oven to 350°.
4. Remove top sheets of plastic wrap; fit dough, plastic wrap side up, into a 9-inch pie plate. Remove remaining plastic wrap. Fold edges under; flute. Line bottom of dough with a piece of foil coated with cooking spray;

arrange pie weights or dried beans on piece of foil. Bake at 350° for 15 minutes. Remove pie weights and foil; cool pastry on a wire rack.
5. To prepare filling, combine sweet potatoes and next 4 ingredients in a food processor; process until blended. Spoon into a large bowl. Add 1% low-fat milk and next 5 ingredients; stir well. Pour filling into pastry. Bake at 350° for 50 minutes or until a knife inserted in center comes out clean. Cool completely on a wire rack. **YIELD:** 8 servings (serving size: 1 wedge).

CALORIES 302 (27% from fat); FAT 9g (sat 5.6g, mono 2.3g, poly 0.5g); PROTEIN 6.2g; CARB 49.4g; FIBER 1.5g; CHOL 24mg; IRON 1.7mg; SODIUM 295mg; CALC 147mg

Plum Tatin

Use red, purple, green, or a combination of plums in this upside-down tart.

½ (15-ounce) package refrigerated pie dough
¼ cup packed brown sugar
1 tablespoon all-purpose flour
¼ teaspoon ground cinnamon
¼ teaspoon ground nutmeg
10 small plums, pitted and cut in half (about 2½ pounds)
½ cup granulated sugar
1 teaspoon lemon juice
1 tablespoon chopped pecans

1. Preheat oven to 425°.
2. Roll dough into a 10-inch circle on a lightly floured surface; set aside.
3. Combine brown sugar and next 4 ingredients. Combine granulated sugar and lemon juice in a 10-inch cast-iron skillet; cook sugar mixture over medium-high heat just until it begins to turn golden.
4. Remove from heat; stir until completely golden. Add pecans and plum mixture. Place dough over plum mixture, tucking dough around plums.
5. Bake at 425° for 25 minutes or until bubbly. Immediately place a plate over pan. Carefully invert tart onto plate. **YIELD:** 6 servings.

CALORIES 328 (30% from fat); FAT 11.1g (sat 3.8g, mono 4.6g, poly 1.3g); PROTEIN 2.4g; CARB 57g; FIBER 1.9g; CHOL 7mg; IRON 0.3mg; SODIUM 136mg; CALC 8mg

Cherry-Apricot Turnovers

Layers of phyllo are brushed with a mixture of melted butter and oil, then sprinkled with graham cracker crumbs and brown sugar. The crumbs help keep the phyllo, which envelops the moist filling, dry and crisp.

1 cup apricot nectar
½ cup chopped dried apricots
⅓ cup packed brown sugar
¼ teaspoon grated lemon rind
2 tablespoons fresh lemon juice
3 (3-ounce) bags dried sweet cherries
2 tablespoons chopped almonds
½ teaspoon vanilla extract
2 tablespoons butter, melted
2 tablespoons canola oil
6 (18 x 14–inch) sheets frozen phyllo dough, thawed
¼ cup graham cracker crumbs
2 tablespoons brown sugar
Cooking spray

1. Combine first 6 ingredients in a saucepan; bring to a boil. Reduce heat, and simmer 20 minutes or until liquid is absorbed, stirring occasionally. Stir in almonds and vanilla. Cool completely.
2. Preheat oven to 375°.
3. Combine butter and oil. Place 1 phyllo sheet on a large cutting board or work surface (cover remaining dough to prevent drying). Lightly brush phyllo sheet with 1 tablespoon butter mixture. Sprinkle with 1 tablespoon crumbs and 1½ teaspoons brown sugar. Repeat layers once. Top with 1 phyllo sheet. Gently press layers together. Lightly coat top phyllo sheet with cooking spray. Cut stack lengthwise into 4 (3½-inch-wide) strips. Cut each strip in half crosswise. Spoon 2 tablespoons cherry mixture onto 1 short end of each rectangle, leaving a 1-inch border. Fold 1 corner of edge with 1-inch border over mixture, forming a triangle; continue folding back and forth into a triangle to end of rectangle. Tuck edges under triangle. Place triangles, seam side down, on a large baking sheet coated with cooking spray; lightly coat triangles with cooking spray. Repeat procedure with remaining phyllo, butter mixture, crumbs, brown sugar, cherry mixture, and cooking spray.
4. Bake at 375° for 15 minutes or until golden brown. Remove from baking sheet; cool on a wire rack. **YIELD:** 16 servings (serving size: 1 turnover).

CALORIES 155 (25% from fat); FAT 4.3g (sat 1.2g, mono 2.1g, poly 0.8g); PROTEIN 1.9g; CARB 27g; FIBER 1.9g; CHOL 4mg; IRON 0.8mg; SODIUM 62mg; CALC 21mg

Mango Macadamia Crisp

Mango Macadamia Crisp

The tangy-sweet taste and velvety texture of the mango contrast nicely with the crunchy nut topping. A bottled refrigerated mango can be substituted for fresh.

FILLING:
- ¼ cup granulated sugar
- 2 teaspoons cornstarch
- 4 cups chopped peeled ripe mango (about 4 pounds)
- 3 tablespoons fresh lime juice
- 2 teaspoons butter, melted
- Cooking spray

TOPPING:
- ⅓ cup all-purpose flour (about 1½ ounces)
- 3 tablespoons granulated sugar
- 1½ teaspoons brown sugar
- ½ teaspoon ground ginger
- 3 tablespoons butter
- 3 tablespoons chopped macadamia nuts

1. Preheat oven to 400°.
2. Combine ¼ cup granulated sugar and cornstarch, stirring well with a whisk. Add mango, juice, and 2 teaspoons butter; toss gently to combine. Place mango mixture in an 8-inch square baking dish coated with cooking spray.
3. To prepare topping, lightly spoon flour into a dry measuring cup; level with a knife. Combine flour, 3 tablespoons granulated sugar, brown sugar, and ginger, stirring well. Cut in 3 tablespoons butter with a pastry blender or 2 knives until mixture resembles coarse meal. Stir in nuts. Sprinkle flour mixture evenly over mango mixture. Bake at 400° for 40 minutes or until browned.
YIELD: 8 servings (serving size: about ½ cup).

CALORIES 238 (31% from fat); FAT 8.1g (sat 3.1g, mono 4.2g, poly 0.3g); PROTEIN 1.7g; CARB 43.7g; FIBER 3.3g; CHOL 14mg; IRON 0.6mg; SODIUM 49mg; CALC 21mg

ORGANIC FACT

There are very few synthetic ingredients that have been included on the "National List of Allowed Substances" that can be included in organic products. The list includes things like baking soda, pectin, and vitamin C.

Source: USDA National Organic Program

Orange Crisp with Coconut Topping

This delicious dessert is sure to please guests on any occasion. The juicy citrus filling is crowned with a buttery layer of crunchy coconut crumbs. Use a shallow baking dish to better distribute the topping.

FILLING:
- 6 large navel oranges
- 1½ tablespoons uncooked quick-cooking tapioca
- 1 tablespoon Grand Marnier (orange-flavored liqueur)
- Cooking spray

TOPPING:
- ⅔ cup all-purpose flour (about 3 ounces)
- ⅔ cup sugar
- ½ teaspoon salt
- ¼ cup chilled butter, cut into small pieces
- ⅔ cup flaked sweetened coconut

1. Preheat oven to 375°.
2. To prepare filling, peel and section oranges over a large bowl, reserving ¼ cup juice. Add tapioca and liqueur to reserved juice; stir until well blended. Add orange sections; stir gently. Let stand 20 minutes, stirring occasionally.
3. Place filling in an 11 x 7–inch baking dish or shallow 2-quart baking dish coated with cooking spray.
4. To prepare topping, lightly spoon flour into a dry measuring cup; level with a knife. Combine flour, sugar, and salt in a large bowl, stirring with a whisk. Cut in butter with a pastry blender or 2 knives until mixture resembles coarse meal. Add coconut; toss well. Sprinkle topping evenly over filling. Bake at 375° for 35 minutes or until crisp is golden and bubbly. **YIELD:** 8 servings.

CALORIES 231 (31% from fat); FAT 7.9g (sat 5.3g, mono 1.8g, poly 0.3g); PROTEIN 2.2g; CARB 40g; FIBER 2.5g; CHOL 15mg; IRON 0.7mg; SODIUM 221mg; CALC 38mg

Santa Rosa Plum Crumble

Santa Rosa Plum Crumble

Santa Rosa plums are great in this dessert, although any juicy plum will work nicely. Because it's good served either warm or at room temperature, this is a choice make-ahead dessert. After scraping the seeds from the vanilla bean, use it to flavor sugar: Bury the bean in a container of granulated sugar, and store for up to six months.

14 plums, each cut into 6 wedges
¼ cup granulated sugar
3 tablespoons dry red wine
1 (4-inch) piece vanilla bean, split lengthwise
Cooking spray
¾ cup all-purpose flour (about 3⅓ ounces)
1 cup regular oats
6 tablespoons brown sugar
1½ teaspoons grated orange rind
¼ teaspoon salt
⅛ teaspoon ground nutmeg
5 tablespoons chilled butter, cut into small pieces

1. Preheat oven to 375°.
2. Combine first 3 ingredients. Scrape seeds from vanilla bean; add seeds to plum mixture. Discard bean. Toss mixture gently to combine. Spoon into a 13 x 9–inch baking dish coated with cooking spray.
3. Lightly spoon flour into a dry measuring cup; level with a knife. Combine flour and next 5 ingredients in a medium bowl; cut in butter with a pastry blender or 2 knives until mixture resembles coarse meal. Sprinkle flour mixture evenly over plum mixture. Bake at 375° for 45 minutes or until plum mixture is bubbly and topping is lightly browned. Serve warm or at room temperature. **YIELD:** 9 servings (serving size: about 1 cup).

CALORIES 284 (26% from fat); FAT 8.2g (sat 4.1g, mono 2.8g, poly 0.7g); PROTEIN 3.8g; CARB 52.5g; FIBER 3.9g; CHOL 17mg; IRON 1.3mg; SODIUM 134mg; CALC 24mg

Bittersweet Chocolate Mousse à l'Orange

Two appliances, the blender and microwave, simplify the preparation of this easy dish. Fresh orange sections are topped with a thick chocolate mousse for a unique presentation. The mild bitterness of orange rind and bittersweet chocolate temper the dessert's sweetness. It can be prepared up to a day ahead.

½ cup sugar
7 tablespoons unsweetened cocoa
2 tablespoons Grand Marnier (orange-flavored liqueur)
1 teaspoon grated orange rind
½ teaspoon vanilla extract
Dash of salt
2 (12.3-ounce) packages reduced-fat silken tofu, drained
3 ounces bittersweet chocolate, chopped
3 oranges, peeled and sectioned
Mint sprigs (optional)

1. Combine first 7 ingredients in a blender or food processor; process until smooth.
2. Place chocolate in a small microwave-safe bowl. Microwave at HIGH 1 minute or until almost melted; stir until smooth. Add chocolate to tofu mixture; process until smooth.
3. Divide orange sections evenly among 6 bowls or parfait glasses, and top each serving with ½ cup mousse. Cover and chill at least 1 hour. Garnish with mint sprigs, if desired. **YIELD:** 6 servings.

CALORIES 241 (27% from fat); FAT 7.1g (sat 3.6g, mono 1g, poly 0.9g); PROTEIN 9.5g; CARB 35.9g; FIBER 4.1g; CHOL 1mg; IRON 2mg; SODIUM 124mg; CALC 79mg

ORGANIC FACT
There are three levels of organic: 100%, 95%, and 70%. Only the first two can carry the USDA organic logo. See page 11 for more details.

Source: USDA National Organic Program

229

Polenta Pudding
with Blueberry Topping

Cooking grains and cereals in the microwave is very simple. There's no clumping, it's quick, and the cleanup couldn't be easier.

  1   cup fresh or frozen blueberries
  ½   cup sugar, divided
  2   cups 2% reduced-fat milk
  6   tablespoons yellow cornmeal
  ¾   teaspoon lemon rind
  ½   teaspoon vanilla extract
  ¼   teaspoon salt

1. Combine blueberries and ¼ cup sugar in a medium microwave-safe bowl. Cover with wax paper; microwave at HIGH 3 minutes or until thoroughly heated and sugar dissolves, stirring after 1½ minutes.
2. Combine ¼ cup sugar, milk, cornmeal, and lemon rind in a 2-quart glass measure; stir with a whisk. Microwave at HIGH 7 minutes or until thick and bubbly, stirring every 2 minutes. Stir in vanilla and salt. Serve with blueberry topping. **YIELD:** 4 servings (serving size: ½ cup pudding and about 3 tablespoons topping).

CALORIES 226 (11% from fat); FAT 2.8g (sat 1.5g, mono 0.8g, poly 0.3g); PROTEIN 5.3g; CARB 45.7g; FIBER 1.7g; CHOL 10mg; IRON 0.7mg; SODIUM 209mg; CALC 153mg

Chocolate-Mint Pudding

Fresh mint leaves steep in fat-free milk to impart the herb's essence; the taste is much better than that of mint extract. Unless milk is stabilized with a thickener, such as flour or cornstarch, it will "break," or curdle, when it becomes too hot; that's why it's important to go no higher than 180 degrees at the beginning of step one.

  3   cups fat-free milk
  ½   cup packed fresh mint leaves (about ½ ounce)
  ⅔   cup sugar
  ¼   cup cornstarch
  3   tablespoons unsweetened cocoa
  ⅛   teaspoon salt
  3   large egg yolks, lightly beaten
  ½   teaspoon vanilla extract
  2   ounces semisweet chocolate, chopped
Mint sprigs (optional)

1. Heat milk over medium-high heat in a small, heavy saucepan to 180° or until tiny bubbles form around edge (do not boil). Remove from heat; add mint. Let stand 15 minutes; strain milk mixture through a sieve into a bowl, reserving milk. Discard solids.
2. Return milk to pan; stir in sugar, cornstarch, cocoa, and salt. Return pan to medium heat; bring to a boil, stirring constantly with a whisk until mixture thickens.
3. Place egg yolks in a medium bowl; gradually add half of hot milk mixture, stirring constantly with a whisk. Add egg mixture to pan; bring to a boil, stirring constantly. Cook 1 minute or until thick. Remove from heat; add vanilla and chocolate, stirring until chocolate melts. Pour pudding into a bowl; cover surface of pudding with plastic wrap. Chill. Garnish with mint sprigs, if desired.
YIELD: 6 servings (serving size: about ⅔ cup).

CALORIES 227 (25% from fat); FAT 6.4g (sat 3.2g, mono 2.5g, poly 0.4g); PROTEIN 6.7g; CARB 39.4g; FIBER 1.2g; CHOL 105mg; IRON 1.1mg; SODIUM 106mg; CALC 173mg

Vanilla Bean Pudding

  2½ cups 2% reduced-fat milk
  1   vanilla bean, split lengthwise
  ¾   cup sugar
  3   tablespoons cornstarch
  ⅛   teaspoon salt
  ¼   cup half-and-half
  2   large egg yolks
  4   teaspoons butter

1. Place milk in a medium, heavy saucepan. Scrape seeds from vanilla bean; add seeds and bean to milk. Bring to a boil.
2. Combine sugar, cornstarch, and salt in a large bowl, stirring well. Combine half-and-half and egg yolks, stirring well. Stir egg yolk mixture into sugar mixture. Gradually add half of hot milk to sugar mixture, stirring constantly with a whisk. Return hot milk mixture to pan; bring to a boil. Cook 1 minute, stirring constantly with a whisk. Remove from heat. Add butter, stirring until melted. Remove vanilla bean; discard.
3. Spoon pudding into a bowl. Place bowl in a large ice-filled bowl for 15 minutes or until pudding cools, stirring occasionally. Cover surface of pudding with plastic wrap; chill. **YIELD:** 6 servings (serving size: ½ cup).

CALORIES 216 (30% from fat); FAT 7.1g (sat 4.1g, mono 2.2g, poly 0.4g); PROTEIN 4.6g; CARB 34.2g; FIBER 0g; CHOL 86mg; IRON 0.2mg; SODIUM 125mg; CALC 142mg

Apple Pie à la Mode Parfaits

4½ cups chopped peeled cooking apple (such as Braeburn)
½ cup sugar
1 tablespoon fresh lemon juice
1 teaspoon apple-pie spice
3 cups oatmeal cookie crumbs, (about 4 ounces, crushed)
3 cups vanilla low-fat ice cream, softened

1. Combine the first 4 ingredients in a medium saucepan, and bring to a boil. Cover, reduce heat, and simmer 5 minutes. Uncover; simmer 5 minutes or until tender, stirring occasionally. Spoon into a bowl; cover and chill.
2. Spoon 1 tablespoon cookie crumbs into each of 8 (8-ounce) glasses; top each with ¼ cup apple mixture and 3 tablespoons ice cream. Repeat the layers once, ending with ice cream. Serve immediately. **YIELD:** 8 servings (serving size: 1 parfait).

CALORIES 284 (24% from fat); FAT 7.7g (sat 2.3g, mono 3.7g, poly 0.9g); PROTEIN 4.4g; CARB 51.4g; FIBER 3g; CHOL 9mg; IRON 0.9mg; SODIUM 129mg; CALC 83mg

ORGANIC QUOTE

"We believe rural vitality can be enhanced by transitioning more acres to organic production. More organic consumers translates to more organic farmers."

—Bob Scowcroft, Executive Director, OFRF

Cranberry-Orange Trifle

The cranberries and pastry cream can be made up to three days ahead. Then, simply assemble and refrigerate the trifle up to 24 hours before you plan to serve it.

CRANBERRIES:
¾ cup sugar
¾ cup fresh orange juice
¼ cup Grand Marnier (or other orange liqueur)
1 (12-ounce) package fresh cranberries
PASTRY CREAM:
½ cup sugar
5 tablespoons cornstarch
2½ cups 2% reduced-fat milk
2 large eggs, lightly beaten
2 teaspoons vanilla extract
⅛ teaspoon salt
REMAINING INGREDIENTS:
1 (10.75-ounce) loaf pound cake (such as Sara Lee), cut into ½-inch cubes
1 teaspoon orange rind

1. To prepare cranberries, combine ¾ cup sugar, orange juice, and Grand Marnier in a medium saucepan over medium-high heat; cook 3 minutes until sugar dissolves, stirring occasionally. Add cranberries to pan; bring to a boil. Reduce heat; simmer 8 minutes or until cranberries pop. Spoon mixture into a bowl; cover and chill.
2. To prepare pastry cream, combine ½ cup sugar and cornstarch in a medium, heavy saucepan over medium heat. Gradually add milk to pan, stirring with a whisk until blended; bring to a boil. Cook 1 minute, stirring constantly. Remove from heat. Gradually add half of hot milk mixture to eggs, stirring constantly with a whisk. Return milk mixture to pan; cook over medium heat 1 minute or until thick, stirring constantly. Remove from heat. Stir in vanilla and salt. Place pan in a large ice-filled bowl until custard cools to room temperature (about 25 minutes), stirring occasionally.
3. Arrange half of cake cubes in the bottom of a 2-quart trifle dish. Spoon 1½ cups cranberry mixture over cake; top with 1½ cups pastry cream. Repeat layers. Garnish with rind. Cover loosely with plastic wrap, and chill at least 4 hours. **YIELD:** 12 servings (serving size: about ¾ cup).

CALORIES 265 (21% from fat); FAT 6.2g (sat 3.2g, mono 1.9g, poly 0.4g); PROTEIN 4.6g; CARB 46.5g; FIBER 1.7g; CHOL 75mg; IRON 0.5mg; SODIUM 155mg; CALC 84mg

Cinnamon-Orange Crème Brûlée

Bake and refrigerate this dessert the night before, so all you'll need to do is add and caramelize the sugar topping before serving dinner.

1 cup 2% reduced-fat milk
6 tablespoons nonfat dry milk
Dash of salt
1 (1-inch) orange rind strip
1 (1-inch) piece cinnamon stick
¼ teaspoon vanilla extract
¼ cup granulated sugar, divided
2 large egg yolks

1. Preheat oven to 300°.

2. Combine milk, dry milk, and salt in a small saucepan over medium heat. Heat to 180° or until tiny bubbles form around the edge (do not boil), stirring occasionally. Remove from heat; stir in orange rind and cinnamon stick. Cover and let steep 10 minutes. Strain milk mixture through a sieve into a bowl; discard solids. Stir in vanilla extract.

3. Combine 2 tablespoons sugar and egg yolks in a medium bowl; stir well with a whisk to combine.

4. Gradually add milk mixture to egg mixture, stirring constantly with a whisk. Divide milk mixture evenly between 2 shallow (6-ounce) dishes. Place dishes in a 13 x 9–inch baking pan; add hot water to pan to a depth of 1 inch. Bake at 300° for 40 minutes or until center barely moves when dish is touched. Remove dishes from pan; cool completely on a wire rack. Cover and chill at least 4 hours or overnight.

5. Sift remaining 2 tablespoons sugar evenly over the top of brûlées. Holding a kitchen blowtorch about 2 inches from the top of each custard, heat sugar, moving torch back and forth, until sugar is completely melted and caramelized (about 1 minute). Serve within 1 hour. **YIELD:** 2 servings (serving size: 1 brûlée).

CALORIES 301 (21% from fat); FAT 7g (sat 3.2g, mono 2.7g, poly 0.8g); PROTEIN 15.6g; CARB 44.1g; FIBER 0g; CHOL 219mg; IRON 0.6mg; SODIUM 273mg; CALC 479mg

Honey Crème Brûlée
with Raspberries

Honey Crème Brûlée with Raspberries

You can check your local farmers' market to find honey produced in your area; it will add pleasantly complex flavor. If you don't have shallow dishes for the crème brûlée, use 6-ounce ramekins instead.

    2   cups 2% reduced-fat milk
    ¾   cup nonfat dry milk
    2   tablespoons sugar
    2   tablespoons honey
    5   large egg yolks
Dash of salt
    3   tablespoons sugar
    24 fresh raspberries

1. Preheat oven to 300°.
2. Combine first 4 ingredients in a large saucepan. Heat mixture over medium heat to 180° or until tiny bubbles form around the edge (do not boil), stirring occasionally. Remove from heat.
3. Combine egg yolks and salt in a medium bowl; stir well with a whisk. Gradually add hot milk mixture to egg mixture, stirring constantly with a whisk. Divide milk mixture evenly among 4 shallow (6-ounce) custard dishes. Place dishes in a 13 x 9–inch baking pan; add hot water to pan to a depth of 1 inch. Bake at 300° for 1 hour or until center barely moves when dish is touched. Remove dishes from pan; cool completely on a wire rack. Cover and chill at least 4 hours or overnight.
4. Sift 3 tablespoons sugar evenly over custards. Holding a kitchen blowtorch about 2 inches from top of each custard, heat sugar, moving torch back and forth, until sugar is completely melted and caramelized (about 1 minute). Top evenly with raspberries. Serve immediately. **YIELD:** 4 servings (serving size: 1 crème brûlée and 6 raspberries).
NOTE: If you don't have a kitchen blowtorch, you can make the sugar topping on the stove top. Place ¼ cup sugar and 1 tablespoon water in a small, heavy saucepan. Cook over medium heat 5 to 8 minutes or until golden. (Resist urge to stir, since doing so may cause sugar to crystallize.) Immediately pour sugar mixture evenly over cold custards, spreading to form a thin layer.

CALORIES 275 (26% from fat); FAT 7.9g (sat 3.4g, mono 3.1g, poly 1g); PROTEIN 12.6g; CARB 39.2g; FIBER 0.8g; CHOL 265mg; IRON 0.8mg; SODIUM 185mg; CALC 364mg

Blueberry Granita with Berry Compote

The more frequently you stir the granita, the slushier it will be. The less you stir, the icier it will be. Both types can be made up to a day ahead.

GRANITA:
    2   quarts fresh blueberries (about 1½ pounds)
    1½ cups water, divided
    ¾   cup sugar
    3   tablespoons lemon juice
COMPOTE:
    2   cups quartered small strawberries, divided
    ½   cup water
    ⅓   cup sugar
    1   (2-inch) piece lemon rind
    ¾   cup fresh blueberries
    1   teaspoon lemon juice

1. To prepare granita, place 2 quarts blueberries in a food processor or blender; process until smooth. With food processor still on, slowly pour 1 cup water through food chute; process until well blended. Strain blueberry mixture through a fine sieve into a bowl; discard solids.
2. Combine ½ cup water and ¾ cup sugar in a small saucepan over high heat, stirring until sugar dissolves. Stir sugar mixture and 3 tablespoons juice into blueberry mixture. Pour mixture into a 13 x 9–inch glass baking dish; let cool to room temperature. Freeze 1½ to 2 hours or until ice crystals begin to form. Remove mixture from freezer; stir well with a fork. Return dish to freezer; freeze 2 hours, stirring every 30 minutes or until slushy. Cover and freeze 1 hour.
3. To prepare compote, place 1 cup strawberries in a food processor or blender; process until smooth. Strain strawberry mixture through a fine sieve into a bowl; discard solids.
4. Combine ½ cup water, ⅓ cup sugar, and rind in a medium saucepan over medium-high heat; bring to a boil. Cook 1 minute; remove from heat. Discard rind. Add pureed strawberries, quartered strawberries, ¾ cup blueberries, and 1 teaspoon juice to pan; stir gently to combine. Let cool to room temperature. Cover and chill. Spoon compote into each of 8 bowls; top with granita.
YIELD: 8 servings (serving size: ⅔ cup granita and about ⅓ cup compote).

CALORIES 174 (3% from fat); FAT 0.5g (sat 0g, mono 0g, poly 0.1g); PROTEIN 0.9g; CARB 44.5g; FIBER 3.5g; CHOL 0mg; IRON 0.3mg; SODIUM 7mg; CALC 12mg

Citrus Tea Sorbet

Citrus Tea Sorbet

Use an unflavored black tea, or substitute your favorite tea. This refreshing sorbet makes a great ending to a spicy meal. If you use loose tea, strain it and discard any solids before adding the sugar.

2¼   cups boiling water
4   black tea bags or 4 teaspoons loose black tea
2   cups sugar
4   cups grapefruit juice (about 8 grapefruit)
1   tablespoon grated orange rind
1   cup fresh orange juice (about 2 oranges)

1. Pour boiling water over tea bags in a large saucepan; steep 5 minutes. Remove and discard tea bags. Add sugar to pan; cook over medium heat 5 minutes or until sugar dissolves. Cool completely.
2. Combine tea mixture, grapefruit juice, rind, and orange juice in freezer can of an ice-cream freezer; freeze according to manufacturer's instructions. Spoon sorbet into a freezer-safe container; cover and freeze 1 hour or until firm. **YIELD:** 8 servings (serving size: about ¾ cup).

CALORIES 252 (1% from fat); FAT 0.2g (sat 0.1g, mono 0.1g, poly 0g); PROTEIN 0.8g; CARB 63.8g; FIBER 0.3g; CHOL 0mg; IRON 0.3mg; SODIUM 2mg; CALC 15mg

Nectarine and Raspberry Sorbet

Fresh peaches also work well for this frozen treat. Garnish with nectarine slices, if you wish.

2   cups chopped peeled nectarines (about 1½ pounds)
1⅓   cups raspberries (about 6 ounces)
2½   cups apricot nectar
½   cup honey
1   tablespoon fresh lemon juice

1. Combine chopped nectarines and raspberries in a food processor; process until smooth. Stir in apricot nectar, honey, and lemon juice. Strain mixture through a sieve into a large bowl; discard solids.
2. Pour mixture into freezer can of an ice-cream freezer; freeze according to manufacturer's instructions. Spoon sorbet into a freezer-safe container; cover and freeze 1 hour or until firm. **YIELD:** 5 servings (serving size: 1 cup).

CALORIES 218 (2% from fat); FAT 0.6g (sat 0.1g, mono 0.2g, poly 0.3g); PROTEIN 1.4g; CARB 56.7g; FIBER 3.4g; CHOL 0mg; IRON 0.9mg; SODIUM 5mg; CALC 21mg

Raspberry Melba

Peach melba—the classic dessert of sliced peaches and pureed raspberries—is reversed with pureed peaches and whole raspberries for an unusual but equally pleasing effect.

¼   cup peach nectar
2   tablespoons sugar
2   teaspoons fresh lemon juice
1   pound ripe peaches, peeled and coarsely chopped
2   cups raspberry sorbet
1   cup fresh raspberries

1. Combine first 4 ingredients in a food processor; process until smooth. Let mixture stand at room temperature 5 minutes.
2. Spoon ¼ cup peach puree into each of 4 parfait glasses; top each serving with ¼ cup sorbet and 2 tablespoons raspberries. Repeat layers with remaining puree, sorbet, and raspberries. **YIELD:** 4 servings.

CALORIES 179 (2% from fat); FAT 0.4g (sat 0g, mono 0.1g, poly 0.2g); PROTEIN 2.3g; CARB 45g; FIBER 4.3g; CHOL 0mg; IRON 0.5mg; SODIUM 5mg; CALC 18mg

Sautéed Apples over Ice Cream

Fuji apples hold their texture during cooking and are so naturally sweet that they need very little additional sugar. Galas are a good substitute.

1   tablespoon butter
1½   cups sliced peeled Fuji apple
1   tablespoon sugar
3   tablespoons brandy
¼   teaspoon fresh lemon juice
⅛   teaspoon ground ginger
1   cup vanilla reduced-fat ice cream

1. Melt butter in a small nonstick skillet over medium heat. Add apple; cook 5 minutes or until lightly browned, stirring frequently.
2. Add sugar, brandy, juice, and ginger; cook over medium-low heat 2 minutes or until apple is tender, stirring occasionally. Serve warm over ice cream. **YIELD:** 2 servings (serving size: about ½ cup apples and ½ cup ice cream).

CALORIES 316 (23% from fat); FAT 8.2g (sat 4.7g, mono 1.7g, poly 0.4g); PROTEIN 3.3g; CARB 46.9g; FIBER 3.8g; CHOL 21mg; IRON 0.2mg; SODIUM 104mg; CALC 108mg

Cherries Jubilee Ice Cream Pie

Cherries Jubilee Ice Cream Pie

All the flavors of the classic dessert combine in this easy-to-prepare pie. Since the cherries are cooked, frozen ones work just fine, especially when fresh ones are not in season—and they save you the trouble of pitting.

- ⅓ cup water
- ¼ cup sugar
- 1 tablespoon cornstarch
- 2 tablespoons brandy
- 1 (12-ounce) package frozen pitted dark sweet cherries
- 2 tablespoons butter, melted
- 2 tablespoons honey
- 1½ cups graham cracker crumbs (about 9 cookie sheets)
- 4 cups vanilla low-fat ice cream, softened

1. Preheat oven to 375°.

2. Combine first 5 ingredients in a medium saucepan. Bring to a boil; cook 2 minutes or until thick, stirring constantly. Cool completely.

3. Combine butter and honey in a medium bowl. Add graham cracker crumbs, stirring to blend. Press mixture into bottom and up sides of a 9-inch pie plate. Bake at 375° for 8 minutes. Cool completely.

4. Place ½ cup cooled cherry mixture in a food processor; process until smooth. Place remaining cherry mixture in an airtight container; cover and chill.

5. Place softened ice cream in a large bowl; beat with a mixer at medium speed until smooth. Add pureed cherry mixture, and gently fold in to achieve a swirl pattern. Spoon mixture into cooled crust. Cover and freeze 4 hours or until firm. Top wedges with reserved cherry sauce just before serving. **YIELD:** 8 servings (serving size: 1 wedge and 3 tablespoons sauce).

CALORIES 277 (23% from fat); FAT 7g (sat 3.4g, mono 2.4g, poly 0.8g); PROTEIN 5g; CARB 47.3g; FIBER 1.6g; CHOL 24mg; IRON 0.7mg; SODIUM 165mg; CALC 88mg

Mascarpone-Stuffed Apricots

Can't find mascarpone? Substitute crème fraîche for similar rich flavor and creamy texture.

- ⅓ cup (3 ounces) block-style fat-free cream cheese
- 2 tablespoons (1 ounce) mascarpone cheese
- 2 tablespoons honey
- 3½ teaspoons lemon juice, divided
- ⅛ teaspoon ground nutmeg
- 2 tablespoons coarsely chopped walnuts, toasted
- 10 small apricots, halved and pitted
- Chopped fresh mint (optional)

1. Combine cheeses, honey, ½ teaspoon lemon juice, and nutmeg, stirring well. Stir in walnuts. Chill 1 hour.

2. Sprinkle cut sides of apricots evenly with 1 tablespoon lemon juice.

3. Spoon about 1 teaspoon cheese mixture into each apricot half, and chill 1 hour. Garnish with chopped fresh mint, if desired. **YIELD:** 10 servings (serving size: 2 apricot halves).

CALORIES 61 (37% from fat); FAT 2.5g (sat 0.9g, mono 0.3g, poly 0.6g); PROTEIN 2.2g; CARB 8.4g; FIBER 0.8g; CHOL 4mg; IRON 0.3mg; SODIUM 49mg; CALC 26mg

ORGANIC TIP

September is Organic Harvest Month™, introduced in 1992 by the Organic Trade Association to draw attention to organic food and agriculture. Check out www.ota.com for local and regional events.

Source: Organic Trade Association

Glazed Peaches in Phyllo Baskets

This delightful dessert is stunning enough to serve at a dinner party but simple to prepare as an everyday treat. The pastry baskets can be made a few days ahead and stored in an airtight container at room temperature.

½ cup whole-milk ricotta cheese
3 tablespoons granulated sugar, divided
1 teaspoon vanilla extract
3 tablespoons chopped hazelnuts, toasted and ground
6 (18 x 14–inch) sheets frozen phyllo dough, thawed
1½ tablespoons butter, melted
Cooking spray
3 cups chopped peeled ripe peaches (about 2 pounds)
½ cup apple jelly, melted and slightly cooled
1 tablespoon powdered sugar

1. Preheat oven to 350°.
2. Place ricotta, 1 tablespoon granulated sugar, and vanilla in a medium bowl, and beat with a mixer at medium speed until well blended. Cover and chill.
3. Combine remaining 2 tablespoons granulated sugar and hazelnuts. Stack 2 phyllo sheets on a large cutting board or work surface (cover remaining sheets to prevent drying); brush with half of butter. Sprinkle phyllo stack with half of hazelnut mixture. Repeat procedure with 2 phyllo sheets, remaining butter, and remaining hazelnut mixture. Top with remaining 2 phyllo sheets. Gently press phyllo layers together. Lightly coat top phyllo sheets with cooking spray. Cut phyllo stacks into 6 (7 x 6–inch) rectangles. Carefully place 1 layered rectangle into each of 6 (8-ounce) ramekins coated with cooking spray. Gently press rectangles into ramekins to form baskets (phyllo will extend about 1 inch over tops of ramekins). Place ramekins on a baking sheet. Bake at 350° for 20 minutes or until lightly browned and crisp. Cool in ramekins on a wire rack. Carefully remove phyllo baskets from ramekins.
4. Just before serving, spread about 1 tablespoon cheese mixture into bottom of each phyllo basket. Combine peaches and melted jelly, tossing to coat. Spoon about ½ cup peach mixture into each phyllo cup. Sprinkle evenly with powdered sugar. Serve immediately.
YIELD: 6 servings (serving size: 1 filled phyllo basket).

CALORIES 264 (29% from fat); FAT 8.5g (sat 3.5g, mono 3.8g, poly 0.7g); PROTEIN 5g; CARB 42.9g; FIBER 2.4g; CHOL 18mg; IRON 0.8mg; SODIUM 201mg; CALC 93mg

ORGANIC FACT

Peaches are the number-one produce item containing traces of pesticides, so be sure to incorporate organic peaches when preparing a dish. See "The Dirty Dozen" on page 14.

Source: Environmental Working Group

Gruyère and Cherry Compote

This is a great introduction to cheese for dessert. Gruyère is a Swiss cheese that has a rich, sweet, nutty flavor. Domestic Swiss and Emmental also work well in this recipe. Gruyère is not overly sweet; a sparkling wine, champagne, or even a dessert wine would be a nice complement to this course.

½ cup sugar
½ cup water
1 pound sweet cherries, pitted
¼ cup fresh lemon juice
5 (1-inch-thick) slices Italian bread (about 5 ounces)
4 ounces Gruyère cheese, cut into 15 thin slices

1. Combine sugar and ½ cup water in a medium, heavy saucepan over high heat. Bring to a boil; cook 1 minute. Add cherries, and cook 1 minute. Reduce heat to medium-low; cook 20 minutes. Remove cherries from pan with a slotted spoon.
2. Cook cherry liquid until reduced to ¼ cup (about 15 minutes). Remove from heat. Add cherries to pan; stir in lemon juice. Cool.
3. Preheat broiler.
4. Cut each bread slice crosswise into 3 strips. Arrange in a single layer on a baking sheet, and broil 1 minute on each side or until bread is toasted. Cool completely.
5. Cut each cheese slice in half diagonally. Arrange 3 bread strips on each of 5 plates. Top each bread strip with 2 slices cheese and about 1 tablespoon compote. **YIELD:** 5 servings.

CALORIES 324 (26% from fat); FAT 9.3g (sat 4.8g, mono 2.8g, poly 1.1g); PROTEIN 10.6g; CARB 51.7g; FIBER 3g; CHOL 25mg; IRON 1.3mg; SODIUM 258mg; CALC 281mg

Figs with Ricotta, Honey, and Walnuts

Fresh figs need little adornment. But a drizzle of honey, a good-quality ricotta, and some fresh cracked walnuts conspire to make an enjoyable summer dessert.

15 fresh figs, trimmed (about 1½ pounds)
½ cup whole-milk ricotta cheese
⅓ cup honey
⅓ cup chopped walnuts

1. Cut each fig into 4 wedges, cutting to, but not through, base of fig. Spread wedges slightly apart; place 3 figs on each of 5 dessert plates. Spoon about 1½ teaspoons cheese into each fig, and spoon about 1 tablespoon honey evenly around each serving of figs. Sprinkle each serving with about 1 tablespoon walnuts. **YIELD:** 5 servings.

CALORIES 273 (27% from fat); FAT 8.3g (sat 2.4g, mono 2g, poly 3.4g); PROTEIN 6g; CARB 49.9g; FIBER 6.1g; CHOL 13mg; IRON 1mg; SODIUM 23mg; CALC 110mg

Baked Figs and Nectarines

This fruit mixture is great over shortcakes.

12 medium fresh figs, halved (about 1¼ pounds)
3 nectarines, pitted and quartered
¼ cup late-harvest riesling or other sweet white wine (such as Gewürztraminer)
2 tablespoons honey
3 tablespoons sugar
3 cups vanilla reduced-fat ice cream

1. Preheat oven to 425°.
2. Arrange fresh figs and nectarines in a single layer in a 13 x 9–inch baking dish. Pour wine over fruit; drizzle with honey. Sprinkle evenly with sugar. Bake at 425° for 25 minutes or until fruit begins to brown. Serve warm with vanilla ice cream. **YIELD:** 6 servings (serving size: about ½ cup fruit mixture and ½ cup vanilla ice cream).

CALORIES 271 (9% from fat); FAT 2.6g (sat 1.1g, mono 0.7g, poly 0.2g); PROTEIN 4.3g; CARB 58.3g; FIBER 5.3g; CHOL 5mg; IRON 0.6mg; SODIUM 47mg; CALC 136mg

Strawberry Sauce with Caramelized Sugar and Pink Peppercorns

An immersion blender goes directly into the strawberry mixture to smooth the sauce, eliminating the transfer of the warm liquid to a stand-up blender. The caramelized sugar enhances the strawberries' sweetness, while the peppercorns add a surprising zing. Serve this sauce over frozen vanilla yogurt, pound cake, or sliced fresh strawberries. This recipe can be prepared up to four days in advance and refrigerated in an airtight container.

⅔ cup sugar
¼ cup water
1 pound hulled strawberries, quartered
½ teaspoon crushed pink peppercorns

1. Combine sugar and water in a large saucepan; bring to a boil. Cook until sugar dissolves; do not stir. Brush down any crystals that form on edges of pan with a wet pastry brush. Cook 2 minutes or until sugar caramelizes and turns pale amber, swirling pan occasionally. Remove pan from heat; let cool 3 minutes. Add strawberries; cover and let stand 10 minutes or until strawberries are tender. Cook over low heat until caramel is liquefied. Stir in peppercorns. Using an immersion blender in pan, puree sauce until smooth. (Sauce will thicken as it cools.) **YIELD:** 1¼ cups (serving size: about 1½ tablespoons).

CALORIES 83 (2% from fat), FAT 0.2g (sat 0g; mono 0g; poly 0.1g); PROTEIN 0.4g; CARB 21.1g; FIBER 1.2g; CHOL 0mg; IRON 0.3mg; SODIUM 1mg; CALC 10mg

Poached Pears with Raspberry-Balsamic Sauce

2 cups frozen unsweetened raspberries
1 tablespoon balsamic vinegar
2 teaspoons honey
⅛ teaspoon freshly ground black pepper
4 peeled firm Bosc pears (about 1¾ pounds)
1 tablespoon lemon juice

1. Place raspberries in a 3-quart casserole. Cover with lid; microwave at HIGH 2½ minutes or until thoroughly heated. Press raspberries through a fine sieve over a small bowl, reserving liquid; discard solids. Add vinegar, honey, and pepper to reserved raspberry liquid.

2. Rub pears with lemon juice. Place pears in casserole, and drizzle with raspberry sauce. Cover with lid. Microwave at HIGH 8 minutes or until pears are tender, stirring and spooning sauce over pears after 4 minutes. **YIELD:** 4 servings (serving size: 1 pear and 2 tablespoons sauce).

CALORIES 239 (3% from fat); FAT 0.9g (sat 0g, mono 0.2g, poly 0.3g); PROTEIN 1.5g; CARB 61.1g; FIBER 4.4g; CHOL 0mg; IRON 1.3mg; SODIUM 2mg; CALC 38mg

Tropical-Fruit Pizza

1 (18-ounce) package refrigerated sugar cookie dough
Cooking spray
⅓ cup sugar
1½ teaspoons grated orange rind
1 teaspoon coconut extract
1 (8-ounce) block fat-free cream cheese, softened
1 cup (1-inch) pieces peeled ripe mango
1 cup sliced banana (about 1 large)
6 (½-inch) slices fresh pineapple, cut in half
2 kiwifruit, each peeled and cut into 8 slices
¼ cup apricot preserves
1 tablespoon Triple Sec (orange-flavored liqueur) or orange juice
2 tablespoons flaked sweetened coconut, toasted

1. Preheat oven to 350°.
2. Cut cookie dough into 8 slices; firmly press slices into a 12-inch round pizza pan coated with cooking spray. Bake at 350° for 25 minutes or until lightly browned. Cool completely on a wire rack.
3. Combine sugar, orange rind, extract, and cream cheese in a bowl; beat with a mixer at medium speed until blended. Spread cream cheese mixture over cookie crust, leaving a ½-inch margin around edges. Arrange mango, banana, pineapple, and kiwifruit on top of cream cheese mixture. Combine preserves and liqueur in a small microwave-safe bowl, and microwave at HIGH 30 seconds or until melted. Drizzle over fruit pieces; sprinkle with toasted coconut. Chill 1 hour. **YIELD:** 12 servings (serving size: 1 wedge).

CALORIES 283 (24% from fat); FAT 7.4g (sat 2.4g, mono 0.1g, poly 1g); PROTEIN 4.6g; CARB 48.2g; FIBER 1.7g; CHOL 10mg; IRON 1.3mg; SODIUM 203mg; CALC 63mg

Sesame Sweets

In these traditional Indian cookies, both the nut filling and the cookie dough are prepared using a food processor.

FILLING:
- ¼ cup slivered almonds, toasted
- ¼ cup packed brown sugar
- 2 tablespoons sesame seeds, toasted
- 2½ tablespoons honey
- ¼ teaspoon ground cardamom
- ¼ teaspoon ground ginger
- ⅛ teaspoon ground nutmeg

DOUGH:
- 2 cups sifted cake flour (about 8 ounces)
- 3 tablespoons granulated sugar
- ¼ teaspoon salt
- ¼ cup chilled butter, cut into small pieces
- 4 to 5 tablespoons ice water
- Cooking spray
- 2 tablespoons powdered sugar

1. Preheat oven to 325°.

2. To prepare filling, combine first 7 ingredients in a food processor, and pulse 6 times or until combined and almonds are finely chopped. Remove almond mixture from food processor, and set aside. Wipe processor bowl and blade with a paper towel.

3. To prepare dough, lightly spoon flour into dry measuring cups; level with a knife. Combine flour, granulated sugar, and salt in a food processor; pulse 3 times. Add butter; pulse 4 times or just until combined. Add ice water, 1 tablespoon at a time, pulsing just until combined. (Mixture may appear crumbly but will stick together when pressed between fingers.)

4. Shape dough into 24 balls. Place dough 2 inches apart on a baking sheet coated with cooking spray. Press thumb in center of each ball to form an indentation. Fill each indentation with about 1 teaspoon almond mixture. Bake at 325° for 20 minutes or until set. Remove from pan, and cool completely on a wire rack. Sprinkle with powdered sugar. **YIELD:** 2 dozen (serving size: 1 cookie).

CALORIES 81 (33% from fat); FAT 3g (sat 1.1g, mono 1.3g, poly 0.4g); PROTEIN 1.1g; CARB 12.9g; FIBER 0.4g; CHOL 5mg; IRON 0.8mg; SODIUM 40mg; CALC 8mg

Chewy Chocolate-Coconut Macaroons

These cookies store well in an airtight container for up to two days. To freeze, layer cookies between sheets of parchment or wax paper in an airtight container. Let cookies thaw about 30 minutes before serving.

 2 ounces unsweetened chocolate, chopped
 ½ cup sifted cake flour (about 2 ounces)
 2 tablespoons unsweetened cocoa
 ⅛ teaspoon salt
 2½ cups lightly packed flaked sweetened coconut
 1 teaspoon vanilla extract
 1 (14-ounce) can fat-free sweetened condensed milk

1. Preheat oven to 250°.
2. Line a large baking sheet with parchment paper; secure with masking tape.
3. Place unsweetened chocolate in a small microwave-safe bowl. Microwave at HIGH 1 minute or until almost melted. Remove from microwave; stir until chocolate is completely melted.
4. Spoon flour into a dry measuring cup; level with a knife. Combine cake flour, unsweetened cocoa, and salt in a large bowl. Add coconut; toss well. Stir in melted chocolate, vanilla, and sweetened condensed milk (mixture will be stiff). Drop by level tablespoons 2 inches apart onto prepared baking sheet. Bake at 250° for 45 minutes or until edges of cookies are firm and centers of cookies are soft, rotating baking sheet once during baking time. Remove from oven; cool 10 minutes on pan on a wire rack. Remove cookies from parchment paper; cool completely on rack. Store in an airtight container. **YIELD:** 3 dozen (serving size: 1 cookie).

CALORIES 84 (38% from fat); FAT 3.7g (sat 3.3g, mono 0.3g, poly 0g); PROTEIN 1.9g; CARB 11.7g; FIBER 0.9g; CHOL 1mg; IRON 0.2mg; SODIUM 45mg; CALC 33mg

ORGANIC HISTORY

"Excluding the last few decades, organic agriculture has been the only form of agriculture practiced on the planet."

Source: Organic Consumers Association

Maple-Walnut Spice Cookies

Store these frosted cookies between layers of parchment paper or wax paper to keep them from sticking together. You can bake and freeze the unfrosted cookies up to a month in advance; bring the cookies to room temperature before frosting them.

COOKIES:
 1½ cups all-purpose flour (about 6¾ ounces)
 ½ teaspoon baking soda
 ½ teaspoon ground ginger
 ½ teaspoon ground cinnamon
 ¼ teaspoon salt
 ⅛ teaspoon ground nutmeg
 ⅛ teaspoon ground cloves
 ¾ cup packed dark brown sugar
 ¼ cup butter, softened
 2 tablespoons maple syrup
 1 large egg
FROSTING:
 1 cup powdered sugar
 2 tablespoons maple syrup
 1 tablespoon fat-free milk
 2 teaspoons butter, softened
REMAINING INGREDIENT:
 ½ cup finely chopped walnuts, toasted

1. Preheat oven to 350°.
2. To prepare cookies, lightly spoon flour into dry measuring cups; level with a knife. Combine flour and next 6 ingredients in a medium bowl, stirring well with a whisk.
3. Place brown sugar and ¼ cup butter in a large bowl; beat with a mixer at high speed until light and fluffy (about 4 minutes). Add 2 tablespoons maple syrup and egg; beat until well blended. Beating at low speed, gradually add flour mixture; beat just until combined.
4. Spoon cookie batter evenly into 30 mounds (about 1 tablespoon) about 2 inches apart on baking sheets. Bake at 350° for 14 minutes or until lightly browned. Cool on pans 5 minutes. Remove from pans; cool completely on wire racks.
5. To prepare frosting, combine powdered sugar, 2 tablespoons syrup, milk, and 2 teaspoons butter, stirring with a whisk until smooth. Spread frosting evenly over cooled cookies. Working quickly, sprinkle cookies with walnuts. **YIELD:** 2½ dozen (serving size: 1 cookie).

CALORIES 98 (30% from fat); FAT 3.3g (sat 1.1g, mono 1g, poly 1.1g); PROTEIN 1.2g; CARB 16.3g; FIBER 0.3g; CHOL 12mg; IRON 0.5mg; SODIUM 58mg; CALC 12mg

Macadamia and Ginger Cookies

½ cup self-rising flour (about 2¼ ounces)
½ cup macadamia nuts
¼ to ½ cup crystallized ginger
2 large egg whites
¾ cup sugar
1 teaspoon honey
1 teaspoon grated orange rind

1. Preheat oven to 300°.
2. Line 2 baking sheets with parchment paper; secure with masking tape.
3. Lightly spoon flour into a dry measuring cup, and level with a knife. Place flour and nuts in a food processor, and pulse 10 times or until mixture resembles coarse meal. Reserve 1 tablespoon flour mixture in food processor; set remaining flour mixture aside. Add ginger to food processor; pulse 8 times or until finely minced. Stir into remaining flour mixture; set aside.
4. Place egg whites in a large bowl; beat with a mixer at high speed 1 minute or until soft peaks form. Beating at high speed, gradually add sugar and honey; beat 4 minutes or until thick and glossy. Gently fold in flour mixture and rind. Drop dough by level tablespoons 2 inches apart onto prepared baking sheets. Bake at 300° for 18 minutes or until set. Remove from baking sheets; cool on a wire rack. **YIELD:** 30 cookies (serving size: 1 cookie).

CALORIES 51 (30% from fat); FAT 1.7g (sat 0.3g, mono 1.3g, poly 0g); PROTEIN 0.6g; CARB 8.7g; FIBER 0.2g; CHOL 0mg; IRON 0.2mg; SODIUM 37mg; CALC 11mg

Maple-Date Bars

Wrap these moist bars individually, or place them in a cookie tin between layers of wax paper or parchment paper.

1¾ cups finely chopped pitted dates (about 12 ounces)
¾ cup water
⅓ cup maple syrup
1 teaspoon grated lemon rind
⅔ cup sugar
½ cup butter, softened
1 cup all-purpose flour (about 4½ ounces)
1 cup regular oats
¼ teaspoon baking soda
¼ teaspoon salt
Cooking spray

1. Combine dates, water, and maple syrup in a heavy saucepan over medium heat. Bring to a boil; cook 12 minutes or until most liquid is absorbed, stirring frequently. (Mixture will look like jam.) Stir in rind; cool completely.
2. Preheat oven to 400°.
3. Beat sugar and butter with a mixer at medium speed until smooth. Lightly spoon flour into a dry measuring cup; level with a knife. Combine flour, oats, baking soda, and salt. Stir flour mixture into sugar mixture (mixture will be crumbly). Press 2 cups flour mixture into bottom of a 13 x 9–inch baking pan coated with cooking spray. Spread date mixture over flour mixture. Sprinkle with remaining flour mixture. Bake at 400° for 20 minutes or until golden brown. Cool completely in pan on a wire rack. **YIELD:** 20 servings (serving size: 1 bar).

CALORIES 162 (28% from fat); FAT 5g (sat 2.3g, mono 2g, poly 0.3g); PROTEIN 1.6g; CARB 29.5g; FIBER 1.8g; CHOL 12mg; IRON 0.7mg; SODIUM 78mg; CALC 14mg

Maple-Date Bars

Orange Fig Bars

DOUGH:

- 6 tablespoons butter, softened
- ¼ cup sugar
- ¼ cup honey
- 1 teaspoon vanilla extract
- 1 large egg
- 1¾ cups all-purpose flour (about 7¾ ounces)
- 1 teaspoon baking powder
- ¼ teaspoon salt

FILLING:

- 2 cups dried figs (about 12 ounces)
- 1 tablespoon grated orange rind
- ¼ cup boiling water
- 2 tablespoons sugar
- 2 tablespoons honey
- 2 tablespoons fresh orange juice

REMAINING INGREDIENTS:

- Cooking spray
- 1 teaspoon fat-free milk
- 1 large egg yolk, lightly beaten

1. To prepare dough, beat butter with a mixer at medium speed until smooth. Add ¼ cup sugar; beat 2 minutes. Add ¼ cup honey, vanilla, and egg; beat well. Lightly spoon flour into dry measuring cups; level with a knife. Combine flour, baking powder, and salt in a medium bowl. Add flour mixture to egg mixture, stirring just until moist. Divide dough in half, and gently press each half of dough into a piece of heavy-duty plastic wrap. Cover dough with additional plastic wrap; chill 8 hours.

2. Preheat oven to 375°.

3. To prepare filling, place dried figs and orange rind in a food processor; process until minced. Combine ¼ cup boiling water, 2 tablespoons sugar, and 2 tablespoons honey, stirring until sugar dissolves. Stir in fresh orange juice. With processor on, slowly add orange juice mixture to fig mixture through food chute. Process until well blended, scraping sides of bowl occasionally; set aside.

4. Working with 1 portion of dough at a time (cover remaining dough to keep from drying), roll each portion into a 9-inch square on a heavily floured surface. Fit 1 portion of dough into a 9-inch square baking pan coated with cooking spray. Spread filling evenly over dough in pan. Place remaining square of dough on top of filling. Combine 1 teaspoon milk and egg yolk in a small bowl, stirring with a whisk. Brush milk mixture over top of dough.

5. Bake at 375° for 30 minutes or until top is golden. Cool 30 minutes on a wire rack. Remove from pan; cool completely. Cut into bars. **YIELD:** 20 servings (serving size: 1 bar).

CALORIES 156 (25% from fat); FAT 4.3g (sat 0.9g, mono 1.8g, poly 1.3g); PROTEIN 2.2g; CARB 28.9g; FIBER 3.2g; CHOL 22mg; IRON 1mg; SODIUM 100mg; CALC 45mg

Streusel-Topped Key Lime Squares

If you can't find Key limes, you can use regular Persian limes.

- ¼ cup butter, softened
- ¼ cup granulated sugar
- 1 teaspoon grated lime rind
- ⅛ teaspoon salt
- ⅛ teaspoon lemon extract
- 1 cup all-purpose flour (about 4½ ounces)
- Cooking spray
- ⅔ cup granulated sugar
- 3 tablespoons all-purpose flour
- ¾ teaspoon baking powder
- ⅛ teaspoon salt
- ½ cup fresh Key lime juice
- 3 large eggs
- 1 tablespoon powdered sugar

1. Preheat oven to 350°.

2. Place first 5 ingredients in a medium bowl; beat with a mixer at medium speed until creamy (about 2 minutes). Lightly spoon 1 cup flour into a dry measuring cup; level with a knife. Gradually add 1 cup flour to butter mixture, beating at low speed until mixture resembles coarse meal. Gently press two-thirds of mixture (about 1⅓ cups) into bottom of an 8-inch square baking pan coated with cooking spray; set remaining ⅔ cup flour mixture aside. Bake at 350° for 12 minutes or until mixture is just beginning to brown.

3. Combine ⅔ cup granulated sugar, 3 tablespoons flour, baking powder, and ⅛ teaspoon salt in a medium bowl, stirring with a whisk. Add lime juice and eggs, stirring with a whisk until smooth. Pour mixture over crust. Bake at 350° for 12 minutes. Remove pan from oven (do not turn oven off); sprinkle remaining ⅔ cup flour mixture evenly over egg mixture. Bake an additional 8 to 10 minutes or until set. Remove pan from oven; cool in pan on a wire rack. Sprinkle with powdered sugar. **YIELD:** 16 servings (serving size: 1 square).

CALORIES 121 (29% from fat); FAT 3.9g (sat 1.7g, mono 1.5g, poly 0.3g); PROTEIN 2.2g; CARB 19.9g; FIBER 0.3g; CHOL 47mg; IRON 0.6mg; SODIUM 93mg; CALC 21mg

Streusel-Topped Key Lime Squares

Nutritional Analysis

HOW TO USE IT AND WHY

Glance at the end of any *Cooking Light* recipe, and you'll see how committed we are to helping you make the best of today's light cooking. With chefs, registered dietitians, home economists, and a computer system that analyzes every ingredient we use, *Cooking Light* gives you authoritative dietary detail like no other magazine. We go to such lengths so you can see how our recipes fit into your healthful eating plan. If you're trying to lose weight, the calorie and fat figures will probably help most. But if you're keeping a close eye on the sodium, cholesterol, and saturated fat in your diet, we provide those numbers, too. And because many women don't get enough iron or calcium, we can help there, as well. Finally, there's a fiber analysis for those of us who don't get enough roughage.

Here's a helpful guide to put our nutrition analysis numbers into perspective. Remember, one size doesn't fit all, so take your lifestyle, age, and circumstances into consideration when determining your nutrition needs. For example, pregnant or breast-feeding women need more protein, calories, and calcium. And men older than 50 need 1,200mg of calcium daily, 200mg more than the amount recommended for younger men.

IN OUR NUTRITIONAL ANALYSIS, WE USE THESE ABBREVIATIONS:

sat	saturated fat	**CHOL**	cholesterol
mono	monounsaturated fat	**CALC**	calcium
poly	polyunsaturated fat	**g**	gram
CARB	carbohydrates	**mg**	milligram

DAILY NUTRITION GUIDE

	women ages 25 to 50	women over 50	men over 24
Calories	2,000	2,000 or less	2,700
Protein	50g	50g or less	63g
Fat	65g or less	65g or less	88g or less
Saturated Fat	20g or less	20g or less	27g or less
Carbohydrates	304g	304g	410g
Fiber	25g to 35g	25g to 35g	25g to 35g
Cholesterol	300mg or less	300mg or less	300mg or less
Iron	18mg	8mg	8mg
Sodium	2,300mg or less	1,500mg or less	2,300mg or less
Calcium	1,000mg	1,200mg	1,000mg

The nutritional values used in our calculations either come from The Food Processor, Version 7.5 (ESHA Research), or are provided by food manufacturers.

Metric Equivalents

The information in the following charts is provided to help cooks outside the United States successfully use the recipes in this book. All equivalents are approximate.

EQUIVALENTS FOR DIFFERENT TYPES OF INGREDIENTS

Standard Cup	Fine Powder (ex. flour)	Grain (ex. rice)	Granular (ex. sugar)	Liquid Solids (ex. butter)	Liquid (ex. milk)
1	140 g	150 g	190 g	200 g	240 ml
¾	105 g	113 g	143 g	150 g	180 ml
⅔	93 g	100 g	125 g	133 g	160 ml
½	70 g	75 g	95 g	100 g	120 ml
⅓	47 g	50 g	63 g	67 g	80 ml
¼	35 g	38 g	48 g	50 g	60 ml
⅛	18 g	19 g	24 g	25 g	30 ml

LIQUID INGREDIENTS BY VOLUME

¼ tsp =				1 ml
½ tsp =				2 ml
1 tsp =				5 ml
3 tsp =	1 tbl =		½ fl oz =	15 ml
	2 tbls =	⅛ cup =	1 fl oz =	30 ml
	4 tbls =	¼ cup =	2 fl oz =	60 ml
	5⅓ tbls =	⅓ cup =	3 fl oz =	80 ml
	8 tbls =	½ cup =	4 fl oz =	120 ml
	10⅔ tbls =	⅔ cup =	5 fl oz =	160 ml
	12 tbls =	¾ cup =	6 fl oz =	180 ml
	16 tbls =	1 cup =	8 fl oz =	240 ml
	1 pt =	2 cups =	16 fl oz =	480 ml
	1 qt =	4 cups =	32 fl oz =	960 ml
			33 fl oz =	1000 ml = 1 l

DRY INGREDIENTS BY WEIGHT

(To convert ounces to grams, multiply the number of ounces by 30.)

1 oz =	¹⁄₁₆ lb =	30 g
4 oz =	¼ lb =	120 g
8 oz =	½ lb =	240 g
12 oz =	¾ lb =	360 g
16 oz =	1 lb =	480 g

LENGTH

(To convert inches to centimeters, multiply the number of inches by 2.5.)

1 in =			2.5 cm
6 in =	½ ft =		15 cm
12 in =	1 ft =		30 cm
36 in =	3 ft =	1 yd =	90 cm
40 in =			100 cm = 1 m

COOKING/OVEN TEMPERATURES

	Fahrenheit	Celsius	Gas Mark
Freeze Water	32° F	0° C	
Room Temperature	68° F	20° C	
Boil Water	212° F	100° C	
Bake	325° F	160° C	3
	350° F	180° C	4
	375° F	190° C	5
	400° F	200° C	6
	425° F	220° C	7
	450° F	230° C	8
Broil			Grill

index

TIPS FOR BUYING AND USING NONSTICK PANS

- Choose a pan with multiple coats. This suggests the base metal has been carefully prepared and the nonstick layer is thick enough to be durable.
- Nonstick skillets need to be replaced more frequently than just about anything else in your kitchen because the nonstick surface will wear down over time.
- Take care not to overheat nonstick pans, especially when they're empty. The coatings on these pans can be damaged by excess heat.
- Use wooden or nylon utensils, and hand-wash pans so the coating performs better and lasts longer.
- Follow the manufacturer's instructions for care because various coatings have different compositions and require different care.
- For safety, throw out a nonstick pan at the first sign of scratches or chips to the nonstick surface.